Risk Treatment

THE FERMA-RIMAP® SERIES

The FERMA-rimap® Series serves as a proactive, continuous and dynamic learning and research platform to respond to risk managers' present and future educational and professional needs. The volumes set a flexible and dynamic measurable standard taxonomy for European Risk Managers and essential reading for students gaining their qualification. The scope of *The FERMA-rimap® Series* is to reach out to experienced or junior risk professionals, whatever their background is, and wherever their career is heading. All risk professionals have a duty to stay in contact with the evolution of the risk landscape.

Risk Treatment

EDITED BY

SIMON GRIMA
University of Malta, Malta

MARÍA ISABEL MARTÍNEZ TORRE-ENCISO
Universidad Autónoma de Madrid, Spain

AND

MAURIZIO CASTELLI
Augustas Risk Services SpA, Italy

emerald
PUBLISHING

United Kingdom – North America – Japan – India – Malaysia – China

Emerald Publishing Limited
Emerald Publishing, Floor 5, Northspring, 21-23 Wellington Street, Leeds LS1 4DL.

First edition 2025

British Library Cataloguing in Publication Data
A catalogue record for this book is available from the British Library

ISBN: 978-1-83662-307-6 (Print)
ISBN: 978-1-83662-306-9 (Online)
ISBN: 978-1-83662-308-3 (Epub)

Contents

Preface

Risk treatment is a fundamental aspect of the risk management process, encompassing strategies to mitigate, transfer, avoid, or accept risks in a structured and effective manner. As businesses and institutions navigate increasingly complex risk landscapes, the need for well-defined risk treatment mechanisms becomes essential to ensuring resilience and continuity.

This volume, *Risk Treatment*, is part of the *FERMA-rimap® Series*, a dynamic and evolving body of knowledge designed to support risk professionals in their pursuit of excellence. It provides a comprehensive exploration of risk treatment principles, frameworks, and methodologies, making it a valuable resource for both seasoned professionals and newcomers to the field. By bridging theoretical foundations with practical applications, this book enables risk managers to design and implement effective risk treatment strategies tailored to their organisational needs.

Throughout this volume, key aspects of risk treatment are examined, such as risk control and reduction techniques, risk financing, including insurance and reinsurance, business continuity planning, and alternative risk transfer mechanisms. Each chapter presents real-world insights, case studies, and best practices to illustrate how risk treatment contributes to sustainable and robust risk management frameworks.

We extend our gratitude to the esteemed contributors who have dedicated their expertise and research to this publication. Their collective insights ensure that this volume remains relevant and invaluable to practitioners, educators, and policymakers.This book series is a testament of FERMA's (Federation of European Risk Management Associations) unwavering commitment to promoting excellence in risk management through education, research, and professional development.[1]

As you engage with this material, we encourage you to view risk treatment as not just a compliance exercise but a strategic enabler of business sustainability and success. We hope this book serves as a valuable guide in your journey to mastering risk treatment and contributing to a more resilient business environment.

---

[1]To know more FERMA's commitment to risk management, please visit www.ferma.eu

Acknowledgements

The structure of the following document is based on the FERMA rimap® Body of Knowledge developed in 2015 by a team of European risk managers representing their national risk management associations, members of FERMA, to serve as a basis for a European Risk Management certification. The FERMA rimap® Body of Knowledge was designed under the supervision of Prof. María Isabel Martínez Torre-Enciso, Doctor in Business and Economics by UCM, Professor of Corporate Finance in UAM, MBA, RIMAP.

Prof. Jean-Paul Louisot, Docteurès Sciences de Gestion de la Sorbonne, MBA, ARM, FIRM, acted as FERMA's subject matter expert to ensure greater consistency among the numerous chapters of the Body of Knowledge, the FERMA existing learning materials and the new content developed to enrich the document.

Disclaimer

This subject matter is provided by FERMA for study, on the understanding that no person should act on the basis of the material contained in this publication without considering and taking professional advice. In particular:

- FERMA, its directors, authors, or any persons involved in this publication expressly disclaim any and all contractual, tortious, or other forms of liability to any person in respect of the publication and any consequences arising from its use, including any omission made, by any person in reliance upon the whole or any part of the contents of this publication.
- FERMA expressly disclaims any and all liability to any person in respect of the consequences of anything done or not done by any person in reliance upon the contents of this subject material.

Chapter 1

General Aspects of Risk Treatment

Introduction

Once risks have been identified and assessed, they need to be treated. Treating risks means that the risk event either does not occur or occurs but has a limited impact (the potential for damage is reduced or the losses are compensated). The risk treatment stage can be thought of as being the stage of the risk management process that solves the issues identified.

Treating risks appropriately requires a number of steps, including defining the organisation's risk appetite, identifying which risks it could tolerate and which would damage it and identifying how much treatments might cost.

It is important to understand where risk treatment fits in the enterprise-wide risk management process, and to understand why it is so important.

This chapter will introduce you to the general aspects of risk treatment and provide some case studies describing risk treatment failures and the damage that resulted to the organisations involved.

Learning Outcomes

By the end of this chapter, you should be able to:

- identify appropriate risk treatments for identified risks;
- describe the differences between risk treatment methods;
- assign risks to tolerable and intolerable categories;
- describe how risk treatment fits into the risk management process;
- explain why risk treatment is important;
- identify the costs involved in risk treatments.

Risk Treatment, 1–26

Published under exclusive licence by Emerald Publishing Limited
doi:10.1108/978-1-83662-306-920251002

Introduction to Risk Treatment

Risk treatment means actively addressing the risks that were identified earlier in the risk management process, leading to reduced or removed uncertainty of outcomes.

It involves:

- selecting and assessing a range of options for treating risk exposures;
- preparing risk treatment plans; and
- implementing the risk treatment plans.

Risk treatment options include accepting/retaining, modifying/reducing, avoiding/suppressing and transferring/sharing the risk exposure. Most organisations use a combination of treatment options to cover all identified risk exposures.

There are two major methods to treat risk:

- Risk reduction aims at changing the level of exposure to reduce the likelihood and/or the consequences.
- Risk financing aims at planning compensation for the organisation for any losses incurred.

This block will cover the reduction of risk, and Block 4 will cover the financing of risk. Therefore, when this block uses the expression 'risk treatment', it is referring to risk reduction measures.

EXAMPLE

Credit Control Function

The following example outlines a common way of treating risk through risk reduction in many organisations.

When an organisation invoices a customer company for goods or services after those goods or services have been delivered, the organisation extends credit to the customer company, which becomes a trade debtor.

A risk to the organisation is that the trade debtor may be unable to pay for the goods or services when the money becomes due.

Before doing business with the potential customer company, an organisation could employ some or all of the following measures to manage this risk:

- Credit check – this requires companies to provide details that clearly identify the legal entity that is purchasing the goods and its registered business address to see if it is financially responsible and stable.
- References – this involves seeking references from three or more organisations that have already extended credit to the company purchasing the goods or services to anecdotally check their delivery and payment history.
- Third-party credit risk reports – these can be compiled from various sources of data to see if there are any legal actions against the company for bad debts.

In this example, the risk identified is the non-payment of monies due and the potential cost of recovery. The risk treatment strategy is credit control, which is aimed at reducing the uncertainty of payment by the debtor. The risk treatment tactic is requiring references and reports before the customer company becomes a trade debtor.

As there are various options for risk treatments, organisations tend to categorise risks to help identify how to treat them. To think about risk management (and risk treatment, as one of its components) as part of organisational management as a whole, every part of the process works towards the achievement of the overall goals of the organisation.

Self-Help Question 1.1

Which of the following are risk treatments to reduce the risk of a motor vehicle accident occurring or to reduce the consequence of an accident?

1. airbags
2. road rules
3. driving licences
4. GST on motor vehicle insurance policies
5. traffic lights
6. roundabouts
7. in-car satellite navigation systems.

Answers to self-help questions are provided at the end of each section.

Activity | Identifying Risk Treatments

Identify five key business processes in your organisation that are risk treatments. For each, state the risk that is being managed by the process and how the treatment modifies the potential outcome of the risk event. For example:

Business process	Password protection when the user logs in to the mainframe system.
Risk	Theft of information resulting from unauthorised access to a user account.
Modification	Reduces the likelihood of theft of information by making it more difficult for unauthorised access to occur.

Risk Treatment and Risk Management

Risk management is the entire process of thinking about business goals, defining success, understanding risks (threats and opportunities) and then managing them to help reach the goals.

As explored in Block 1, there are five major steps in the risk management process.

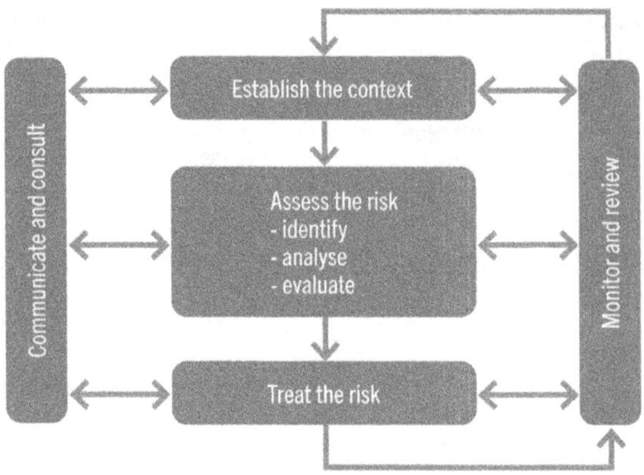

The Risk Management Process

The 'Treat the risk' step is essentially a planning and implementation phase where risk treatment options are considered and put into practice. The 'Establish the context' and 'Assess the risk' steps define the problems, and the treatment step is where solutions are assessed, chosen and put into action. Types of risk treatment options will be covered later in this section.

Activity | Risk Treatment Within the Risk Management Process

In the previous activity, you identified five risk treatments used in your organisation and explained how each treatment influenced the outcome of a risk event.

For this activity, select two of these previously identified risk treatments and analyse them using the complete risk management process; that is, note in which business context the risks have been identified, make an estimate of how the organisation analysed the risk level and evaluated the risks, and how the risk and risk treatments are being monitored (or not, as the case may be). For example:

Business process	Password protection when the user logs in to the mainframe system.
Business context	Protection of information that helps sustain the competitive advantage of the business.

Risk level	In the absence of controls to block unauthorised logins it would be highly likely that unauthorised access would occur and, depending on who the person was and for what reason, the consequences could be catastrophic – for example, if competitors obtained key customer information.
Risk evaluation	Unacceptably high.
Risk treatment	Introduce password protection on all user logins and require passwords to be changed monthly.
Monitoring	The system auto-generates a request for the new password each month and locks out the user if the password is not changed within three days.

Why Is Risk Treatment Important?

Risk treatment is the phase in the risk management process where solutions are designed to resolve defined problems or challenges. Leaving a risk untreated means leaving a problem or challenge unresolved, which, if a problem arises, can expose an organisation to operational failure.

It is often the case that organisations fail to deliver on risk treatments after having been through the earlier phases of the risk management process. This can be due to the following reasons:

- poorly formed context for the risk assessment process resulting in a lack of commitment to, or acceptance of, the need for action;
- inability to manage change;
- management being distracted by other business issues that arise, leading to a lack of monitoring and review;
- poor communication.

If organisations do not identify risks and prepare and implement suitable risk treatments, a risk may become a reality and could potentially destroy the organisation. Look at the following case study as an example of a known risk not being properly managed.

Case Study – National Australia Bank Rogue Trading Case

Introduction

In banking terms, trading describes the process of buying and selling financial instruments such as shares and foreign currency.

Options, in banking terms, are contracts that give the holder the right to buy or sell securities at a set price or within a set period of time. Investors often use them to protect or hedge an existing investment. An option is part of a class of securities called derivatives, so named because these securities derive their value from the worth of an underlying investment (for example, a parcel of shares or a number of Australian dollars or US dollars). If the price moves in the direction anticipated (either up or down) a profit is made. If the price moves in the opposite direction, a loss is made. Usually, these types of trades have stop-loss provisions where if the price moves too far against the trader, the size of the loss is capped. 'Rogue trading' is a term used to describe the situation when an employee of a financial institution abuses their position and trades outside of company guidelines.

The National Australia Bank (NAB) rogue trading case is a prominent example of how risks that are not appropriately treated can have a major impact on an organisation. In the case of NAB, the banking industry regulator APRA (Australian Prudential Regulation Authority) shut down its foreign exchange trading desk and imposed on the NAB Board a number of directives that had to be adhered to in order for NAB to continue to be an authorised banking business. The CEO of NAB resigned over the scandal along with a number of other senior executives, while others were moved into different positions. Two of the traders involved were sentenced to jail for criminal misconduct for their role in the scandal.

As you read through the following outline of the events, you will become aware that not implementing risk treatments is highly dangerous. Risk treatments need to be appropriately planned and implemented to ensure risk levels are within an organisation's defined risk appetite.

The events

In September 2003, traders on the NAB currency options trading desk decided that, on the balance of probabilities, the Australian dollar would begin to fall against the US dollar over the following few months. They put into place a strategy for NAB to profit from this move in currency exchange rates. Over the following few months, the Australian dollar actually gained against the US dollar.

As the currencies moved against the NAB traders, they fraudulently created a series of fictitious trades to hide the true position of their currency options trading book of business (the technical detail of how they affected these fictitious trades is beyond the scope of this case study). As the currencies continued to move against them, they created even more fictitious trades.

On 13 January 2004, NAB announced that they had lost A$180 million on their currency trading desk from rogue trading. By the end of the month, they had revised that figure to A$360 million.

NAB's risk controls

NAB, like all banks, knew the risks associated with trading in currency options and had in place a series of risk controls. These included the following:

Market limits – there were guidelines in place that placed limits on the size of individual and cumulative options trades.

Segregation of responsibilities – the traders operated in the front office while those responsible for reconciling options trades to the financial accounts resided in the back office.

Risk management oversight – a business unit called the Market Risk and Prudential Control unit within NAB's Risk Management Division had the role of overseeing the risks against rewards being taken by the front office, to ensure they were within the risk appetite of the bank.

Internal audit – regular reviews of the currency trading desk and the back-office systems.

External audit – NAB's external auditors conducted limited additional reviews of the trading desk and back-office systems.

APRA investigations

The Australian Prudential Regulation Authority (APRA) oversees banks, credit unions, building societies, general insurance and reinsurance companies, life insurance, private health insurance, friendly societies and most members of the superannuation industry. APRA is funded largely by the industries that it supervises.

Because of the serious nature of a regulated bank losing large sums of money, despite having a reportedly robust approach to risk management, APRA investigated the events and the corporate structures of the bank to identify causes and to make directives and recommendations to the NAB Board to take actions that would help ensure the bank was appropriately stable.

The following selection of quotations taken from the APRA report sums up their findings. It becomes clear why the CEO of NAB and other senior executives resigned or were moved into other positions (APRA: Report into Irregular Currency Options Trading at the National Australia Bank, 23 March 2004).

> The losses ultimately incurred by the National Australia Bank (NAB) on currency options were caused by four currency options traders, possessed of an abundance of self-confidence, who positioned the NAB's foreign currency options portfolio in the expectation that the falls in the US dollar that occurred mid last year would reverse and volatility would stabilise. Rather than closing their positions as

> the market moved against them, the traders chose to conceal their true positions – allowing those positions to deteriorate unchecked over a period of three months before they were finally discovered. By that time, the positions held were totally out of control ...
>
> That this was possible was, first and foremost, due to the collusive behaviour of the traders themselves. However, it can also be attributed to an operating environment characterised by lax and unquestioning oversight by line management; poor adherence to risk management systems and controls; and weaknesses in internal governance procedures ...
>
> There are many layers to NAB's internal control framework: line management; back office; middle office; risk committees; internal audit; and the Principal Board and its subcommittees. While the collusive behaviour of the traders involved succeeded in suppressing many of the bank's early warning signals, NAB's internal control systems failed at every level to detect and shut-down the irregular currency options trading activity ... (p. 5).

The final result

Ultimately, NAB operated for many months under a number of strict APRA directives. A new CEO was appointed, structures changed, and new systems were implemented.

It took NAB 15 months, until April 2005, to gain APRA's confidence and approval to reopen its options trading desk to business.

The purpose of this case study is to demonstrate the importance of effective risk treatments. Two final quotations from the APRA report sum up their importance:

> [...] The control failures in this case have more to do with poor implementation than poor design. On paper, NAB's existing control framework – despite its weaknesses – should have been able to identify and contain the risk positions of the traders ... (p. 5).
>
> The culture that predominated in CIB at NAB was one in which risk management controls were seen as trip-wires to be negotiated rather than presenting any genuine constraint on risk-taking behaviour ... (p. 6).

Other Examples

Toyota 2011 Recall

Toyota is a Japanese automobile maker that has been the number one automaker in the world most years since 2008 (the exception was 2011, when it suffered losses in the wake of the tsunami). It has been plagued since 2009 by lingering issues with sticky accelerator pedals and electronic faults.

In 2009, it was found that the floor mats in eight models were slipping around the driver foot well, trapping the accelerator pedal and causing uncontrollable acceleration. In 2010, it was also found that some accelerator pedals were sticking, again causing uncontrollable acceleration.

In 2010, while still recalling cars with the accelerator pedal issues, Toyota's anti-lock brake software was discovered to be faulty, resulting in brake failure.

By mid-2010, Toyota had recalled over eight million vehicles from all over the world, including the US, Europe and Asia, due to these three issues. It also paid a $16.4 million fine (a record at the time) for responding too slowly to the accelerator pedal issue and was facing lawsuits from the crash victims and from people who claimed their vehicles were improperly repaired following the recall.

The National Highway Traffic Safety Administration (NHTSA), a US agency dedicated to improving automobile safety, and NASA investigated Toyota's electronic systems and announced in 2011 that the acceleration issue was caused by mechanical defects, not electronic ones. However, in 2013, a US jury overrode this investigation, having found that the uncontrolled acceleration could have been caused by an electronic fault in the throttle systems. In those proceedings, a software engineer, Michael Barr of the Barr Group, testified that NASA had not actually completed its examinations of the throttle systems and that a processing error could easily result in unintended acceleration. He also argued that Toyota had not followed best practice guidelines when developing its software. As a result, Toyota began negotiations with plaintiffs.

In March 2014, Toyota was required to pay a US$1.2 billion penalty following an agreement reached with the US Justice Department that Toyota would pay the fine but not face trial over allegations that it had intentionally lied about its safety issues to protect its reputation.

During the crises, it was estimated that Toyota and its dealers could lose $54 million a day in revenue due to production and sales freezes. Despite this, Toyota has maintained its position as the world's biggest car manufacturer (as of mid-2017).

Risk Management Professional Comment. For a while during the crisis, Toyota leadership tried to buy time to reach a unanimous decision and did not take into account the impact of social media where a battle raged in the US. The delays in finding a solution for the problem in 2010 could have jeopardised Toyota's reputation – which had been built on utmost quality – but the explosion of the Deepwater Horizon deep water oil drill platform in October 2010 diverted social media attention from Toyota's issues.

Furthermore, in the automotive industry, product recalls have become a regular process, and a sign of reliability and responsiveness, rather than a lapse in quality. Toyota may have become the leader in product recalls, but this seems not to have affected its status as a successful automaker.

Fukushima Daiichi Nuclear Disaster

On 11 March 2011, a major earthquake struck Japan's north-eastern coast, near Tōhoku. The 9.0–9.1 magnitude earthquake, known as the Great East Japan Earthquake, was the most powerful ever recorded in Japan (and one of the largest ever recorded in the world). It triggered a 15-metre tsunami, which in turn triggered a level7 nuclear meltdown at the Fukushima Daiichi nuclear power plant. Level 7 is the highest classification and is the same level as the Chernobyl 1986 disaster.

The earthquake and tsunami not only cut off electrical power to the plant but also damaged the emergency generators. This meant the cooling systems for three of the six reactors failed. After a few days, a fourth reactor overheated and caused fires that led to radiation being released. Officials attempted to cool the reactors using seawater, which was subsequently contaminated and caused a new problem as it leaked from the plant.

The Fukushima Nuclear Accident Independent Investigation Commission (NAIIC) found that the disaster was 'manmade', and that:

> The operator (TEPCO), the regulatory bodies (NISA and NSC) and the government body promoting the nuclear power industry (METI), all failed to correctly develop the most basic safety requirements – such as assessing the probability of damage, preparing for containing collateral damage from such a disaster, and developing evacuation plans for the public in the case of a serious radiation release.

In October 2012, Tokyo Electric (Tepco) admitted that it had deliberately downplayed the safety risks. In 2017, a claim against Tepco was being heard in a US court. The plaintiff was asking for US$5 billion compensation.

The nuclear accident itself didn't kill many people (though some were injured) but it displaced hundreds of thousands of citizens because of fears of radiation contamination. The UN reported in 2014 that it expected no increase in future cancer rates or birth defects due to the accident, but that thyroid cancer risk in children could be increased.

Risk Management Professional Comment. The costs to TEPCO and the Japanese economy, including the loss of trust TEPCO suffered in Japan, are enduring. However, there were two more consequences that touched organisations worldwide:

- **Loss of support for nuclear-generated energy:** The traction nuclear energy was gaining in the climate change context, at least as an interim alternative to fossil energy until renewable energy sources are fully efficient and economical, was suddenly halted, as nuclear energy tumbled in public opinion. This resulting in a withdrawal of projects worldwide and even the early shutdown of existing nuclear power plants, including in Germany.

- **Drastic review of contingent loss of revenues by reinsurers:** Many leading manufacturers discovered in the wake of the tsunami and nuclear accident that they suffered business interruptions despite having never identified key suppliers/subcontractors in that country. As a result, reinsurance companies that covered most of the major losses caused by contingent business interruption, i.e. interruption resulting from events taking place outside of the insured premises, required a full dependencies analysis to expand their coverage. As a result, there has been since then a flourish of procurement network risk management efforts.

Self-Help Question 1.2

The Hillsborough disaster at a soccer stadium in Sheffield, England, resulted in the deaths of 96 fans from a crowd crush.

Study the description of the Hillsborough disaster incident in Appendix and answer the following questions.

1. What was the risk treatment commonly used at soccer stadiums in the UK at the time of the incident to help manage the risk of hooliganism such as pitch invasions by the crowd?
2. What role did this risk treatment play in the disaster?
3. What was the risk that was not adequately treated in the disaster? Had this risk been identified by the stadium operators?
4. What did the government enquiry identify as the most significant failure that caused the disaster? What else contributed to the disaster?
5. After your analysis of this failure, what step in the risk management process do you think was overlooked?
6. Describe the risk treatment strategy that was designed and implemented for future soccer matches because of the Hillsborough disaster.

Answers to self-help questions are provided at the end of each section.

Risk Appetite and Risk Tolerance

As defined in Block 1, the organisation's risk appetite and tolerance determine the type and amount of risk an organisation is willing and able to accept in the pursuit of its objectives.

The organisation's interpretation of its risk appetite denotes how the board or senior executives:

- set organisational objectives
- pursue those objectives with regards to the degree of the environment's volatility.

EXAMPLE

Risk Appetite and Tolerance Interpretation

A context analysis aims to provide the organisation with a better appreciation of its operating environment. The outcome of this context analysis informs the organisation about whether it is having a conservative, neutral or progressive year. In summary, an organisation's risk appetite and tolerance inform the kind of objectives the board sets.

Risk appetite

Depending on the type of year the board decides the organisation is having, the board will consult the risk appetite to convey the tone about how the organisation should proceed.

For example, the board would set very conservative objectives if it decides it is a conservative year (for example, due to budgetary constraints). Conversely, the board may 'stretch' the organisation's objectives if it decides the organisation is having a progressive year (because of the appetite to consume more risk in the pursuit of the organisation's objectives).

Risk tolerance

In a progressive year, the organisation might be able to tolerate a larger loss in the pursuit of its objectives due to the environment being more prosperous.

Conversely, in a conservative year, an organisation would endeavour to reduce any loss due to the less prosperous environment.

The Risk Appetite Statement

The board determines the organisation's risk appetite and tolerance in the risk appetite statement. The risk appetite statement reflects the board's view on what degrees of risk are acceptable (or unacceptable) to the business to meet its stated strategy.

The following table defines:

- acceptable and unacceptable risks;
- the tolerance levels assigned to the risks by way of tolerance (or target) levels.

Acceptable or Unacceptable Risks

Risk Type	Definition	Allocated Tolerance Level
Acceptable	Forms part of the necessary strategic elements required to meet the organisation's vision or goals	Rated on a sliding scale
Unacceptable	Does not realise the strategic vision of the company	Low tolerance level

Design

The design of the risk appetite statement is based on the existing risk management framework. The key difference is that thinking about risk has moved from **a risk is bad and should be minimised** approach to a **portfolio management, pick risks that are good** advisory function. The risk appetite framework should align risk with the elements in the following table.

Key Determinants of an Organisation's Risk Appetite

Element	Description
Shareholder expectations	Align the target risk and earnings profile with: • shareholder demands; or • the board's performance expectations
Strategy	Align capacity and tolerance for risk taking with capital allocation for profitable growth
Finance	Shape aggregate risk levels through decisions on balance sheet structure (leverage) and risk transfer (hedging or insurance)
Business operations	Aligning the acceptability and volume of risks actually taken by business lines with the desired risk profile
Regulatory standing	Ensuring business activities align with licencing and legislative obligations

Risk Criteria

The risk management context enables the organisation to establish and classify the types of risks to which it is exposed. The primary objective of risk management is to manage the effects of unexpected events.

Note: Despite an organisation's best efforts, it is not always possible to reduce the consequences of risk to zero.

Risk Appetite/Risk Tolerance

Whether or not the organisation takes any further action to alleviate its risks depends on the organisation's risk appetite or risk tolerance. A tolerable risk is one which, if the risk should occur, the organisation can still achieve its objectives. It is therefore necessary for the organisation to use its appetite for risk as a yardstick for developing its risk criteria.

Developing risk criteria involves the organisation determining the benchmarks against which it evaluates risks. The organisation needs to set risk criteria to enable it to effectively identify, analyse, evaluate and treat its risk exposures.

Organisations need to continually review their risk appetite as they evolve, regardless of means they use to communicate their risk tolerance.

Risk Tolerance Categories

An organisation's risk appetite must be tailored to its own specific needs. Risks can be divided into two clearly defined risk tolerance categories – those an organisation is prepared to accept (tolerable risks) and those it is not prepared to accept (intolerable risks).

Organisations are generally prepared to tolerate some risk exposures if a benefit can be derived from being exposed to the risk in question.

For example, the risks associated with a certain project may be significant but the financial and reputational returns associated with undertaking the project may be substantial. In this case, the organisation may be prepared to tolerate these risk exposures and take on the project, subject to agreed risk management initiatives.

Tolerable Risks

Defining an organisation's risk appetite is a fundamental part of developing a risk management programme. What an organisation deems as a tolerable level of risk depends on a number of factors, including:

- financial strength (the ability to withstand the financial consequences of the risk exposure);
- the attitude of the board and management (whether they are risk takers or risk averse);
- the measure/s necessary to handle the risk of loss and minimise consequences;
- the relative size of the risk exposure in terms of the organisation's activities.

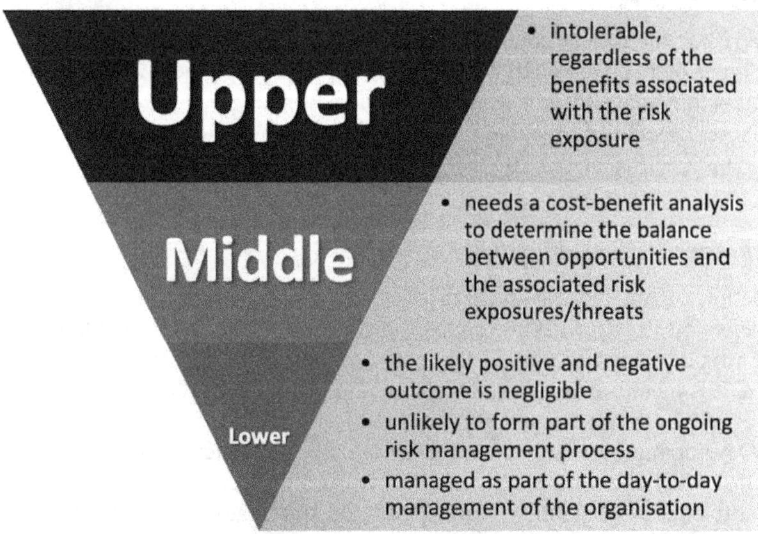

Three Groups of Risk Exposures

Classifying Risks According to Tolerance. A common means of addressing how much risk an organisation is prepared to tolerate is by classifying the risk exposures into the following three distinct groups.

Subjectivity. Groupings such as these often rely on subjective value judgements of risk exposures. For example, what one organisation regards as an intolerable (upper group) exposure, another organisation might regard as tolerable (middle group) depending on the organisation's particular situation.

EXAMPLE

Ministry of Transport

The following table provides a hypothetical analysis of some of the Ministry of Transport's risk exposures according to each of the previous three tolerance groupings.

Group	Example of Risks
Upper	train derailment (or other accident) resulting in injuries or fatalities complete system failure for an extended period system capacity cannot meet the demand
Middle	on-time performance below set standards level of individual service cancellations above set standards late delivery of major infrastructure initiatives fare evasion increases
Lower	on-time performance less than 100% but exceeds minimum benchmarks minor station vandalism minor and non-systemic non-core equipment failure (such as a ticket vending machine)

Note: These examples are hypothetical and may not reflect the actual views of the Ministry of Transport.

Statements of Acceptable Risk Levels

Some organisations often find it difficult to identify a 'comfortable' level of risk (tolerance and/or appetite) and they can rarely express this as a single statement. However, using quantitative and qualitative statements regarding what is not an acceptable level of risk is often a useful start.

The following table provides examples of quantitative and qualitative statements indicating risks an organisation is not willing to accept.

Quantitative and Qualitative Statements

Quantitative Statements	Qualitative Statements
• A loss of assets exceeding € X • Incurring non-budgeted liabilities exceeding € X • An inability to operate for a period exceeding five days	• Damaging reputation to a level where stakeholders begin to frequent other organisations • The death or serious injury of an employee • Failing to achieve board-mandated key strategic initiatives • Non-compliance with legal obligations

Overall Risk Levels

In addition to making quantitative/qualitative statements, determining which overall risk levels are acceptable or unacceptable is another useful way to express risk appetite information and decide whether risks of a certain level are acceptable or unacceptable. Overall levels of risk take into account a combination of the likelihood and consequence of a risk.

Importantly, every organisation will have its own risk tolerance levels and its appetite will therefore be individual.

Economics of Risk Treatment

The first stage of risk treatment involves evaluating risk exposures against their residual risk to determine which ones the organisation needs to actively treat. The key factor in ranking is the relative size of the risk as determined by its likelihood and consequence.

Note: Residual risk exposures remain after an organisation has determined risk treatment options and established treatment plans.

The following practical considerations affect this ranking:

- What are the organisation's corporate objectives and board priorities?
- What is the public perception of the organisation?
- What are the managers' priorities?
- What are the stakeholders' expectations?
- What resources does the organisation require to manage the risk exposure?
- What are the budget constraints?

As part of the risk evaluation process, decisions need to be made about:

- whether a particular exposure requires any treatment;
- whether an activity or project should be undertaken (and under what circumstances);
- priorities for treating individual risk exposures.

If the organisation is well managed, the decision-makers should find that many risks already have an appropriate level of control, i.e. efficient treatment measures. The key is to identify material risks requiring additional action.

Note: The evaluation may also conclude that existing risk treatments are excessive.

Identifying Risk Treatments

Once risks have been evaluated, potential treatments need to be identified and assessed against organisational aims. This involves:

- determining the effectiveness of existing risk treatment measures or controls;
- assessing the strengths and weaknesses of each of these measures;
- determining potential new treatments.

The following table provides examples of risk treatment measures.

Examples of Risk Treatment Measures

Risk	Controls
Bad debts	Credit limits New customer approvals Monitoring of debt ageing
Building fire	Fire sprinklers No smoking policy Flammable materials storage Insurance
Failure to achieve product growth goals	Marketing plan Advertising Customer surveys
Employee injury	Workplace health and safety (WHS) committee Workplace health and safety (WHS) audits Training
Printing errors	Proofreading Page scanning (including spell check)
Fraud	Segregation of duties Reconciliations System security

Assessing Risk Treatment Options

After identifying possible risk treatment strategies, the organisation needs to choose which risk treatment option is suitable for each identified risk. These options are:

- accepting/retaining
- modifying/reducing

- avoiding/suppressing
- transferring/sharing.

All options should be considered when the organisation is assessing risk treatments as they can be applied either individually or in combination.

Section 6.5.2 of ISO 31000:2018 states that selecting the most appropriate risk treatment options involves:

> [...] potential benefits derived in relation to the achievement of the objectives against costs, effort or disadvantages of implementation.

Risk treatment options are not necessarily mutually exclusive or appropriate in all circumstances. When assessing risk treatment options, organisations need to consider the following factors:

- consequences of not treating the risk;
- the risk appetite and the risk tolerance of the organisation;
- potential benefits or opportunities;
- the extent of risk reduction;
- costs of implementation.

The chosen risk treatment/s will need to take each of these factors into account, and appropriate treatments will vary from organisation to organisation due to differences in risk exposures and risk appetite/tolerance. Essentially, what is appropriate for one organisation may not necessarily be appropriate for another.

In practice, it is not often that organisations employ only one risk treatment option to treat a risk exposure and its likely effects; combinations of treatments are more common. Additionally, one risk treatment may address multiple risks – disaster recovery plans (DRPs) are a good example as they normally address a wide range of interruption scenarios (risks). Furthermore, some risk treatments may create new risks that must be considered, i.e. a sprinkler system will control a fire but may cause water damage even without a fire if there is a malfunction in the system.

Costing Treatment

Once an organisation decides on its risk treatment options, it needs to acquire information on how much it will cost to implement, both as investment and ongoing recurring costs, as the case may be.

The following table provides examples of risk treatment measures and their associated costs.

Risk Treatment Measure	Associated Cost
Insurance policy	The annual premium
Additional supervision of production	The wages of additional required staff

Additional security	The one-off cost of additional security fencing The ongoing cost of a security service
Project management	The project management resource Any additional measures the project manager identifies as a result of their work

Note: Calculating costs versus benefits is often subjective as there is often insufficient information to appropriately cost certain controls/risk treatments.

Cost-Benefit Analysis

Management is unlikely to approve the expenditure for a risk treatment measure without a detailed cost-benefit analysis. Organisations need to weigh the cost of implementing the risk treatment option against the potential benefits.

Risk managers who do not take this approach are unlikely to be successful in convincing key stakeholders to implement an 'eliminate-risk-at-all-costs' approach. Remember, risk management is not about eliminating risk; rather, it is about reducing risk to an acceptable level at a reasonable cost. Ultimately, risk treatment selections are financial decisions that reflect the risk appetite and financial resources of the organisation while taking into consideration stakeholders' expectations.

It is not economically viable to:

- spend more on treating a risk exposure than the potential cost of the associated loss;
- choose an expensive treatment option when a cheaper alternative would reduce the risk to an acceptable level (residual risk).

In many situations, when compared with the potential consequences of the corresponding risks, the costs of implementing risk treatments may be insignificant; however, there are other situations when these costs may be significantly greater than the associated benefit/s in real terms. The following example contextualises such a situation.

EXAMPLE

Building fire

Making a building totally fireproof would reduce the risk but it would be too expensive. Rather, the organisation would reduce the likelihood by:

- using sensible construction methods;
- using safe building materials;
- installing sprinkler systems and alarms;
- developing policies around the storage of flammable materials.

Self-Help Question 1.3

GPG is concerned about the increasing number of motor vehicle accidents their delivery drivers are experiencing. Marjorie Crawford, the finance manager, wants to consider how their risk management program can help reduce both the number (likelihood) and magnitude (consequence) of accidents.

Using a combination of risk treatment options, what prelimivwnary advice would you give GPG to help reduce the likelihood and consequence of the motor vehicle accidents?

Answers to self-help questions are provided at the end of each section.

Costs

The costs of a risk treatment can include, but are not limited to:

- WHS programs (for example, defensive driving);
- physical devices to reduce losses (for example, sprinklers and security alarms);
- controlling business risks (for example, financial reviews and market research);
- different techniques for handling losses (for example, crisis management and contingencies);
- capital purchase costs;
- additional labour for supervision or review (for example, accident feedback interview, pre-emptive maintenance);
- security systems (for example, speed limitation devices, antilock brake system [ABS])
- training (for example, first aid courses, accident report filling);
- developing IT systems.

Once-Off Versus Continual Costs

Once an organisation has incurred the high initial cost of a physical control measure (such as the installation of a machine guard), the organisation generally has the continuing benefit of these measures for little or no extra cost.

Conversely, insurance, when considering risk financing measures, and other risk mitigation measures often only provides a benefit for a limited period (usually 12 months). In the case that a control/treatment requires additional supervision, the cost is also ongoing, as may happen if a different process is called for to reduce the risk that increases the cost of operations.

Direct and Indirect Costs

One other aspect that needs to be considered when selecting a risk treatment measure is that there are numerous indirect costs and long-term effects associated with every accident or event. Analysing the total costs of any incident reveals:

- the direct cost of the physical loss or injury (when relevant)
- the indirect costs associated with:
  - repairing or replacing the loss
  - rehabilitating the injured person/s
  - the administrative processes
  - pain and suffering
  - lost production
  - downtime disruption

Case Study – Glamour Financial

Glamour Financial is a prestigious investment banking group that prides itself on hiring top executives. It is a high-achieving organisation and it rewards staff with social events.

A major social event is the staff's Christmas party held in a rented venue outside of the organisation's premises. This party is exclusively for staff and no customers or spouses are invited. The party includes spectacular entertainment, outstanding cuisine and plentiful alcoholic and non-alcoholic beverages. The bank has grown from a few dozen people to 800 employees and the parties have become opportunities for binge drinking and bad behaviour. Each year the number of alcohol-fuelled incidents of bad behaviour increases.

The Group Risk Manager has highlighted for senior management some high-profile sexual harassment and injury cases that resulted from similarly rowdy office Christmas parties at other organisations. She has especially highlighted the judicial trend that holds directors of companies more and more accountable for these risk events. She has put together a comprehensive list of options, not all of which are practical or palatable. The options are:

- leave the parties as they are;
- cancel the staff party;
- restrict the availability of alcohol, e.g. serve only light beer and wine and ask venue staff to closely monitor alcohol consumption;
- invite spouses to the party on the basis that spouses will have a sobering influence on staff;
- reduce the duration and entertainment of the party to moderate the party atmosphere, but still thank staff for their efforts.

The senior executive met with the Group Risk Manager and discussed the options. The Finance Director realised that extending the invitation to spouses would incur additional cost to the organisation. The other options reduce cost to the organisation.

The Manager of Sales and Marketing supported the option of keeping the party in its present format. She supported her opinion by explaining that staff saw the party as a major reward and it would be sorely missed. She put forward the proposition that the bank should appeal to staff to moderate their behaviour.

Eventually, the Group Risk Manager listed the positives and negatives of the options. These included the impact on staff morale, the overall reduction in risk to directors and staff, and the impact on corporate image as the parties were talked and written about in the industry media. While the parties were spectacular and incident free, the media coverage had been positive and helped attract quality staff.

The senior executive chose to extend the party to include spouses. He also decided to shift the focus of the party by providing top-class entertainment and reduce the amount of alcohol available. He decided to turn this risk into an opportunity and make the party even more talked about by staff and their spouses. He felt the increased cost was appropriate because it helped ensure a safe event for staff and reduced the risk of liability costs, while maintaining staff morale and improving corporate image.

Self-Help Question 1.4

Many motor vehicle accidents involve younger drivers. One risk treatment option government regulators have considered to help reduce the incidence of these accidents is to limit the number of passengers a young driver is allowed to carry.

Analyse this treatment strategy and list the potential advantages (benefits) and disadvantages (costs). Remember, these can be monetary or otherwise.

Answers to self-help questions are provided at the end of each section.

- wasted labour cost;
- time spent on:
    - accident investigation
    - legal proceedings

- the cost of management being redirected to deal with the loss and its related problems rather than future operations;
- the long-term costs of diverting money and resources from other intended uses or investments to repair, replace or rehabilitate the results of the incident;
- possible damage to the organisation's reputation;
- the loss of customers or potential growth as a result of customers having to find alternative suppliers during the resumption of production/services.

Summary

Please keep the following points from this chapter in mind:

- Risk treatment means actively addressing the risks that were identified, analysed and evaluated earlier in the risk management process, leading to reduced or removed uncertainty of outcomes.
- There are two major methods to treat risk:
  - risk reduction
  - risk financing
- Risk treatment is the phase in the risk management process where solutions are designed to resolve defined problems or challenges.
- If organisations do not identify risks and prepare and implement suitable risk treatments, a risk may become a reality and could potentially destroy the organisation.
- Risks can be divided into two clearly defined risk tolerance categories – those an organisation is prepared to accept (tolerable risks) and those it is not prepared to accept (intolerable risks).
- Risk exposures can be classified into three groups:
  - Upper: intolerable, regardless of the benefits associated with the risk exposure
  - Middle: needs a cost-benefit analysis to determine the balance between opportunities and the associated risk exposures/threats
  - Lower: the likely positive and negative outcome is negligible, it's unlikely to form part of the ongoing risk management process and can be managed as part of the day-to-day management of the organisation.
- Once risks have been evaluated, potential treatments need to be identified and assessed against organisational aims.
- After identifying possible risk treatment strategies, the organisation needs to choose which risk treatment option is suitable for each identified risk. These options are:
  - accepting/retaining
  - modifying/reducing
  - avoiding/suppressing
  - transferring/sharing.

- Risk treatment measures may be classified into three categories: physical, procedural and managerial.
- In practice, it is not often that organisations employ only one risk treatment measure to treat a risk exposure and its likely effects; combinations of treatments are more common.
- Management is unlikely to approve the expenditure for a risk treatment measure without a detailed cost-benefit analysis. Organisations need to weigh the cost of implementing the risk treatment option against the potential benefits.

Answers to Self-Help Questions

Self-help question 1.1

The GST on motor vehicle insurance policies and the in-car satellite navigation systems would not be considered risk treatments. The GST is collected into general revenue and is not specifically redirected into road safety initiatives. The navigation system may reduce the stress of being lost or running late; however, the use of the system can be distracting, hence it would not be considered an aid for reducing the risk of a motor vehicle accident.

The others are all risk treatments as they either reduce the consequence of an incident (airbags for injury, traffic lights and roundabouts for the speed at which an accident may happen) or the likelihood (road rules, licensing, traffic lights and roundabouts).

Self-help question 1.2

1. The risk treatment commonly used at soccer stadiums was a high steel fence between the spectators and the pitch.
2. The high steel fence did not allow spectators to escape the crush of oncoming fans.
3. The risk that was not adequately treated was the risk of overcrowding, which could result in a crowd crush. This risk had been identified by the stadium operators because the stadium included crushed barriers and used police and stewards to direct the crowd.
4. The most significant failure identified by the Government enquiry was not monitoring the entrances to central pens 3 and 4 on the terraces. This meant that more and more people entered the already overcrowded pens and were not aware of the crush they were creating at the front of the pens. Also, the terraces lacked seating, which allowed overcrowding.
5. The risk management process that was overlooked was monitoring and review – most likely there was no policy or procedure for cross-checking that police and or stewards were in their appropriate positions at critical times.

→

6. As a result of the inquiry, fences in front of fans were removed and stadiums were converted to become all-seated.

Self-help question 1.3

As part of their risk management program, GPG could reduce the likelihood and consequence of motor vehicle accidents by implementing the risk treatment options listed in the following table.

Risk Treatment Option	Description
Reduce accident likelihood (prevention)	GPG could send delivery drivers on a driver education program The program could develop skills to help drivers avoid accidents and improve vehicle maintenance If the organisation has a driver education program, insurance premium savings are likely to be an added benefit
Reduce accident consequences (protection)	The driver education program can help delivery drivers employ skills to help lessen the consequences of accidents on the vehicles GPG could also buy safer vehicles, including: – safety devices, such as driver and passenger airbags – passenger safety cells
Risk transfer/sharing	Instead of owning delivery vehicles, GPG could lease the vehicles and the lessor could assume responsibility for vehicle damage
Purchase additional vehicles	GPG could purchase additional vehicles to ensure standby vehicles are available for use when delivery vehicles are not operational
Improving the quality of their fleet	GPG could spend more money on improving the quality of their fleet to have safer cars and a regular repair and maintenance cycle

Self-help question 1.4

The potential advantages (benefits) and disadvantages (costs) of limiting the number of passengers carried by young drivers are as follows.

Advantages (benefits) would include:

- reduced amount of distraction to drivers caused by the passengers;
- reduced number of people involved in any given accident. →

→

Disadvantages (costs) would include:

- increased number of young drivers on the road to transport the same number of people – i.e. two drivers would be needed to take four people to a party – and this could double the risk of accidents due to inexperienced or drink/drug-affected drivers;
- potential increased risk-taking because young drivers may 'race' each other during the journey;
- potential increased effect on police resources by having more cars on the roads;
- potential increased effect on the environment by having more cars on the roads.

Chapter 2

Identifying and Designing Risk Treatments

Introduction

Now that the general principles of risk treatment have been described, it is time to explore more specific aspects of risk treatment.

Risks can vary from year to year, organisation to organisation and context to context. Therefore, not all risks can or should be treated, and not all can be treated the same way. Additionally, different organisations have different risk appetites, and risks that are tolerable to one organisation could cause another to collapse.

Risk managers must be able to first identify which risks need to be treated and then to identify all potential treatments for those risks. They must then evaluate the options to ensure the most appropriate treatments are chosen. It is important to balance the effectiveness of the risk treatment with its cost, and to ensure that the risk treatment selected will not give rise to another, potentially worse, risk.

This chapter will describe the process for identifying and designing risk treatments and outline the various factors risk managers need to take into account to ensure treatments are suitable, cost-effective and successful.

Learning Outcomes

By the end of this chapter, you should be able to:

- identify potential risk treatments;
- design risk treatments to suit risks and organisational criteria;
- evaluate the likelihood and consequences of risks to determine which risks to treat and how;
- categorise risk treatments;

Risk Treatment, 27–51

Published under exclusive licence by Emerald Publishing Limited
doi:10.1108/978-1-83662-306-920251004

- allocate risks, as required;
- perform a cost-benefit analysis (CBA) of tangible and intangible costs and benefits;
- calculate benefit-cost ratios;
- select appropriate risk treatments.

Identifying and Designing Risk Treatments

Identifying and designing appropriate risk treatments is a key step in the risk treatment process and occurs after risks have been collated, reviewed in the context of the risk appetite of the organisation, and possibly ranked. Risks that are unacceptably high are targeted for risk treatments. In practical terms, identifying risk treatments may be easy, but designing the risk treatment can present challenges.

Consider the operational level risk of fire posed from allowing smoking in a warehouse. It is obvious that banning smoking in the warehouse is a sound risk treatment; but less obvious are the challenges that implementing the ban may pose for the organisation. For example, where will smokers now smoke? When will they smoke? What effect will not smoking have on their productivity? What cultural effect will the absence of smokers during work time have on non-smokers? Will this affect productivity? This example clearly shows the potential for the less obvious effects of an identified risk treatment.

Risk management practitioners have developed a range of tools and techniques for identifying and designing risk treatments. The options for risk treatment have been outlined in ISO 31000:2018 and in ISO 31010. The following four broad categories apply to risk treatments.

- Avoiding/suppressing – consciously engaging or disengaging from the opportunity, objective, strategy, operation, task or activity.
- Modifying/reducing – reducing the likelihood (prevention) and/or consequences of a risk event (protection).
- Transferring/sharing – working with other parties to treat identified risks, which usually includes some contractual arrangements, hence the name sometimes used 'contractual risk transfer'. These parties may in turn choose to modify the risk allocated to them.
- Accepting/retaining – allocating risk to remain with the organisation and taking appropriate action to monitor and review retained risk against the risk appetite of the organisation.

Categorising risk treatments is the first step in developing a range of risk treatment options. Each category prompts a risk analyst to think about treating any particular identified risk by asking questions such as the following.

- How can this risk be avoided/suppressed?
- How can this risk be modified/reduced?
- How can we transfer/share all or part of this risk?
- Should we accept/retain this risk?

In theory, all risk treatment categories are options for any identified risk; however, in practical terms, there will be instances where some categories are simply not available or palatable to an organisation and would not be considered. For example, in the pharmaceutical industry, avoiding testing a new drug because of unknown risks to human health would render research into new drugs pointless. However, the precaution principle would require an investigation into the potential consequences of the proposed new drug and in many countries laws and regulations will dictate the research to be conducted.

The following case study looks at options for treating risks.

Case study – Larry's Lawn Mowing Services

Larry owns a lawn mowing business and operates it himself. A key risk for Larry is personal injury, which could result in him being unable to mow lawns and earn any income.

Possible risk treatments for Larry's risk of personal injury in each of the risk treatment categories are as follows:

Avoiding – assuming Larry does not perceive any opportunity from being injured with respect to his income, an option to avoid risk would be subcontracting the work to one or more workers. An injured contractor could be replaced.

Modifying/reducing – Larry could only mow level lawns that are generally free of debris and he could inspect each lawn and clear it as necessary to reduce the likelihood of injury. He could also wear protective clothing to reduce both the likelihood and consequence of an injury.

Transferring/sharing – Larry could go into partnership with others and share the risk of someone being injured; alternatively, he could purchase income protection insurance.

Accepting/retaining – Larry could continue to operate as he always has done.

In this case study, each category is covered, and each is perfectly viable; however, each will have costs and benefits associated with implementation.

It is evident from the case study of Larry's Lawn Mowing that identifying and designing risk treatments requires thought. More complex risks may need more complex thinking to identify the most appropriate option for an organisation. In order to assist in the risk treatment process, risk managers have utilised a range of tools and techniques to assist in considering complex problems, including brainstorming. The next part of this block will consider creative thinking and root cause analysis (RCA) as tools to aid practitioners of the risk treatment process.

Creative Thinking

When identifying risk treatment options, there is a range of creative thinking techniques that can be used to 'think outside the box' and help design effective solutions. For example, creative thinking can be stimulated by the following techniques.

- **Brainstorming** – allowing any idea to be proffered by any member of a group without criticism or comment. Allowing any idea to be discussed means good ideas are not stifled and great ideas may be developed by considering a brainstorming idea.
- **Random word** – words are chosen at random and are considered in the context of the problem at hand. It forces the group to approach the problem from a different angle. For example, a marketing executive for a winery that supplies exclusive wines may be asked by the owners to expand sales by selling wine over the Internet. One of the risks the executive identifies is that the winery's premium brand may be devalued because most sales have been through liquor stores specialising in premium wines. The executive needs to consider how to manage this risk if online selling is to proceed.

  Using the random word technique, the executive could pick up a dictionary and randomly choose the word 'familiarity'. The executive could draw associations between this word and the risk of devaluing the brand. This may lead the executive to think of opportunities such as paying to link the winery's website to premium products that the target market may be familiar with, such as prestige cars or high-end golf equipment vendors. The executive can repeat this process several times as not every word chosen will prompt new ideas for managing the risk.
- **Challenge facts** – identify what information is true and current, and what is hearsay, conjecture or based on situations that have since changed.
- **Scenario analysis** – choose an identified risk to analyse, imagine the risk has occurred and take the event through a series of steps to consider what the outcomes of the risk event may be. Each step could have a number of 'event' or 'decision' options to choose from and different scenarios run where a different event is considered to occur, or a different decision is made.

Each technique is aimed at redirecting thinking away from the most obvious solution and encouraging people to think outside the box. The human brain is good at making sense out of chaos by identifying, collating and ordering or indexing information for later use. When seeking a solution to a problem, the brain scans its memory set or index of information and looks for fast solutions that have previously been effective. This is useful when seeking a quick solution but not the best tactic when trying to find a creative response to a complex problem.

Techniques of creative thinking cause the human brain to disconnect from its normal mode of indexing and retrieving information so that seemingly unrelated items of information are matched. Matching information this way may lead to new and potentially valuable solutions to organisational problems. As with any business challenge or opportunity, the greater the threat or opportunity, the more such creative techniques should be used. For the best outcomes, the use of external facilitators experienced with the techniques should be considered.

Root Cause Analysis

Another technique used in the risk management industry to assist with identifying and designing treatment options is RCA. RCA is also a form of creative thinking. RCA forces participants to think differently about a situation, just as creative thinking techniques used in business do. The following example shows how RCA is designed to identify the true cause of an incident.

Incident	Product sells poorly online
Direct cause	Insufficient consumers purchased the product
Indirect cause	Insufficient consumers visited the website
Indirect cause	Advertising campaign failed to attract consumers to the website
Root cause	Used organisation's current advertising agency, which does not have any experience in online selling

Analysis can continue to find the root cause of a problem; for example, the root cause of the previous example might be analysed further to highlight HR problems of not hiring staff competent to achieve organisational aims. This would not necessarily be very helpful when trying to design risk treatment options for the future; however, it would be necessary to identify and treat poor hiring practices.

The RCA technique was developed further to help identify reasons why a particular risk event had the ultimate effect it did. The following example shows how the RCA technique has been further developed.

Incident	Product sells poorly online
Direct effect	Poor sales figures for the year
Indirect effect	Negative impact on profitability
Indirect effect	No bonuses paid due to poor profitability
Indirect effect	Several key personnel decide to leave the organisation

This type of analysis may at least lead to identifying the need to minimise the fall-out from poor product sales by ceasing the advertising and production campaigns earlier to minimise the effect on profitability.

When identifying risk treatment options, it is essential that the true cause of an identified risk is being treated. RCA is a useful tool for identifying true causes; however, the organisation must be prepared to accept that root causes can sometimes be cultural or can, in fact, lead all the way back to the senior management of the organisation and their approach to certain aspects of the business. In the above example, the organisation may not have been able to source appropriately skilled people to manage the new product launch because of a hiring freeze.

Butterfly Approach

Some organisations find it difficult to explain the RCA to risk owners and may use another technique, a simplified version known as the butterfly approach.

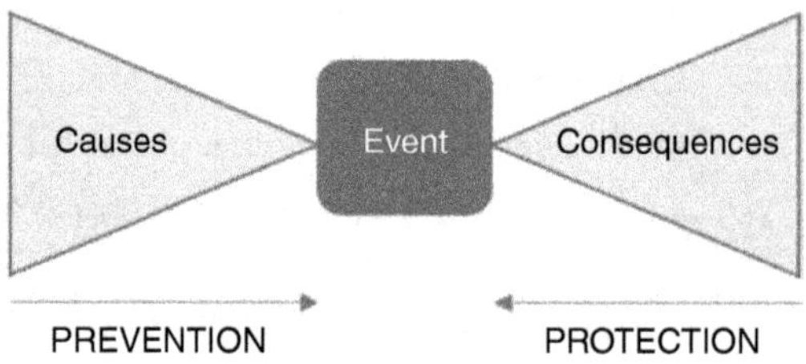

The Butterfly Approach

This traditional version does not take into account the level of control the organisation may have over the risk exposures depending on where the causes originate, and where the consequences are experienced.

The revised version below considers:

- internal causes and consequences that the organisation can control to the best of its abilities and therefore choose the risk treatment that best suits its needs;
- causes and consequences that originate with or are experienced by the partners (upstream: suppliers, providers, subcontractors; or downstream: customers, society, etc.) over which the organisation has limited control, mostly through joint brainstorming and contractual arrangements;
- causes and consequences that originate with or are experienced by the environment (society, external stakeholders, consumers, etc.) over which the organisation has little or no control other than communication or lobbying, and event management.

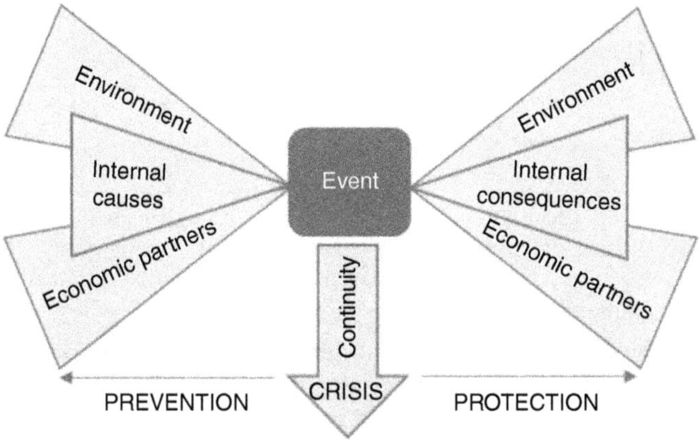

The Revised Butterfly Approach. *Source*: Prof Jean-Paul Louisot.

The Effects of Risk Treatments

Creative thinking and RCA techniques are both valuable in identifying and designing risk treatment options. In addition to designing a treatment that will be effective, a risk manager also needs to be aware of the potential for unintended effects on the organisation as a result of its implementation. The potential effect on organisational culture from banning smoking in a warehouse has been previously explored. Two other examples are:

- effect on staff morale from cost cutting;
- effect on staff morale from acquiring a company with new technology.

Cost cutting is a risk treatment if the company is not performing financially; however, staff may be adversely affected during its implementation. Similarly, if an organisation acquires new technology, employees may see this as a threat to their positions and be intimidated rather than seeing the opportunities. The potential effect of a risk treatment should be identified, and strategies included in the risk treatment plan to manage it. In a situation where the risk treatment may demoralise staff, an additional treatment will be required to manage that risk.

These two examples demonstrate why it is necessary to consider the potential broader effects of risk treatment. When designing risk treatments, the potential for new risks being created needs to be considered and creative thinking techniques can assist in identifying and solving these risk problems.

Self-Help Question 2.1

Consider each of the following proposed treatments and list some of the challenges you can see in implementing them.

	Risk	Treatment
1	Incompetent project management	Train personnel in project management
2	Insufficient workplace planning	Introduce individual performance agreements with annual work plan objectives and major tasks

Answers to self-help questions are provided at the end of each section.

Principles of Risk Allocation

Principles of risk allocation cover two areas:

- Allocation – risk must be someone's responsibility;
- Principles – how organisations develop an allocation process.

Allocation

Monitoring and reviewing is part of the risk management process in ISO 31000:2018 because it is often necessary to remind people of their responsibilities to manage specific risks and because risks may change over time. Day-to-day responsibilities of staff may prevent them from considering or being prepared for events that may happen in the future. Monitoring and reviewing the risk management process highlights risks that need attention even if they seem unlikely or remote.

Another reason for allocating risk to specific staff, or risk-owners, is to guarantee there is a person responsible for managing the risk before and after the event and how much of the responsibility is shared. A typical example of risk allocation is an insurance policy. In its simplest form, an insurance policy is a contract between the insured and the insurer stating that the insurer is responsible for the financial consequences of a risk event occurring. For taking on this risk the insurer is paid a premium by the insured.

However, insurers have long been in the business of managing risk and they allocate some risk back to the insured; hence the overall risk is shared. A typical example is in a standard property insurance policy where, as a condition of insurance, the insured must keep their property well maintained due to an insurer not wanting to repair a property damaged because of lack of maintenance. Insurance is for unexpected events.

Principles

Beyond internal allocation, there is also risk allocation between partner organisations. The principles or the science behind allocating risk have entered mainstream risk management through the use of commercial contracts. A commercial contract is a legal agreement between two or more parties, generally where one party seeks goods and services and the other provides them. Principles concerning risk allocation were developed in high-risk contract areas; for example, in the construction industry such as in contracts between the developer and builder for the construction of a high-rise apartment building, or in defence procurement in contracts between the Department of Defence and a ship manufacturer for the construction of a naval frigate. In high-risk projects, the more clearly risks are allocated, the better they are managed. Also, when risks have been allocated according to clearly defined principles, it is less likely that contracts will attract legal battles over which party should bear the consequences.

Note: In some instances, there is a binding responsibility that cannot be modified by contractual clauses and any attempt to contract out of it would be deemed null and void. An example of this is decennial liability in France, which requires every building contract to be insured and cannot be waived.

There are no universally accepted principles of risk allocation, but the following can be used as a guide.

- Risk versus reward – risk is related to reward and in allocating risk between parties, there should be equal reward. The new owner of the risk should be able to gain substantial benefits if the risk is managed well. If the 'risk versus reward' equation is unbalanced, the owner of the risk may suffer unexpected losses or may choose to take a chance and not manage the risk appropriately as the owner perceives no benefit to themselves. An example of risk balanced with reward is when an insurance company charges a premium that it believes is an equal reward for the financial risk it takes on.
- Capability – the party allocated a risk should be in the best position to manage the risk. The party should be able to retain, transfer or modify the risk. For example, there is no point in allocating the risk of breaching copyright to a bookseller when the author and editor/publisher have control over the content of the book.
- Capacity – if a risk event occurs, the party allocated that risk must have the capacity to bear the consequences of the risk. For example, if the consequences are financial, they must have the ability to meet the cost, either from existing resources or from an appropriate insurance policy or other risk financing arrangement.

- Clarity/transparency – it is essential that all parties entering into a contract where risk is involved understand the risks and each other's objectives in managing risks allocated to them. Without this clarity, it is likely that the risk allocation will be flawed, and the following adverse outcomes may occur.

  - By allocating a risk to a party the 'risk versus reward' equation is not balanced and the person transferring the risk (the transferor) is overcharged or undercharged. Being overcharged is financially damaging but being undercharged can be potentially more damaging. For example, the party accepting the risk (the transferee) may not be able to manage the risk because they do not have sufficient funds and look to find shortcuts that may lead to failure to manage the risk adequately.
  - A party may ignorantly pass on a risk that would be more appropriately managed by them. For example, it would be more rewarding for the government to manage the media in relation to announcing the opening of a new bridge than it would be for the construction contractor. The reward for the contractor is the profit from successfully building the bridge and the prestige of being associated with the bridge at the time of the opening. Using the media, the government can promote how they wisely spend money on infrastructure development to benefit the public. Ultimately, risk managers need to think about risk allocation in terms of which party has the most vested interests in ensuring the successful management of a risk.
  - A party may underestimate a risk that they later find out they do not have the capability or capacity to manage. Using the previous example of opening a bridge, a contractor may believe that there are low risks involved in opening a bridge. However, there may be political or environmental sensitivity over the opening that incites protest and increases the amount of risk the contractor faces.

Implications for Categories of Risk Treatment

The principles of risk allocation evolved out of the commercial contracting arena where the risk treatment of risk sharing is defined between the principal to a contract and the contractor. The principles do however have application to the other categories of risk treatments of seeking, avoiding, modifying, transferring and retaining.

- Avoiding – in avoiding risk, the principles of risk allocation do not apply, except that the risk that the decision may be seen to be a bad one will remain with the decision-makers.
- Transferring – When seeking out an opportunity, the principles of risk allocation apply. When assigning a person or organisation to manage the opportunity, it should be ensured that:

  - there is a balanced 'risk versus reward' equation
  - there is the capability or skill required to manage it

  - there is access to sufficient resources (capacity) to realise the opportunity
  - the assignee has similar perceptions to senior management regarding the 'risk versus reward' equation for the organisation and has clear goals and objectives.

- Modifying – when modifying a risk, the same issues apply as for seeking an opportunity. The risk must be allocated to someone to manage and they must meet the principles of 'risk versus reward', capability, capacity and clarity.
- Retaining – when an organisation chooses to retain risk it is allocating risk as it is to itself. As the risk continues to exist, there is a need to monitor and review it against the risk appetite of the organisation. When assigning a person to be responsible for the retained risk, the principles of risk allocation apply. The person responsible must have the knowledge, skills, the authority and potential for reward for the risk to be successfully retained.

Methods of Allocating Risk

Risk may be allocated, or transferred, through insurance policies and common law contracts. Both of these types of contracts define which risks are owned by which party and to what extent. There are several methods used for allocating risk that can be internal or external to a contract. However, a distinction must be made between two types of risk allocating to third parties: for risk financing like an insurance policy, or risk reduction like subcontracting.

Risk managers need to be aware of these methods, how they work and any implications that may be attached to them. Some examples are given below.

- Indemnities – an indemnity is the obligation of one party to reimburse another party for losses that have occurred. The most common method of risk allocation is an indemnity. Most contracts will have an indemnification clause where the principal will seek to ensure the contractor indemnifies them for any loss the principal incurs because of the contractor's negligence in performing its duties under the contract. The risk of contractor negligence is clearly assigned to the contractor.

  There are many variations on the wordings of indemnity clauses. Some are onerous on the contractor and others are clearly restricted to negligence of the contractor. For inexperienced contract negotiators, legal advice on the implications of indemnity clauses is necessary to ensure clarity of risk allocation.
- Warranties – a warranty is where one party confirms to another party the way in which particular goods or services should be expected to perform once purchased. In some cases, one party to a contract requires the other party to express certain warranties so that they can be held liable if certain outcomes are not achieved. For example, when one organisation buys another organisation, it is common for the purchaser to require the seller to warrant that the financial statements provided are true and proper.
- Limitation of liability – limitation of liability means that the amount of risk a contractor or organisation is exposed to under a specific obligation is limited.

Most indemnities in a contract are open-ended in that if a claim on the indemnity is made, the indemnified party can keep claiming for any loss up to the ability to pay of the party who granted the indemnity, including any available insurance. Understandably, the party who grants indemnity may seek to limit its liability.

When seeking to limit liability, it is common for the wording of the limitation clause to include, 'to the extent permitted by law'. Interpreting this wording precisely is outside the scope of this module; it is sufficient to be aware that there may be laws that override the clause, depending on circumstances. For example, in Australia, the *Trade Practices Act 1974* seeks to protect consumers from organisations trying to contract out of their responsibilities to provide a product that works as advertised. Another common method of limiting liability is for the wording of the limitation clause to include 'to the limit of insurance cover'. For inexperienced contract negotiators, legal advice on the implications of a limitation of liability clause should be sought to ensure clarity of risk allocation.

All member countries of the European Union must transpose into national legislation all the European directives. Several are linked to consumer protection and the management of financial markets, notably the Solvency II directive for insurers, and the new directive on the protection of personal data. These directives restrain the limitation of liability that organisations marketing goods and service to consumers may insert in their contracts.

- Letters of comfort – according to the Australian Department of Financing and Administration (DOFA), a 'letter of comfort is essentially an instrument that is used to facilitate an action or transaction but is constructed with the intention of not giving rise to a legal obligation' (Financial Management Guidance No. 6, 2003). A letter of comfort documents intent, and this intention may be to manage or bear the consequences of a particular risk event. Although not intended to be legally binding, letters of comfort create moral obligations for the parent companies. Letters of comfort are a legal practice in most countries and in international contracts.

Case Study – Pages and Pages Publishing

Pages and Pages Publishing is negotiating a contract with an author to prepare an unauthorised biography of a prominent European. The publisher has identified the following risks and opportunities.

- Defamation – the risk that the prominent European may claim defamation and seek damages through the courts.
- Breach of copyright – the risk that some part of the book is found not to be original as the author may plagiarise work to save themselves time and effort.

- Ethical misconduct – the risk that the public sees the book as overstepping the bounds of human decency. For example, there may be concerns about invasion of privacy.
- Marketing – the risk that sales and, hence, profit or loss, will be affected by the quality of the book's marketing.
- Distribution – the more prominently the book is located on shelves in major book stores, the higher the sales. There is an opportunity to increase sales by convincing major book stores to display the book prominently.
- Additional books – the opportunity that, if the book is a success, there will be a demand for a sequel to the biography or additional books on different topics by the same author.

The publisher and the author agreed the following allocation of these risks.

- Defamation – the publisher decided to allocate this risk primarily to itself because it has the financial capacity to fund a legal review of the book, the source material and to defend any defamation case brought against it. However, Pages and Pages did not want to assume all the risk and did not grant an indemnity to the author. An indemnity would have protected the author from any damages awarded against Pages and Pages from a successful defamation case. This will help ensure the author is responsible with the information he uses and will not intentionally make false or misleading statements to increase the sensational appeal of the book.
- Breach of copyright – this risk was allocated to the author and a warranty was requested from the author stating that all of the work was his own. It would be impossible for a publisher to know all the sources of material written about the subject of a book, which makes them unable to check for plagiarism.
- Ethical misconduct – Pages and Pages assumed this risk. The publisher utilises an ethics committee of external authors, journalists, academics and other people of note to advise them on the ethics of a book. The damage to the publisher's reputation over one book is not worth the potential gain in revenue from a sensationist publication.
- Marketing – Pages and Pages assumed this risk as marketing is part of its core business. However, the contract required the author to attend a book launch and a number of books signing sessions to promote the book in book stores. Distribution – Pages and Pages assumed this risk as it is part of its core business to have and manage distribution relationships.
- Additional books – no one can predict the success of a book so it can be hard to decide whether to contract authors for more books before the release of their first. In this case, the author and publisher entered into a contract for revenue sharing of future books. This was reasonably favourable to the author but locked out other publishers.

The case study shows how the principles of risk allocation apply in enterprises of a different kind from the high-risk high-reward arenas of major infrastructure projects and major defence supply contracts.

Although sources of guidance such as ISO 31000:2018 do not explicitly define the process of risk allocation, there is sufficient literature on the subject to support risk allocation as having a set of principles. This section of the module has demonstrated how principles of risk allocation are applicable in broad and mainstream commercial contracting.

Self-Help Question 2.2

Consider the employment agreement between a long-distance truck driver and their employer.

What are the key risks in long distance truck driving and how should they be allocated between the driver and the employer?

Answers to self-help questions are provided at the end of each section.

Cost-Benefit Analysis

CBA is the analysis of the potential costs and benefits of a project to allow fair comparison of the returns from alternative forms of investment. CBA is a key step in the evaluation phase of the risk treatment process and involves a risk analyst assessing whether all of the benefits that may or will flow from a particular risk treatment initiative will exceed the cost of implementation.

CBA is sometimes referred to as benefit-cost analysis because the ratio for determining whether a particular activity is cost-effective or not is obtained by dividing the total of all benefits by the total of all costs (b/c). When the ratio is greater than 1.0, the benefits outweigh the costs. For example, if the dollar savings (the benefits) of implementing a new way of producing widgets is €200 and the cost of implementing the new way of producing is €100 then the ratio b/c is 200/100, which is 2.0 or 2:1

CBA evolved as a means to assess the worth of a particular activity; for example, a project to develop a new highway. In building a road for the community, many issues need to be taken into account and some issues may conflict with each other. For example:

- People wishing to travel on the highway want to travel the most direct route at maximum speed.
- Local residents prefer the highway to be as far from their houses as possible and do not want it to interfere with their access to local shops and recreational areas or access to other roadways.

- Environmental groups want the highway to have zero or minimal effect on the local environment.

In determining whether or not a highway should be built, how it should be built and the size and route it should take, not everyone's wishes can be taken into account. Decision-makers would introduce CBA to help consider all options. Options may range from not building the road to suit local residents to building the best road for road users. An organisation's decision-makers would consider which option provides the greatest net benefit to their stakeholders. It is a challenging task because determining which benefit is greatest – access for residents to amenities, protection of the local environment or shorter travel time for road users – is not easily done.

Costs and benefits tend to be closely related. Although it costs money to train managers, this cost is likely to be offset as managers will then be able to more effectively assess the risks involved, which means delays and budget overruns can be avoided.

A complication in CBA is that analysts are considering the future. All organisations face uncertainty regarding future costs and benefits. Even though organisations consider the implementation of a risk treatment, there is the risk that assumptions are incorrect, and the benefits do not outweigh the costs.

Just as an analyst applies likelihood in a risk assessment, it is necessary to consider the likelihood for the costs and benefits in a CBA. For example, we may list as a benefit for a risk treatment that it creates an opportunity to increase sales in a new market segment. In assessing various risk treatment options using CBA, it is necessary to consider whether the potential new opportunity has a low, medium or high likelihood of materialising. This may be based on our ability to implement a risk treatment or it may be based on incomplete knowledge of how the target market may respond once the treatment is implemented.

The CBA Process

There is no universally accepted CBA process; however, for the purpose of evaluating a risk treatment initiative, the process will generally include the following steps.

1. Establish the context. State the risk criteria against which costs and benefits will be assessed.
2. Define the treatment and any options to be considered. Try to ensure all viable options are included.
3. Gather data about costs and benefits. This requires collation and analysis of both direct and indirect costs. There may be incremental costs and benefits connected to a risk treatment; for example, the cost of phone calls to improve relationships with suppliers. Collectively, all the indirect costs and benefits can be significant; however, usually at least 80% of costs or benefits will be associated with direct costs and benefits.
4. Express the cost and benefit data in a standard and measurable way; for example, relate all data back to the financial cost.

5. Calculate the benefit-cost ratio. This means adding up the costs and benefits and dividing the sum of the benefits by the sum of the costs. This will show whether a benefit is worth the cost to the organisation.
6. Sensitivity analysis. This is the process of varying the parameters in a given model to assess the level of change in its output. A sensitivity analysis is conducted to determine which elements (usually referred to as variables) of the cost-benefit equation appear to have the most influence on the ratio. Having this detailed information about the value of variables reduces uncertainty and clarifies actions to be taken during implementation to limit uncertainty; for example, negotiating a labour rate to contain the cost of labour.
7. Consider likelihood. Analyse the risks underlying the analysis by considering the probabilities of the various outcomes on the cost and benefit sides of the equation. For CBA with a high degree of numeric data, consider using statistical simulation techniques such as 'Monte Carlo' to determine the expected outcome.
8. Include qualitative factors. Consider all of the qualitative factors that could not be expressed in dollars. Qualitative factors are observations that do not involve measurements or numbers.
9. Weigh up options. Decide on an option and document the decision. Documentation is essential to explain the decision in the future as well as to allow later analysis of decisions to test the accuracy of research and assumptions.
10. The extent to which each step in this process is followed is determined by the scale of the risk treatment initiative and its importance in managing risk and opportunity to enable an organisation to achieve its objectives.

Key Issues in CBA

A risk analyst must consider a number of issues to ensure results of a CBA are legitimate and appropriately interpreted. The key issues are as follows:

- **Intangible costs and benefits** – tangible costs and benefits are those easily identified and quantified; for example, decreasing or increasing the amount of cash in the bank or profit for the year. The intangibles are less easy to define and may include benefits or costs accruing to reputation, workforce morale or the perception of the media regarding management competency.

  How an analyst deals with intangibles may determine the success of the risk treatment implementation. Step 8 of the CBA process, weighing up options, including qualitative factors, is how intangibles are considered.
- **Rating intangibles** – one option for dealing with intangibles is to develop risk criteria for them and to rate them alongside tangible criteria. An example is a risk treatment that reduces the risk to the environment from 'Localised and medium-term impact' to 'Localised and short-term impact' that also reduces the risk of profit reduction in monetary terms.

This method is particularly valuable for comparing options that have significant non-financial benefits and costs. For example, a risk analyst can give each of the intangibles an average dollar cost and/or benefit and then sum all the costs and benefits to provide an overall assessment for each option.

- **Quantifying the unquantifiable** – more effort is required to quantify intangible costs and benefits than those that are tangible; for example, when an initiative is going to cost a large sum of money but may save lives, how is it possible to quantify the benefit of saving one or many lives? It is easy for a stakeholder to say that human life has immeasurable value; however, as public servants and economists have had to recognise, it is impossible to fund every project that promises to save human life and that some rational basis is needed upon which to select what projects are approved and what projects are turned down.

  People do voluntarily accept increased risks in return for higher pay; for example, in mining and construction. High-risk choices that lead to financial gain can be used as examples to calculate the value of reduced risk; for example, an unskilled worker in a low-risk office environment may be paid significantly less than a similarly skilled worker in a high-risk occupation. The difference between the two salaries is the value of reduced risk.
- **Interpreting benefit-cost ratio** – if a benefit-cost ratio is greater than 1.0, the benefits outweigh the costs; however, interpreting benefit-cost ratios strictly on the numeric outcome is not wise, given the potential for inaccuracies in the CBA and peoples' perception of risk. For example, a risk treatment to reduce injury to workers may be given the benefit-cost ratio of 0.9, but this does not mean that government authorities believe the employer provides a safe place of work. Government authorities are looking for risk to be reduced as low as is reasonably practicable and this can be difficult for organisations to interpret. Risk analysts and managers should consider all intangible costs and benefits when interpreting BCA results.

When considering the results of a CBA, management needs to:

- carefully interpret the results;
- consider the likely accuracy of the construction of the CBA and the accuracy of the key components;
- consider how their decision may be perceived by key stakeholders after the event, because they judge management with the benefit of hindsight.

It is also important to remember that an approach based on expected costs and expected benefits may not be enough. Like in any risk-management decision, there is a need to take into account the comparative volatility of various decisions. A post-optimal analysis like a stress test or a value at risk analysis could be conducted to complement the CBA.

Case Study – Glamour Financial

In Section 2, the case study about Glamour Financial introduced you to a prestigious investment banking group that prides itself on hiring top executives and rewarding achievement with lavish social events.

Glamour Financial was considering the risk of sexual harassment, employee injury and third-party injuries at staff Christmas parties. These parties are exclusively for 500 staff and no customers or spouses are invited.

The parties supply spectacular entertainment, outstanding cuisine and plentiful alcoholic and non-alcoholic beverages.

The Group Risk Manager highlighted for senior management the following options as risk treatments for the legal liability risk to the organisation and its directors and officers:

- allow the parties to remain as they are – base option;
- cancel the party;
- restrict the availability of alcohol – serve only light beer and do not serve beer or wine during entertainment;
- invite spouses to the party on the basis that spouses will have a sobering influence on staff;
- reduce the duration and entertainment of the party to moderate the party atmosphere, but still thank staff for their efforts.

Earlier in the case study, the Group Risk Manager conducted a CBA and listed the positives and negatives of the options. Organisational executives chose their preferred option. Now consider a more analytical CBA.

In the following pages, we develop a more sophisticated CBA for risk treatments for Glamour Financial's Christmas parties. The main aim of this strategy is to demonstrate the effect indirect costs, benefits and intangible items can have on a CBA.

The direct monetary cost of the Christmas party is the amount of money paid by the organisation to hold the party. These costs include the venue, food, beverages, entertainment and any transport provided for staff. Direct monetary benefits are the reduction in legal liability risk to the organisation its directors and officers, which is the reason risk treatments are being considered.

The following table shows the direct monetary costs and benefits of the proposed risk treatment to Glamour Financial. There is a need to document the information behind the monetary amounts. This will allow senior management to understand the assumptions made by analysts in building the CBA and assist them in their interpretation of the results.

Direct Monetary Costs and Benefits

Option	Costs	Benefits
Base option	€0 – there are no additional costs to the organisation and the expected cost of the liability remains the same	€0 – there is no reduction in the expected cost of legal liability
Cancel party	−€250,000: cancelling the party has saved on direct costs	€100,000 – i.e. the expected legal liability cost p.a. based on one €1,000,000 payout every 10 years
Restrict alcohol	€25,000 – a savings on the drinks bill	€50,000 – i.e. the likelihood of an event is halved to 1 in 20 years with the same €1,000,000 consequence
Invite spouses	€150,000 – the extra cost of feeding spouses and hiring a larger venue with lower alcohol consumption per head	€80,000 – the likelihood of an event has reduced to 1 in 50 years with the same €1 million consequence giving an expected cost of risk of €20,000, which is an €80,000 reduction from the original cost
Reduce scale	−€200,000 – e.g. if the party was changed to a one-hour 'thank you' with finger food provided	€90,000 – the likelihood of an event has reduced to 1 in 100 years with the same €1,000,000 consequence giving an expected cost of risk of €10,000, which is a €90,000 reduction from the original cost

As you can see from the above table, a straight direct Euro CBA is potentially flawed. In this case, many of the 'costs' are actually savings; therefore a CBA cannot properly be applied. If there are no costs, only savings, the option with the highest savings (highest benefits) should be implemented. This does not require the calculation of a benefit-cost ratio.

The option with the greatest benefit is 'Cancel party', which would result in a saving of €350,000. However, to cancel the party would be very unpopular with staff. Risk managers need to consider the indirect and intangible costs and benefits of risk treatments before implementing a risk treatment.

CBA – Indirect and Intangible Costs and Benefits

Once the monetary costs and benefits are established, a risk manager will list the indirect costs and benefits and the intangible costs and benefits. In the case study, the risk manager identified:

- the effect on staff morale;
- the effect on corporate image as the parties were talked about and written about in the industry media.

Other indirect and intangible items include:

- staff productivity the day of and the day after the party;
- management time to organise the party;
- the effect on staff turnover due to increased/decreased admiration for the company;
- the effect on productivity due to the increase or decrease in staff morale;
- health impact on staff – e.g. alcohol abuse.

In the next step of the CBA process, all options should be weighed up by introducing all of the qualitative factors that could not be quantified. A good start in this process is to decide what could be reasonably easily quantified from the previous list.

Easier-to-Quantify Risks

Easier-to-Quantify	Comments
Staff productivity on the day of and the day after the party	Based on past experience, estimate the % hours lost per person because of being distracted from work while discussing and/or preparing for the party
Management time to organise	Allocate an hourly rate and estimate hours to organise the party based on past experience
Effect on staff turnover	HR may well have a Euro cost estimate for staff turnover. Based on this number, estimate the likely increase or decrease in staff turnover

'Difficult to quantify' Risks

More Difficult to Quantify	Comments
Staff morale and the consequent shift in productivity	Would need to have measured staff morale over a period and simultaneously monitored productivity. Would need to take into account impacts on productivity unrelated to morale, such as process improvements
Corporate image and the effect on profit from the ability, or not, to attract good staff or charge clients' high prices	Would need to have measured corporate image over a period and simultaneously monitored profit. Would need to take into account impacts on profit unrelated to image, such as the entry or exit of a competitor from the industry
Health effects on staff	Not being health researchers, this information would not be easily available although some research may well have been conducted that could be used

In the original case for Glamour Financial, it was sound judgement to include intangibles; however, it would have been preferable to build a more advanced CBA. In order to do so, the first thing a risk analyst would need to decide is which of all the listed items are worthwhile including in the analysis, and which items would only have a negligible or incremental effect. For example, an analyst might decide the following:

- The effect of staff productivity on the day of and the day after the party is insignificant compared to the effect on productivity throughout the year because of decreased staff morale.
- Management time spent in organising the party is insignificant when compared to the overall costs and benefits of the party.
- The health effect on staff is likely to be minimal as heavy drinking will be prevented causing no long-term damage to staff.

If this type of analysis was accepted by management, it reduces the number of variables that need to be included in the CBA.

A typical method of including these additional costs and benefits in the CBA is to apply monetary ranges to high, medium and low levels of effect. The following table demonstrates this.

Applying Monetary Amounts in a CBA

Rating	Staff Turnover (€50,000 Cost Per Person)	Annual Productivity (€50 Million Payroll)	Corporate Image (€20 Million Profit)
High	5% change = €1.5 million	10% change = €5 million	10% change = €2 million
Medium	3% change = €750,000	5% change = €2.5 million	5% change = €1 million
Low	1% change = €250,000	1% change = €500,000	1% change = €200,000

In the case of Glamour Financial, the net effect of the indirect and intangible costs and benefits on the various options are presented in the following table.

Net Effect of Indirect and Intangible Costs and Benefits

Option	Staff Turnover	Annual Productivity	Corporate Image	Net Cost
Base option	No change	No change	No change	€0
Cancel party	Negative high	Negative high	Negative low	€1.5m + €5m + €200,000 = €6.7m
Restrict alcohol	Negative low	Negative low	No change	€250,000 + €500,000 = €750,000
Invite spouses	Positive medium	No change	Positive low	(−€750,000) + (−€200,000) = –€950k
Reduce scale	Negative low	No change	Negative low	€250,000 + €200,000 = €450,000

Now that the tangible and intangible costs have been quantified, the CBA, including calculation of a benefit-cost ratio, can go ahead.

This analysis shows that the only option with a benefit-cost ratio greater than 1.0 is the option to invite spouses. This is dependent on assumptions about inviting spouses being correct. It would be appropriate at this stage to conduct a sensitivity analysis to decide which assumptions most influence the results. It is also necessary to decide whether assumptions made are correct or whether more research and analysis needs to be undertaken to come to a conclusion. The assumptions include the expected cost of legal liability per annum and the effect decisions will have on the three key indirect or intangible items.

A Typical CBA Analysis

Option	Costs	Benefits	Benefit-Cost Ratio
Base option	€0 – there are no additional costs to the organisation and the expected cost of legal liability remains the same	€0 – there is no reduction in the expected cost of legal liability	0/0 = 0
Cancel party	−€250,000 + €6.7m (intangibles) = €6.45m	€100,000 – i.e. the expected legal liability cost per year based on one €1mpayout every 10 years	€100,000/ €6.45m = 0.02
Restrict alcohol	−€25,000 + €750,000 (intangibles) = €725,000	€50,000 – i.e. the likelihood of an event has halved to 1 in 20 years with the same €1m consequence	€50,000/ €725,000 =0.07
Invite spouses	€150,000	€80,000 (the change in legal liability) + €950,000 (improved staff turnover and corporate image) = €1.03m	€1.03m/€150,000 = 6.9
Reduce scale	−€200,000 + €450,000 (intangibles) = €250,000	€90,000 – the likelihood of an event has reduced to 1 in 100 years with the same €1m consequence	€90,000/€250,000 = 0.36

Summary

Please keep the following points from this chapter in mind:

- Identifying and designing risk treatments is a key step in the risk treatment process and occurs after risks have been collated, reviewed in the context of the risk appetite of the organisation, and possibly ranked. Risks that are unacceptably high are targeted for risk treatments.
- Categorising risk treatments is the first step in providing developing a range of risk treatment options.

- In order to assist in the risk treatment process, risk managers have utilised a range of tools and techniques to assist in considering complex problems.
- When identifying risk treatment options, there is a range of creative thinking techniques that can be used to 'think outside the box' to help design effective solutions, including, but not limited to:
  - Brainstorming
  - Random word
  - Challenge facts
  - Scenario analysis
- Another technique used in the risk management industry to assist with identifying and designing treatment options is RCA.
- In addition to designing a treatment that will be effective, a risk manager also needs to be aware of the potential for unintended effects on the organisation as a result of its implementation.
- When designing risk treatments, the potential for new risks being created needs to be considered and creative thinking techniques can assist in identifying and solving these risk problems.
- Principles of risk allocation cover two areas:
  - Allocation – risk must be someone's responsibility
  - Principles – how organisations develop an allocation process.
- Risk is allocated, or transferred, in insurance policies and common law contracts. Both of these types of contracts define which risks are owned by which party and to what extent.
- CBA is the analysis of the potential costs and benefits of a project to allow comparison of the returns from alternative forms of investment. It evolved as a means to assess the worth of a particular activity.
- CBA is sometimes referred to as benefit-cost analysis because the ratio for determining whether a particular activity is cost-effective or not is the division of the total of all benefits by the total of all costs (b/c). When the ratio is greater than 1.0, the benefits outweigh the costs.
- Once the monetary costs and benefits are established, a risk manager will list the indirect costs and benefits and the intangible costs and benefits.
- When contrasting costs and benefits after a CBA analysis, it is useful to conduct a post-optimisation analysis or stress test to assess the impact of the volatility of the various alternatives.

Answers to Self-Help Questions

Self-help question 2.1

1. Challenges:

    - time involved for attendees, which may affect their work schedules. The benefits of training would need to be conveyed to the attendees
    - designing the right training program for the organisation – different programs may suit different types of organisations
    - ensuring the training matches organisational goals and objectives – in particular, for risk management. The risk criteria and risk assessment tools need to be consistent with organisational guidelines.

2. Challenges:

    - employee concern about the effect of performance agreements on job security
    - employee concern about the effect on promotion, pay raises and bonuses
    - potential for agreements to be perceived as inflexible and not explicitly allowing for change of work plans to suit the changing work environment over the year
    - potential for organisation to become outcome focused, which can lead to the introduction of unsatisfactory processes that are justified by stating that the ends justify the means.

Self-help question 2.2

- **On-time delivery** – risk should be shared between the driver and the company. The company should agree to reasonable timeframes for delivery that do not require speeding; allow for appropriate rest breaks; account for traffic in major centres and waiting times at freight pick-up points. Drivers should agree to drive a certain number of hours per day.
- **Occupational health and safety** – this is a responsibility that the employer cannot allocate to the driver; but the driver also has a responsibility to operate in a safe manner.
- **Road safety** – in order to help maintain a safe workplace, the company should instruct the driver to obey all traffic laws and regulations as well as assist with driver training programs where appropriate. Drivers should remain responsible for their actions.
- **Safe vehicle** – the employer should allocate maintenance of the truck to themselves and require drivers to carry out regular pre-trip vehicle inspections and notify them of any maintenance issues.
- **Cost of delivery** – a major cost of delivery will be petrol consumption. This risk is outside the control of the employer once the vehicle is maintained. The employer could set petrol consumption targets and monitor driver performance, which may have an effect on fuel consumption.

Chapter 3

Risk Control/Reduction Techniques

Introduction

As the previous chapter suggested, there are numerous different types of risk treatment strategies, and all serve a particular purpose. Not all categories of risk treatments are appropriate for all risks, and it is important to understand the distinctions between them.

Risk control is a category of risk treatment that involves trying to change the nature of the risk exposure itself to reduce threats as much as possible and maximise opportunities for the organisation. Risk reduction involves reducing the threat.

This chapter will discuss certain risk control and reduction treatments in more detail.

Learning Outcomes

By the end of this chapter, you should be able to:

- evaluate which risk control or reduction technique is appropriate;
- understand the differences between techniques;
- determine whether avoidance is practical;
- consider the risks an organisation could be exposed to if it chooses to avoid risk altogether;
- apply diversification, segregation and duplication techniques.

Risk Avoidance/Suppression

Risk avoidance/suppression is a treatment strategy based on a conscious and informed decision to avoid exposure to a particular risk and its likely effects. Risk avoidance eliminates any possibility of an event occurring by either abandoning or not undertaking an activity because the risk exposure is considered excessive.

Risk Treatment, 53–68

Published under exclusive licence by Emerald Publishing Limited
doi:10.1108/978-1-83662-306-920251006

Avoidance may be the most appropriate technique when the costs and potential outcomes associated with accepting the risk exposure are significantly higher than the associated benefits. Avoidance is the term used when a project is rejected; when it comes to stopping an existing activity, it can be called suppression.

EXAMPLE

Manufacturing

A manufacturer could decide that the potential cost of product liability claims arising from a proposed product will be so high that it would not be economical to produce the product.

The decision to avoid an exposure to risk must, at times, be considered in contrast to losing an opportunity for organisational or market growth and market visibility.

EXAMPLE

Balancing Threats and Opportunities

A manufacturer could decide that the threats associated with building a new factory are less than the risk of missing out on the opportunity to expand.

Legislation and Codes

In most countries, government legislation and industry practice codes have made risk avoidance compulsory for some specific dangerous activities, meaning some activities are forbidden or very strictly regulated. The risk management process aims to comply with legislation and industry codes related to risk avoidance/suppression.

EXAMPLE

Dangerous Goods Transport and Storage

Some chemicals (for example, highly corrosive or toxic substances) cannot be transported in tunnels or highly populated areas.

Limitations

While avoidance can eliminate the likelihood of a loss by reducing its probability to zero, there are certain limitations and certain instances where it is not practical:

- avoidance may not be possible;
- avoidance may not be feasible;
- avoidance may not be desirable;
- avoiding one exposure may create another.

Avoidance May Not Be Possible

While everyone seeks to avoid sickness, it cannot be avoided completely; there is no such thing as a completely safe environment.

Avoidance May Not Be Feasible

While it may be possible to avoid some risk exposures – for example, ownership of buildings – it is not feasible to avoid all exposures associated with the occupation of buildings as this would effectively prevent most organisations from operating.

Avoidance May Not Be Desirable

Risk avoidance may be undesirable because of the inherent connection between risk and reward: organisations must take risks if they wish to continue functioning; this is particularly true of speculative risks as illustrated below.

While it may be possible to avoid a specific risk exposure, doing so may cause the organisation to sacrifice a great opportunity or market advantage (for example, a new product development program).

Pursuing opportunities is risky as it usually requires significant investment with no guarantee of success. Organisations take these risks because competitors may threaten their existence and profitability if they remain stagnant. A good example of this is the introduction of a new product.

EXAMPLE

Manufacturing

Organisations cannot avoid the risk of product failure by ceasing to manufacture products. In this case, the organisation must select other options which reduce the risk of product failure such as:

- production line quality control;
- additional design testing controls.

Risk Avoidance May Create Another Risk Exposure

Any substitute method an organisation chooses to avoid risk exposure may involve a new set of risk exposures. The organisation needs to carefully compare this substitute method to the original method to establish whether it increases or decreases the risk exposures they are aiming to avoid.

EXAMPLE

Subcontracting Delivery Services

If an organisation chooses to avoid the risk exposures associated with using its own vehicles to deliver its goods, the organisation must use other methods of delivery, for example, subcontracting to a delivery company.

By subcontracting delivery services, the organisation needs to manage the risk of supplier failure and/or poor performance.

Case study – Pages and Pages Publishing

The following case study provides an example of the type of cost-benefit analysis an organisation needs to undertake when deciding whether to use a risk avoidance strategy.

Timeless Tubing

Timeless Tubing manufactures tubing for a range of different industries and has recently developed a new tubing system with specific applications in the offshore oil and gas industries.

Cost-Benefit Analysis

The manufacturer's cost-benefit analysis of the innovative product begins to raise concerns about the significance of potential consequences of product failure – if the tubing were to fail, the exposure arising from lawsuits could be large enough to threaten the existence of the entire company.

Conclusions

While Timeless Tubing is confident the new tubing system is an excellent product, they decide the risks are too great and that the only alternatives are either to:

- avoid the risk and cease production of the new tubing

or

- find an alternative 'safer' market outside the oil and gas industries.

Self-Help Question 3.1

Review the following list of identified risk exposures then answer the question.

1. Which (if any) of GPG's identified risk exposures could the organisation avoid completely?

Ref	GPG's Risk Exposure	Ramifications
1	Raw materials are stored largely in one area	Leave GPG's stocks vulnerable to: • fire • water damage • other damage
2	GPG's document management system (DMS) stores master copies of clients' work	If GPG's DMS was damaged or destroyed, clients: • would not be able to access master copies of important documents • could take legal action against GPG
3	Hydraulic trolleys/forklifts transport raw materials from the storage area to the printing plant	This business process would be interrupted if the forklift/trolley is damaged or stolen
4	One single printing machine	There is a significant reliance on the single printing machine because print production cannot continue if the printer breaks down
5	Folding machinery	A breakdown of folding machinery could interrupt regular business operations
6	The collation and binding operations' reliance on key pieces of machinery	The collation and binding operations depend on key pieces of machinery that may be difficult to source/replace quickly if damaged or destroyed
7	Reliance on one particular supplier	Reliance on one particular supplier could endanger production
8	Reliance on one particular distributor	Reliance on one particular distributor could endanger distribution
9	The doorways between building one and building two are permanently open	This presents an increased level of risk if there is a fire at the premises

→

→

Ref	GPG's Risk Exposure	Ramifications
10	There is no sprinkler system in building one	The building is only protected by: • fire hose reels • extinguishers
11	GPG's premises are bounded by a river on one side	This could present a significant risk if the river is susceptible to flooding
12	LPG, oil and diesel storage tanks	The LPG, oil and diesel storage tanks present a risk of fire/explosion
13	The LPG, oil and diesel storage tanks are unfenced There is easy access to the tanks from the scrubland	This presents a significant risk to GPG if one tampers with any of the tanks
14	Staff parking their cars on the bitumen at the side of the access roadway near the main plant operations	• Creates traffic congestion • Could cause an accident which: – damages GPG's premises – results in staff/public injury
15	• An absence of gatekeepers • Gates being left open after hours	Leaves GPG vulnerable to theft
16	Miscellaneous equipment and parts: around the waste skip area inside the buildings	• Indicates poor housekeeping standards • Could cause an accident as the skip is adjacent to: – finished products – the flammable liquid store
17	The computer backup is stored onsite in a fireproof cupboard	Although the backup is stored in a fireproof cupboard, one could damage or steal the data
18	Building valuations are outdated	• Current insurances are likely to be inadequate • If a loss occurs, GPG could incur considerable costs because they are underinsured
19	The staff lunchroom is situated next to the materials storage area and the recharger facility There is evidence that staff smoke cigarettes in the lunchroom	This situation poses a significant fire hazard

→

→

Ref	GPG's Risk Exposure	Ramifications
20	There is a fireworks manufacturer situated next to GPG's premises	The adjacent fireworks manufacturer presents a significant risk in terms of fire and explosion
21	Contracts with Commonwealth Government departments	GPG may lose a significant portion of its revenue stream if it is not successful in renewing its contracts
22	Reliance on only one operator for specialty machinery such as: • printers • binders	• Reliance on only one operator could mean deadlines are jeopardised • Clients could take legal action against GPG for delays in production or delivery
23	Government policy change	Government policy change which allows entities to source printing from the private sector exposes GPG to the following negative outcomes through price competition: • lost clients • reduced margins
24	Machinery purchased from China (a new supply source)	GPG has not used this supply source before and the machinery may be: • unreliable; or • not sourced according to schedule
25	Existing client pressure	Existing clients may pressure GPG to: • cut costs; • defer; or • cancel print jobs they would traditionally order
26	Alternate overseas suppliers	• May be unreliable • Product quality may impact on the quality of print jobs
27	A tense union environment	Could result in heated industrial action
28	Failure to successfully penetrate the private sector market	Lost revenue and opportunities

Answers to self-help questions are provided at the end of each section.

Risk Mitigation/Preventive Techniques

Prevention groups all activities that can reduce the frequency or likelihood of a risk, or help to avoid the risk altogether. The objective of prevention is to act on the causes of risks.

The higher the likelihood of the risk before prevention measures are undertaken, the more important prevention becomes. There is very little point in reducing the frequency of accidents for which the likelihood of occurrence is already very low. Thus, it can be said that prevention applies above all to 'frequency risks': risks for which the likelihood is high and the consequence relatively low.

Risk avoidance is the ultimate preventive action. Other useful actions are listed below.

Training

Appropriate training of the organisation's staff, educating them in the approach to risk, is vital. Often, staff who make errors in processing or when giving information to customers were insufficiently trained in legal obligations and processes. Training plans should not only highlight the relevant legislation and regulations but should also emphasise the importance of adhering to the specified procedures. The aim of the latter consideration is to support the risk culture of the organisation; it does not add any significant costs but can have a very rapid beneficial effect.

Establishing Clear Procedures

Explanations or diagrams that clearly show staff what they should and should not do in terms of risk management and prevention procedures are particularly useful. It is certain that having simple and comprehensible instructions about how to implement procedures is a real factor in improving the quality of human interventions in the organisation's processes.

Automating the Points of Interruption of Processes

It is most often where processes (industrialised, computerised or automated) are interrupted that problems are concentrated; for example, multiple and incoherent data entry operations degrade the quality of data, congestion causes losses of documents or information, and shortcomings in controls open the door to malicious actions. It is therefore particularly beneficial to identify these points of interruption and eliminate them when it is possible. However, it is important to ensure that the automation procedures do not create new and greater risks, for example by making the process more opaque or complicated, especially if the procedural documentation is not updated.

Safety and Security Actions

These are probably the oldest and the most widespread prevention activities and include ensuring the safety of the organisation's staff and property and the security of at-risk activities. In general, organisations have specialist staff members who are responsible for managing these aspects, such as accident-prevention engineers, security guards, firemen, and human resource staff. The Health, Safety and Working Conditions Committee (or equivalent) can also play a useful role in this risk prevention component.

Compliance and Quality Checks

Internal control systems and quality approaches are the building blocks of risk prevention. If compliance and quality activities are not enacted for operations, products and services, the organisation could be exposed to numerous potentially damaging or dangerous risk events.

Risk Transfer

Transferring risks can be a useful preventive technique. Transferring a risk (for example) to a subcontractor who is better equipped to manage the risk than the organisation itself can reduce the risk exposure. As previously mentioned, risk transfer can expose the organisation to other risks, so the risks that arise from transfer must be analysed in as much detail as the original risk exposure; for example, outsourcing exposes an organisation to the risk of supplier deficiencies or shortages. Risk can also be transferred to customers or partners, though this should be made explicit in the conditions agreed by both parties to avoid disputes in case of an accident. This contractual transfer of risk for reduction is of a different kind from the risk transfer dealt with in risk financing (see Block 4). A contractual risk transfer for financing, is no longer about transferring the risk and managing it, but about financing the losses that may be caused by any accidents.

Loss Reduction Techniques

Control is about trying to change the nature of the risk exposure itself to reduce the downside as much as possible and maximise the upside for the organisation. Not all risks may be appropriately treated by control strategies.

In respect to the **upside** of exposure to risk, the aim of control is to maximise the possible benefit whilst minimising any adverse effects on the organisation. In respect to the **downside** of exposure to risk, the aim of control is to eliminate or minimise adverse effects by limiting the likelihood of an event occurring (i.e. prevention) or by limiting the consequences of the event (i.e. protection). In many instances, a control strategy will involve a combination of both types of measures. Some control measures may simultaneously reduce the likelihood and consequences of an identified event – for example, a driver education course could effectively reduce both the number of accidents that occur and the severity of these accidents.

Controls can be directed at all exposures to risk – hazard, operational, strategic and financial – and can be achieved by implementing policies, standards, procedures and physical changes to a workplace (such as the installation of equipment and fittings). Management must be committed to control strategies for these strategies to succeed.

Controls should involve treatment programs designed to reduce the likelihood and consequences of exposure to risk. The extent of the control program will very much depend on organisational objectives and the context of the risks identified and may also reflect drivers that are external to the organisation, such as changes in government legislation and regulation or advances in technology.

All physical control measures need to be considered in terms of their cost effectiveness when compared with the value of assets they protect and/or the level of interruption to business and growth. It does not make good business sense to spend more on a control measure than the maximum probable loss associated with the particular risk exposure.

There are a wide variety of techniques that may be used to reduce the likelihood and consequences of a risk exposure. Some of these were explored in the previous section, 'Risk Mitigation/Preventive Techniques'. However, not all risk control measures are **physical measures**, especially when dealing with criminal activity. There are also:

- **procedural measures:** a procedure is developed to limit the possibility of a threat materialising like a double signature for payment in the case of misappropriation;
- **managerial measures:** a culture is developed where criminal activity is considered unacceptable, for example putting signs in the supermarket stressing that shoplifting increases the price you pay for goods by 5% as an attempt to reduce shoplifting.

Reducing the Likelihood of Risk

The following are examples of control measures that are likely to reduce the likelihood of an event occurring (prevention measures):

- audit or compliance programs
- contract conditions and dispositions
- formal reviews of requirements, specifications, design, engineering and operations
- inspection and process controls
- investment and portfolio management
- project management
- preventative maintenance
- quality assurance, management and standards
- research and development, technological development
- structured training and other programs
- supervision
- testing
- organisational arrangements
- technical controls.

EXAMPLE

Controlling the Likelihood of Fire, Security and Fraud Risks

Fire

When there is an identified risk of fire, organisations may employ physical control measures such as:

- good housekeeping
- fireproof materials
- a non-smoking policy.

Security

For security risks, control measures may include:

- physical barriers
- locks.

Fraud

For fraud risks, control measures could include:

- background checks on staff members
- segregation of incompatible duties
- implementing system security to limit access.

Controlling the Consequences of Risk

The following are examples of control measures (protection measures) that are likely to reduce the consequences of risk:

- business continuity planning
- contractual arrangements
- contract conditions
- design features
- disaster recovery plans
- engineering and structural barriers
- fraud control planning
- minimising exposure to sources of risk
- portfolio planning
- pricing policy and controls
- separation or relocation of an activity and resources
- public relations
- ex gratia payments
- training and education – that is, what to do as well as why it needs to be done.

EXAMPLE

Controlling the Consequences of Fire

An example of a physical control strategy designed to reduce the consequences of a fire could be a sprinkler system installed in a building to reduce the damage/cost of repair to the building or any subsequent interruption to normal business activities.

Note: A sprinkler system does nothing to reduce the likelihood of a fire occurring; such systems reduce the expected amount of loss or the consequence.

Case study – Pages and Pages Publishing

The Ministry of Transport is responsible for providing the following public transport services:

- buses
- trains
- trams.

The following table lists the associated risks which the Ministry of Transport must eliminate (or reduce) to an acceptable level in order to function effectively.

Ministry of Transport Risks

Risk	Reduce Likelihood (Prevention)	Reduce Consequences (Protection)
Accident resulting in injury or death	• Duplication of rail lines to eliminate head-on crashes • Dead man devices to stop vehicles in the event of a driver emergency • Signalling systems • Maintenance program • Station attendants • Route planning	Design vehicles to minimise injury
Unpunctual services	• Achievable timetables • Service provider key performance indicators (KPIs) and incentives • Maintenance program • Driver substitution roster	• Back-up vehicles • Station radio interconnections and announcements • Mobile applications (apps) to advise system status to travellers

Risk	Reduce Likelihood (Prevention)	Reduce Consequences (Protection)
Fare evasion	• Station barriers • Ticket inspectors • Advertising program	• Station barriers • Ticket inspectors • Advertising program
Note: In some cases, steps to reduce likelihood and steps to reduce consequences can be the same.		
System capacity	• Forward planning • Crowding surveys • Ticketing system reports	• Vehicle seating configuration options • Timetable reviews • Route substitution

Separation, Diversification and Duplication Techniques

For measures that aim to reduce the consequences of a risk event, there is a specific approach that essentially embodies the old saying, 'Do not put all your eggs in the same basket'. It is mostly used to reduce real estate and property losses or net revenue losses and helps ensure activity can be continued when damage occurs to procurement, production or distribution facilities. It is therefore often seriously contemplated in the process of developing continuity planning (see ISO 22301:2012 – *Societal security and business continuity planning*).

This approach is generally referred to as **segregation of loss exposures**, which is, in practice, a form of diversification – diversification of sources when looking at procurement, of facilities when looking at manufacturing, and of outlets when looking at distribution channels. It should be noted that this approach tends to increase the likelihood of a risk event, but this is more than balanced out as it also substantially reduces the consequences.

It can be separated into two broad categories, depending on whether excess capacity is involved. In all cases, these measures will result in increased investment and operating costs thus reducing the return on capital that must be justified by the benefits expected and will be justified by a specific cost-benefit analysis, including the competitive advantage through improved continuity of service and a potential impact on reputation.

Separation or Segregation Without Redundancy

Separation consists of splitting a large asset into several smaller ones, for example, a site could be divided by firewalls, if fire is the exposure to be treated. It could also be that different operations of the same business are housed in several buildings on the same site rather than in a single building. If machinery breakdown is the problem, several lines or machines could be installed in the same building.

For other perils like social unrest, workers' strike or natural disasters, a different location, another country or another continent may be the answer. For risks induced by economic downturn, it may be another activity with counter-cycle effects.

The idea behind separation is that full capacity is necessary for normal operations. Any business interruption event will disturb the normal level of activity; even the disturbance is limited because of multiple locations/operations. These smaller entities could increase initial investment costs and cause a loss in economies of scale (hence higher production costs). However, in some cases, logistical constraints may justify a multiple-sites approach, like storage for a chain of supermarkets when one warehouse alone would not be able to service a whole country.

It is important to always consider all aspects of an organisation and its functions to ensure sound risk management decisions are made.

When looking at procurement, diversification would involve using several suppliers or subcontractors, usually not more than three, to avoid being dependent on one. There could be also regional suppliers to reduce shipment risks and costs.

When looking at distribution, diversification would involve setting up several channels of distribution, or ensuring that sales are spread out across a range of customers rather than allowing a limited number of customers to purchase a signification percentage of the products.

When looking at product or service offerings, diversification would involve developing a range of products, including innovation efforts, to avoid being dependent on one model or product.

Duplication or Segregation with Redundancy

Duplication or segregation with redundancy is a generic term that refers to any situation where, to protect the organisations' goals and objectives, excess capacity must be purchased that is kept idle and put to use only following damage to the main capacity. It is therefore an additional investment with no other return than reducing uncertainty.

The most frequent case is information systems backup. The main site is doubled with a 'shadow system' and it may go so far as multiplying by two all costs, investments, maintenance and personnel. However, it is rarely the case nowadays when specialised companies offer back-up contracts in which they guarantee 'computer energy' with limited downtime. In a way, these companies share out the risks of their customers to offer their service at a reasonable price.

For the same risk, some use facility management, but this is more closely related to contractual transfer for loss control (see above).

The word duplication is somewhat narrow as it refers to a second site identical to the first and there are situations where a middle solution between separation and duplication may be the best solution. This is the reason why the term 'segregation' is preferred over duplication or separation.

Summary

Please keep the following points from this chapter in mind:

- Risk avoidance/suppression is a treatment strategy based on a **conscious and informed** decision to avoid exposure to a particular risk and its likely effects.
- Risk avoidance eliminates any possibility of an event occurring by either abandoning or not undertaking an activity because the risk exposure is considered excessive.
- The term **suppression** is used when an existing activity needs to be stopped.
- When deciding whether to avoid an exposure to risk, risk managers must consider the potential that an opportunity for organisational or market growth and market visibility may be lost.
- In most countries, government legislation and industry practice codes have made risk avoidance compulsory for some specific dangerous activities.
- Avoidance is not always a solution because there are certain limitations and certain instances where it is not practical

  - avoidance may not be possible
  - avoidance may not be feasible
  - avoidance may not be desirable
  - avoiding one exposure may create another.

- Prevention groups all activities that can reduce the frequency or likelihood of a risk or help to avoid the risk altogether. The objective of prevention is to act on the causes of risks.
- Risk avoidance is the ultimate preventive action.
- Control is about trying to change the nature of the risk exposure itself to reduce the downside as much as possible and maximise the upside for the organisation.
- Diversification involves ensuring that there is no single source, facility and outlet being relied on for all of an organisation's processes. This varies the potential risk exposures.
- Separation consists of splitting a large asset into several smaller ones. The idea behind separation is that full capacity is necessary for normal operations. Any business interruption event will disturb the normal level of activity, but in a limited way as each unit covers only a part of the total production.
- Duplication or segregation with redundancy is a generic term that refers to any situation where, to protect the organisations' goals and objectives, excess capacity must be purchased that is kept idle and put to use only following damage to the main capacity.

Answers to Self-Help Questions

Self-help question 3.1

The following table lists some of the physical risk exposures GPG could completely avoid, which require changes to how and where GPG operates.

→

→

Physical Risk Exposures GPG Could Completely Avoid

Risk Reference	Risk Description
11	GPG could avoid the potential for river flooding by moving their operations to another site
12 and 13	GPG can avoid LPG, oil and diesel storage tank tampering /explosion if it: • removes the storage tanks • obtains petrochemicals from an offsite location as required
20	GPG can only avoid the loss related to the adjacent fireworks manufacturer if: • it moves its operations to another site; or • the fireworks manufacturer moves to another site

Chapter 4

Introduction to Disturbance Management and BIA

Introduction

One of the core missions of risk management is to ensure the resilience of the organisation. That is, risk management must facilitate and organise an efficient response to any level of disturbance that an organisation may be challenged by. It is sometimes called 'event management'. As with its many tools and processes, the risk management objective during event management is to ensure the organisation's strategic goals, and in some cases its survival. This requires all staff to be ready to act not only when a pre-identified event (risk threat) happens but also when an unexpected development creates a surprise (emerging risks).

As a result, risk management should never be limited to controlling only identified risks and preparing plans that will be ready to implement as soon as the event occurs. It must enable the organisation to react in situations beyond its probable or possible range of events so that it is ready to have a positive response even when confronted with the unexpected.

Learning Outcomes

By the end of this chapter, you should be able to:

- understand the role of risk management and risk owners in situations of disturbance (event management);
- explain the different levels in a disturbance situation;
- explain why stabilising a situation is important;
- understand the role of upper management in the case of rupture or chaos;
- develop a BIA analysis to complement the traditional risk assessment step.

Risk Treatment, 69–87

Published under exclusive licence by Emerald Publishing Limited
doi:10.1108/978-1-83662-306-920251009

Levels of Disturbance and Appropriate Responses

As risk management professionals are all too aware, risk management is now applied to systems that are more and more complex, in a web of interdependencies and a volatile context. All stakeholders, especially the operational managers, are constantly watching for and anticipating signs of change so that they can take the actions that will bring the system back into balance. However, over the last decade, it has seemed that organisations' upper management panic when a problem arises, especially if social media are involved, and have been using the term crisis for all events that are out of the range of the predetermined possible. Using crisis to refer to events that clearly can be managed internally, without real impacts on external stakeholders and without attracting media attention, could have negative consequences, such as:

- causing a cascading effect that actually does result in a crisis;
- inducing complacency in staff, who then may not be appropriately reactive when a real crisis happens. (This situation can be compared to Aesop's fable of 'The boy who cried wolf'.)

The condition of 'non-enlightened alarmism' was reported on in a recent publication by Dylan Evans, who stated, 'when [staff] qualify low probability events in quasi-certainty as soon as these events are perceived as highly daunting by stakeholders, this worst-case approach can lead to appalling decisions'. This is precisely why the organisation and its upper management must be reactive but must always be able to assess the level of the disturbance as early as possible, before the event – if possible when warning signs first develop – so that their response is aligned with and in proportion to the nature and potential effects of the disturbance.

Although disturbance levels for any complex system are on a continuum, it is necessary for planning purposes to develop a decision-aid tool to pre-define a set of levels that make sense to decision-makers. The Cynefin framework was defined by David Snowden and Mary Boone in their article, 'A leader's framework for decision making'. Their aim was to describe the different contexts an organisation will find itself in, and to suggest ways to respond to risks that relate to each context. The four contexts, as determined by the authors, are explored here.

- **Level 1 – Simple**

  The nominal state of the organisation as it was designed according to best practices; and it is seldom maintained in the long run. The design was built around the missions assigned by the founders, or the directors, on the basis of the analysis of the context at the time the organisation was set up.

  The major characteristics of the state are:

  - stability
  - clearly identified cause/effect relationships
  - slow evolution, order and accomplishment
  - a wariness of complacency.

It is therefore important for risk managers to remain alert, so they can validate at any time the fundamental hypotheses of their risk management strategies, despite the changes and developments going on around them.

- **Level 2 – Complicated**
  This is a state where experts are essential in order to implement good practices. The operational managers or risk-owners need to tweak the risk management strategies and plans – potentially on a daily basis – to make sure they remain on track, despite daily deviations within the range of the probable.

  This state is characterised by the presence of multiple possible responses, meaning several solutions must be considered and decision-makers must be attentive to non-conventional thinking.

  Note: It is essential to act decisively and make swift decisions, not to wait for the 'best' response to appear. As the nominal simple state is by essence unstable, the system is always deviating from this state, but the complications remain in the range of the expected for which operational manager should be prepared to act.

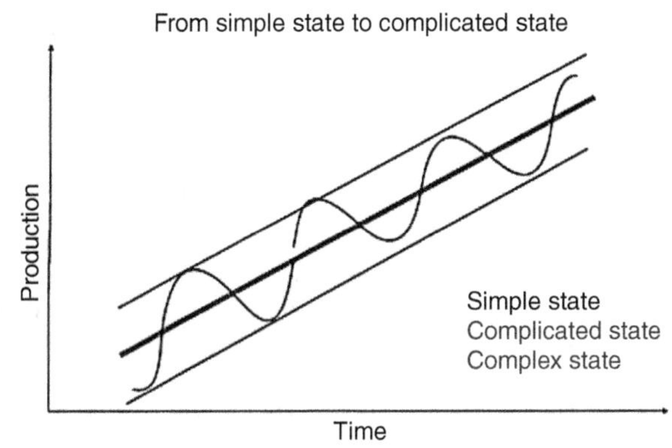

- **Level 3 – Complex**
  This situation requires the operational managers or risk owners to be open to innovative solutions but also to implement solutions that do not lend themselves to improvisation. Planning must occur before a situation arises and this is commonly called **business continuity plan (BCP)**.

  The major characteristics of the state are:

– only feedback loop and forward thinking will enable understanding of the chain of events, and therefore enable finding remedies
– organisations must be aware that there is no return to business as usual because it is necessary to define a new normal (a new simple state) to go forward
– innovation, creativity, new management models and frameworks are the key to a successful continuity planning, beyond management of the event.

These are situations where operational managers can be overtaken by the unfolding event unless they are prepared enough to identify it early and manage their department through the difficulty. If they are responsible for managing the interruption, they must also have the authority to implement the plan without depending on authorisation from upper management or an ad-hoc committee.

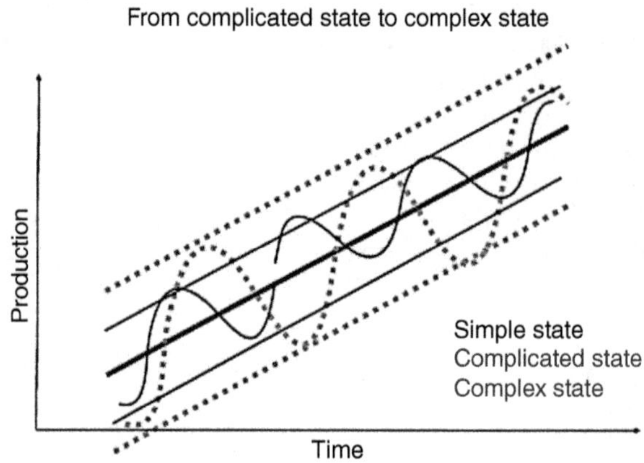

- **Level 4 – Chaos**
  These are exceptional situations where a swift reaction is necessary but the extent of the rupture, proven or potential, requires a global vision that is beyond the local situation that the operational managers have to live through. They are unable to implement the continuity plan with a good chance of reaching the goal of 'acceptable' downtime. This is when it becomes essential to rethink the strategy through a **strategic redeployment plan (SRP)** which supposes that the directors and officers can react swiftly. The major characteristics of the state are:

  - impossibility of discerning stable cause/effect relationships, no general and global schemes to plan management;
  - necessity to find a path to some regulation so that the system is returned to a complex state;
  - top-down communication must be transparent with clear instructions to the operational (this not the time for consultation, which takes place during the feedback effort);
  - ideal for implementing innovation (**change management**).

These are exceptional situations where the scenarios or plots used for developing continuity plans are exceeded and the system would continue to diverge so that more drastic action is needed. The directors and officers must take the time for a strategic effort before restarting the operations. However, time is limited to halt the divergence, hence the strategic exercise must be prepared with the right data available, which can be obtained through analytics and big data, etc.

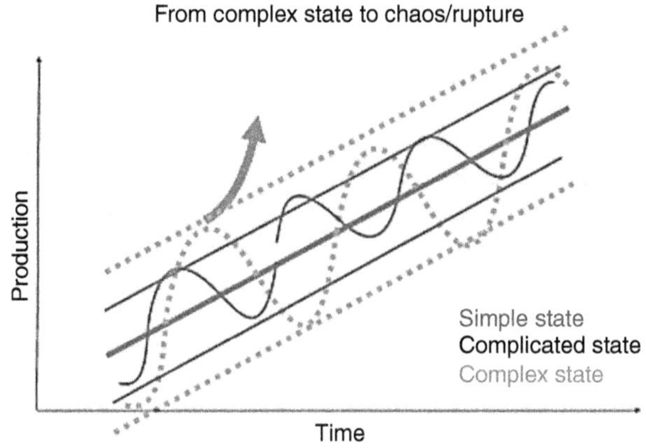

There is also a fifth context – disorder – that applies when the situation is so disordered that it is not clear to the organisation which of the four above contexts it's in. When in this state, the crisis situation must be broken down into smaller parts that can more easily be assigned to a specific context.

Each state of the HBR scale has to be linked with an operational process or a specific risk management tool. As long as the disturbance remains within the range of the expected, local operational managers must be granted the authority to implement the adjustments they deem necessary to maintain the system within the limits of the 'nominal' and avoid divergence, and even any discontinuity in the operations.

When the system deviates more to reach the **possible** range, the operational manager needs to bring the system back to the **probable** range, to stabilise it and avoid further divergence. The manager will need to rely on a pre-established plan to protect people, reputation and assets and implement a specific start-up plan depending on the causes of the event.

Activity | The Cynefin Framework

Read the article at https://hbr.org/2007/11/a-leaders-framework-for-decision-making for more details on the framework and the characteristics of each context.

Note: You will need to register to read the full article. Registration is free.

Mission of the Executive Team and Board in Threat of Rupture

When a situation seems to get out of hand and the risk-owners realise they may not be able to successfully implement the pre-established continuity plan and that the system may diverge into chaos creating ruptures, they must warn upper management without delay. The key consideration here is whether implementing the specific plan might exceed the maximum downtime allowed. In such situations, the future of the organisation, even its survival, may be at stake and operational managers may not be able to envision what should be done beyond their own role and mission.

At this time, an emergency or crisis meeting of the executive committee and/or the board of directors should be called to analyse the situation and decide if the current business model is still viable. In such circumstances, timing is key: leadership has little time to decide and prepare a specific data room and finding ways for early warning will buy time for the decision-makers. To ensure a timely response, staff must be trained to recognise warning signs as far ahead of the actual rupture points as possible. But, as mentioned, upper management decisions can be swift only if they can test scenarios and rely on a sound business analysis for their information and modelling.

During the emergency meeting, the questions that must be answered are:

- Can the organisation remain relevant to its partner networks?
- Can the organisation protect the trust and confidence of all stakeholders?

This strategic process under stress can be called strategic redeployment planning (SRP) and it is efficient only if two conditions are met:

- the leaders are trained in making decisions under stress;
- the organisation's analytics are powerful enough to help rapidly build a number of scenarios to assist decision-makers with a map for the future.

Although the SRP is a new concept that is not broadly accepted throughout the risk management profession under this name, most economic actors and decision-makers recognise that a strategic shift may be commanded by a high disturbance situation. Therefore, the concept provides a clear description of the strategic issues that are linked to risk management and outlines the actions organisations need to take to prevent resources and reputation being irreparably destroyed. The concept is being described here for educational purposes to best enable all risk management professionals to gain a strategic vision of their mission.

At the time of the emergency meeting, the team must be able to think beyond the existing plan, show imagination, and adopt an innovative path for the organisation. In some cases that may require them to redefine the mission so as to maintain resilience.

As far as scenarios and exposures that can generate level 3 and 4 disturbances, some precautions must be met:

- Mechanisms must be developed to ensure business continuity in all departments and services whatever the circumstances, meaning there should be specific plans to restore operations linked to different scenarios. This may improve normal operations as the search for alternatives may uncover improved ways of operating. The thinking process must be extended to envision what alternative courses of action could be taken if the minimal conditions for continuity cannot be met. In France, the first specialist sometimes used the term survival planning to refer to this activity.
- Vital resources must be identified at the level of each operational unit, as must the prevention methods that will have to be implemented to reduce the likelihood of losing the resources and the associated costs (investment, maintenance, and implementation). The approved plan that will be audited by the internal audit must be set up. Vital resources are ones that would allow temporary continuation of operations but would not suffice in the medium term to ensure normal operations.
- Alternative production and office spaces must be located and secured in case the main locations are not available, and alternative procurement sources and routes for all critical processes and activities identified. Conditions and procedures to implement at any time need to be defined, updated and practised regularly. Updates should occur at least annually, but more often when there are noted changes in the context. A cost-benefit analysis must be conducted to justify the process (pre-event) and the extra expenses that would be incurred when if the plan is actually implemented (post-event).
- The communication equipment and temporary resources that may be needed in case of an emergency and the associated costs (crisis communication) must be defined and secured.

All solutions should be approved by upper management, not in detail but at the level of framework and process, so that effort is consistent throughout the organisation. The BCP must be distributed to all internal stakeholders, and even to some key suppliers and subcontractors.

Unlike a BCP, which must be as detailed and specific as an alternative operations plan, a guide for crisis should not attempt to define a detailed plan but should be specific about what warning signs call for a bottom-up warning; this will facilitate the internal flow of information, keep management informed in real time, and avoid the risk of whistle blowing.

This will buy time for upper management to make the necessary decision when a level 4 disturbance becomes a stronger possibility (alarm stage). As mentioned, all channels of communication must be opened, including social media, which means that a blog manager must be on board (whether on staff or hired). The mission of all those involved in crisis management must be clearly defined to avoid lack of assignment, dual assignments and confusion.

For level 3 and 4 emergency readiness, BCPs must be updated regularly, not only for context evolution but also to take into account experience feedback. This will allow an updated cost-benefit analysis to be approved by the finance department.

The development of a systemic process to assess exposures and their potential consequences – to rank the risks – is totally aligned to an ERM programme developed according to the ISO31000 recommendations. There are three fundamental questions to ask to develop a risk management framework and process integrated at all decision levels: strategic, tactic and operational.

- In what context is the organisation operating and are its missions still relevant for its stakeholders? (This analyses the external and internal context including setting risk appetite and risk tolerance.)
- What events could curb, or even interrupt, its development? (This is an exposure diagnostic: risk assessment, including identification, analysis and evaluation.)
- What could prevent such events from happening or limit their consequences so that the organisation's goals and objectives are preserved? (This relates to risk treatment: prevention/protection, continuity and crisis management, and risk financing.)

All risk management professionals, whatever their rank or position, must always keep in mind that the CEO is the ultimate risk manager whereas in governance, the board is the body to define the risk strategy and follow its implementation through the risk committee. This is even more important in level 4 disturbances when the future of the organisation is at stake. Final decisions rest with the CEO and the board. This is why, even if consultants are hired for specific tasks, the overall risk management that a CRO might perform, as risk management facilitator, must be performed by a member of the executive team. Risk management is the natural companion to strategic management to ensure optimum performance of the organisation, including enhancing opportunities and curbing threats.

Furthermore, uncertainties are the drivers of performance provided that risk appetite and risk tolerance are defined by upper management and explained at all levels so that all decision-makers knows what their own limits are to keep organisational risk taking in check within the boundaries set.

It is essential that all measures taken to respond well to an exceptional situation (business continuity event or crisis) must be consistent with all the other risk treatment measures, as well as be at the level of the risk reduction (prevention, protection, segregation, externalisation, contractual transfer, etc.) and at the level of risk financing (internal: retention; or external: transfer to an insurer or another party). In such a scheme, crisis management is the last line of defence of the organisation in case of chaos or rupture to ensure resilience and sustainable development.

To summarise, emergency situations call for the implementation of a BCP that enhances operational performance and allow them to manage complex situations that are beyond their daily missions; thus, the BCP is for a performance enhancer that translates at the organisational level. BCPs are further explored in Chapter 5. However, pre-crisis or crisis situations must be brought without delay to the attention of upper management to immediately trigger the strategic deployment plan (SDP). The elements of crisis management detailed in Chapter 5 are also relevant in these situations.

Best Response When Confronted with a Disturbance

While all organisations must be prepared to navigate smoothly through emergency situations, it is essential to trigger the crisis process only when the organisation's system is diverging beyond control at the operational level. In any disturbance case, a rescue plan must be ready if persons, reputations and/or assets are to be protected from further damages.

In any situation, the first move should be to stabilise the system before any attempt at restoring the production capacity; when the disruption can be contained within the limited deemed necessary to maintain the organisation's relevancy, then the start-up plan is key. Otherwise, if the system cannot be stabilised satisfactorily, and the situation derives towards chaos or rupture, it is high time for upper management to think over the strategy.

A continuous monitoring of the internal and external context is a vital necessity for any organisation operating in a complex and volatile world. This being said, leaders must always keep in mind that refusing risk is not an option, as the definition of risk in the ISO31000 states risk is uncertainty, hence risk is both opportunity and threat.

Rupture situations are not only threats, they also offer opportunities, particularly for risk management professionals as their relevance for a strategy process is highlighted in such occasions, provided they are ready to size the situation and offer their expertise to be put to the test.

These situations illustrate best why the management of risks must be clearly entered into the strategic equation in a global and integrated approach totally aligned with the ERM programme. It is also a unique opportunity to show that RM thinking goes far beyond the operational and the tactic levels, and insurance purchasing.

Obviously, the other lines of defence must also be involved in the process. Internal control must validate that the procedures are repetitive and reliable. Internal auditors must provide the assurance of their implementation and efficiency. But exceptional situations are becoming like a new norm with higher likelihood and severity. The resilience of any organisation is linked to its ability to adapt to the changes, including rapid evolution, and this will require innovation and creative thinking.

These periods when the organisation is navigating troubled waters are precisely also times when the social body, staff and partners, are ready to accept changes, even drastic changes that would not be acceptable in quiet times: what does 'gained benefits' mean when the survival of the organisation is at stake?

At the operational level, risk management must focus on the daily realities of the physical life of the organisation, at the tactical level, where branch managers and function officers are positioned; the language of change must be seen as an opportunity, not a threat. But at the board and executive levels, the issues are mission, strategy, trust and reputation. These are at the heart of risk management at the strategic level, where investors and economic partners are key stakeholders.

Need for a Continuous Strategic Process

With the rapid changes and the increasing complexity of the internal and external context in which the organisations must find their path to success, directors and officers have no other choice but to wade their way through the uncertainties. They have to take measured risks informed by constant adaptation of strategies to perceived realities and emerging evolutions. The price to pay to preserve, and reinforce, the organisation's relevancy as a key knot in its web of partners, and a reference for interested parties, is to adapt and anticipate at all times; continuous innovation is the name of the game and taking chances is not a choice but a necessity.

Under such circumstances, leaders with a vision that can shape the future are instrumental in building the resilience of the organisations they lead. However, for those with a less clear vision, the key is to put in place a process that will bring to their attention the emerging evolution. This process will result from the implementation of a new triangle where a continuous strategic thinking process is fed through a holistic, integrated and systematic management of risk, such as an ERM programme that provides information gathered by all operational staff in their daily interactions with stakeholders and a culture for change for survival.

The SRC Triangle: Continuous Strategic Process

Ultimately, until artificial intelligence can assist them, leaders must develop the capability to discern the major trends through the information they receive. They must instil a culture of change and the elements of change management that will give their staff the means and will to turn their business vision into an economic and social success.

Although there are debates among risk and security professionals and academics who do not agree on a definition of resilience, especially when applied at the societal level, for both private and public organisations, the key is retaining stakeholder trust and confidence. Hence, resilience is the capacity to remain relevant whatever the evolutions of the internal and external context, even when the evolutions reach the level of ambiguity or chaos. To be efficient the reaction to anticipated change must be timely and to the point, that is, resulting from a continuous effort.

Business Impact Analysis

In many organisations, there is an apparent disconnect between the risk management and strategic planning activities. Unfortunately, too often, risk management is viewed as a compliance or regulatory activity that needs to be done to satisfy some external demand for risk management. As a result, risk management is relegated to a lower-level, non-strategic position that addresses important, but not strategy-defeating issues. It seems business leaders continue to struggle to remember the important connection between risk and return. This results in the organisation's risk management efforts being inadequately integrated with strategic planning. This may partially be driven by how risk managers have been leading their risk identification and assessment efforts.

When identifying key risks, rather than beginning the conversation with a discussion about what drives value for the organisation, the conversation could instead begin with identifying what risks are on the horizon (e.g. by asking 'What keeps you up at night?'). By starting the conversation with what is strategically important to the organisation and then asking what might prevent that from being successful, risk professionals might better assist business leaders in seeing how risk management can be positioned to provide strategic value.

Business Impact Analysis

The risk assessment step in the risk management process includes analysing all the consequences of a potential exposure should the risk materialise, including the resulting business interruption.

However, the growing importance of disturbance management, including continuity and crisis management, has led risk management professionals to develop additional investigations into the business impact of interruption including the degree of interruption, the time necessary to restart and the additional costs of continuing business under duress. This additional risk analysis is called business impact analysis (BIA) and it provides one of the tools to demonstrate to upper management the importance of integrating risk management into the strategic process.

Therefore, BIA is a detailed review of business interruption exposures. It identifies, quantifies and qualifies the business impacts of a loss, interruption or disruption of business processes on an organisation, and provides the data from which appropriate continuity strategies can be determined. Generally, a project team should be established to conduct the analysis.

According to the Business Continuity Institute's 'Good practice guidelines', the purpose of a BIA is to achieve the following:

- obtain an understanding of the organisation's most critical objectives, the priority of each and the timeframes for resumption of these, following unscheduled interruption;
- inform a management decision on maximum tolerable outage (MTO) for each function;

- provide the resource information from which an appropriate recovery/restoration strategy can be determined and recommended;
- outline dependencies that exist both internally and externally to achieve critical objectives.

The MTO is the timeframe during which recovery must take effect before an outage compromises the ability of the organisation to achieve its business objectives. Seasonality may affect the MTO. For example, a financial year-end may reduce the tolerable outage for the finance function and a one-off contract with significant time penalties may reduce the tolerable outage for a range of functions within the organisation.

Conducting the BIA

When conducting the BIA, it is necessary to capture both the tangible and intangible effects of a business interruption on the organisation and then to quantitatively and qualitatively analyse the effects.

The methods, tools and techniques to carry out a BIA include the following:

- templates
- checklists
- workshops (facilitated by a BCM professional)
- questionnaires (can be automated)
- interviews.

The 'Good practice guidelines' suggest the information needed to establish how critical a particular activity is in isolation and as part of the whole organisation includes:

- timeframes within which the activity must be resumed (MTO);
- locations from which activity is undertaken;
- influences on the activity – e.g. things that can affect the activity, peak periods, regulatory reporting;
- the impact of not continuing the activity and how long the organisation can last without it (are there any alternatives?);
- volumes – e.g. calls per hour, output on production line;
- contractual, regulatory or legal requirements;
- key tools to achieving continuity of the activity (how many, where and when?), including:

  - people – skill sets
  - equipment – IT, telecommunications, manufacturing/industrial plant
  - data – paper and electronic
  - dependencies – internal and external to organisation.

Steps Involved in the BIA

Communication. The BIA stage is the first time that the majority of staff become involved in the BCM process, therefore effective communication is crucial.

To complete the BIA, process the project team will need to interview a large selection of staff in the middle management and supervisory levels of the organisation – those who have a good understanding of the specific operations of the organisation. At the same time, the BIA will be reviewing the current levels of resourcing in order to determine the minimum needs for emergency and recovery plans.

It is important to remember that the questions being asked during the BIA may be perceived by staff as threatening, and staff may withhold information, cover up deficiencies in the system, exaggerate the importance of the function or their role in it, or inflate the resources necessary to operate critical tasks. This can significantly affect the process, therefore the BIA project team need to educate the relevant staff about the purpose of the BIA, why it is necessary and what the outcomes will be. Complete staff cooperation is key to ensuring a complete and accurate picture of the organisation emerges.

Define Core Business Activities. It is likely that core business activities were defined earlier in the risk analysis process based on input from senior management. These activities now need to be confirmed with the managers and staff who supervise and carry out these activities. It may be found the activity as first defined is not actually critical but that other activities not previously defined are. Often, the significance of an activity or function is overlooked because there may be no direct financial impact. However, the operational impact to the organisation may be just as, if not more, important to the organisation than other activities with financial effects. For this reason, many support activities should be considered in a BCM program, as they affect the efficiency of deployment even if they are not strictly core.

The outcome of this step must be an agreed list of core activities and their broadly included dependencies that should be approved by senior management.

Identify Resource Requirements. For each core business activity, the current resource requirements for people, infrastructure, systems, services and information need to be determined. When this is documented, the minimum resources to conduct the activity under agreed emergency conditions (that is, the minimum activity that is acceptable to maintain the function in the event of a disruption) must be agreed with senior management.

When identifying requirements, the analyst needs to be mindful that in some activities, although the critical functions can be maintained by a skeleton staff for a considerable period, the backlog of non-critical tasks that are not carried out can build up to a point where it is impossible to catch-up, so these tasks also need to be taken into consideration.

Establish Interdependencies. A critical function of a BIA is to map and understand the interdependencies of the various core activities. These dependencies can be between functions and activities within the same business unit; across different departments or business units of the organisation; or with external parties, either as an outsourced function or a supplier of goods and/or services.

Often a critical activity requires the input from another activity that in itself is not critical. If that other activity is not available, the critical activity will fail. This also applies to a key person, for example, someone who is the contact point between interdependent functions.

It must also be understood that, even if an external supplier is a key dependency for your organisation, you may not be their top priority.

At the completion of this stage, all of the interdependencies should be documented, their purpose known, and details obtained of all necessary contacts.

As part of the BIA process, it is useful if process maps or flowcharts can be accessed, or if these are not available it is worthwhile developing them. Not only will they assist in understanding the process and ensuring that no critical function or requirement is missed, they will also assist in identifying alternative workarounds and systems to ensure business continuity.

Determine the Disruption Impacts. It is necessary when discussing the impact of an event on business continuity that everybody interprets the information consistently. Some people tend to trivialise intangible things such as a business interruption event that hasn't happened, while others make a drama out of the same event. It is best to work from a realistic 'worst case' scenario – a major fire destroying head office or a prolonged disruption to electricity supplies, for example. These may not be highly likely, but it will help ensure that managers and staff are consistent in their approach to possible impacts.

Analysing actual business continuity events at other organisations, either in the same geographic area or in the same industry, can assist management and staff in estimating the impacts of such an event on their activities.

Disruption impacts can be either tangible or intangible. Although some consider intangible impacts such as adverse publicity or a compliance breach that invites regulatory attention, to be non-financial impacts, in the long run, these can affect the financial position of the organisation, often more severely than direct financial impacts.

Financial impacts include losses of revenue, increased costs of operating, financial penalties for non-completion of contractual obligations and cash flow impacts caused by lack of liquidity. Non-financial impacts (at least in the short term) include loss of investor/customer/supplier confidence, lowered staff morale, loss of goodwill, loss of reputation and increased regulatory attention.

It is useful to gather information on the disruption impacts after increasing timeframes, such as one hour, one day, one week and one month. These timeframes will vary depending on the organisation. For example, a bank will need to recover its major operations faster than a mining organisation therefore will need to review the impacts of a business continuity event over hours and days rather than weeks and months.

As outlined earlier, seasonality plays a part in many business functions so should be considered when assessing the impacts of a business continuity event. For example, the real estate market may be quiet during December and January therefore banks' home lending units are often quiet as well. However, the EFT-POS and credit card sections of the bank will be very busy over the same period because of Christmas shopping.

In some industries, consideration should also be given to cycles that span several years.

Identify the MTO Times and Recovery Objectives. The MTO is the timeframe during which recovery must take effect before an outage compromises the ability of the organisation to achieve its business objectives. It should be set by the owner of each core business activity and confirmed by operations and senior management to ensure that it is reasonable and accounts for the BCM objectives and the business strategy. A set of agreed criteria should be established to calibrate the owner's perception of the requirement and the business priorities and strategies.

Associated with the MTO is the recovery time objective (RTO), which is the level of capability that the organisation aims to recover within a defined timeframe. This time is usually set by the provider of the service or infrastructure.

The MTO and RTO times do not have to be identical: the MAOMTO is based on what the business decision-makers believe is necessary, the RTO is based on what can currently be delivered. The gap between these two times will be catered for by:

- developing workarounds to provide an acceptable level of continuity during the gap period – this level does not have to be the same level as defined for the MTO;
- developing alternative plans and capabilities, including manual processes, to cover the gap;
- increasing the delivery capability of the supplying function/activity by increased infrastructure expenditure, alternative suppliers, and so on.

The MTOs can be used to prioritise the criticality of functions and the order in which the various core activities should be recovered. This priority will depend to some degree on the relevant RTOs. The MTOs and RTOs can be utilised to develop a triage framework, which is based on the incident response system used by the UK Emergency Services that prioritises which core activity, and at what level, will be recovered when.

An example of a simple triage framework is as follows.

Triage Level	Recovery Criteria
Gold	Recovery back to an acceptable level within 24 hours
Silver	Recovery back to an acceptable level within 48 hours
Bronze	Recovery back to an acceptable level within 5 days

Criteria that can be used to develop a priority triage framework include:

- contribution to critical business objectives;
- level of risk associated with loss of function or process;
- time sensitivities of key success factors;
- time deliverables in service level agreements, contracts and similar items.

Identify the Recovery Point Objective. In the case of an IT disturbance, the recovery point objective (RPO) is the point to which data must be restored to ensure business objectives can be met in line with MTO for the activity following a system, network or computer failure. The RPO determines how often data should be backed up. It often (and in the case of certain organisations must) includes the time needed to reduce the backlog of work to normal proportions.

Self-Help Question 4.1

Mt Barney Bank currently has an IT strategy of having a third party provide a backup computer site in case of a business interruption event. The RTOs for banking computer systems were set as:

- 12 hours if the event occurs between 8 a.m. and 6 p.m. Monday to Friday;
- 24 hours if it occurs outside of this time.

The difference between the two RTOs is due to the overnight batch work that would need to be re-run if the system were to fail during the various batch runs.

The team has agreed on the MTO times as follows:

- Call centre and EFTPOS support and ATMs – 4 hours;
- Branch support – 8 hours;
- Batch processing finished and system availability by 12 p.m.

1. What are the availability gaps between what is required by the MTO and what is being delivered in accordance with the RTO?
2. What steps can be taken to close these gaps?
3. Answers to self-help questions are provided at the end of each section.

Identify Alternative Workarounds and Processes. As part of the BIA process, the analyst should gather information on current or possible workarounds (see Chapter 3, 'Separation, diversification and duplication techniques', for more details). Potential workarounds include:

- **Equipment redundancy** – similar equipment used in different parts of the business, alternative external sources for equipment, or lease arrangements, etc.

- **IT systems redundancy** – similar multiple networks at different locations, transportability between networks, or existence of hot sites, warm sites and cold sites, etc.
- People – availability of trained specialists, and/or contractors, multi-skilling, contractor availability
- **Facilities** – availability of alternative accommodation, or presence of suitable infrastructure (e.g. data cabling), etc.
- **Communications** – arrangements for emergency/disruption communications, e.g. public websites, confidential staff information websites, arrangements with media providers, etc.
- **Data** – resilience of security systems and back-up systems, or off-site storage arrangements, etc.
- **Paper records** – alternative access arrangements, multiple copies, secure storage or electronic copies
- **Suppliers** – existence of multiple suppliers, or supplier's own continuity arrangements (particularly sole suppliers) etc.
- **Assistance** – types of external assistance available – for example, arrangements with competitors (e.g. for customer assistance, inventory sharing) – contractor and lease agreements, or third-party access, etc.

In the current automated world, manual solutions, however simple, are not always available. If recourse to manual operations is the alternative, the analyst needs to confirm the ability of staff to carry out these processes, by asking the following questions:

- Are all the data (e.g. price lists) available?
- Are the appropriate resources (pens, blank invoices etc.) available?
- Has staff been properly trained in the manual process?
- Is there sufficient staff available to carry out the generally more labour-intensive manual operations?

Making assumptions about an organisation's ability to revert to manual systems can be a recipe for escalating a simple business continuity event into a major crisis.

Recognising existing or potential workarounds can give a level of comfort to the organisation as to its ability to withstand a business interruption event and also give ideas on which BCM strategies to develop for the future.

Outcomes

The outcomes from a BIA include the identification and documentation of:

- end-to-end core business activities, their dependencies and single points of failure (including seasonal trends and/or critical timing issues);
- financial and non-financial impacts resulting from the disruption, interruption or loss of one or more core activities over various time periods;

- the BCM objectives for each core activity and its dependencies;
- a prioritised minimum acceptable resource recovery configuration to support the required minimum acceptable level of performance of each core activity and its dependencies;
- details of vital records, information and data;
- details of key employees, customers, suppliers, clients and other stakeholders;
- details of contractual, regulatory or owner-enforced constraints.

Summary

Please keep the following points from this chapter in mind:

- Using **crisisto** refers to events that clearly can be managed internally, and could have negative consequences, such as inducing staff complacency.
- Organisations and their upper management must be reactive but must always be able to assess the level of the disturbance as early as possible so that their response is aligned with and in proportion to the nature and potential effects of the disturbance.
- It is useful for planning purposes to develop a decision-aid tool to define a set of acceptable and unacceptable levels of disturbance that make sense to decision-makers, such as the Cynefin framework.
- When a situation seems to get out of hand, the risk-owners must warn upper management without delay. At this time, an emergency or crisis meeting of the executive committee and/or the board of directors should be called.
- The strategic process under stress, needed in the case of ruptures in the context, can be called SRP.
- Unlike a BCP, which must be as detailed and specific as an alternative operations plan, a guide for crisis should not attempt to define a detailed plan but should be specific about what warning signs call for a bottom-up warning.
- There are three fundamental questions to ask to develop a risk management framework and process integrated at all decision levels:

  - In what context is the organisation operating and are its missions still relevant for its stakeholders?
  - What events could curb, or even interrupt, its development?
  - What could prevent such events from happening or limit their consequences so that the organisation's goals and objectives are preserved?

- While all organisations must be prepared to navigate smoothly through emergency situations, it is essential to trigger the crisis process only when the organisation's system is diverging beyond control at the operational level.
- In any situation, the first move should be to stabilise the system.
- The resilience of any organisation is linked to its ability to adapt to the changes, including rapid evolution, and this will require innovation and creative thinking.

Answers to Self-Help Questions

Self-help question 4.1

Based on the RTO and MAO set out in the question, the current worst-case gaps are:

- business continuity event occurs during working day – requirement 4 hours, delivery 12 hours – gap 8 hours;
- business continuity event occurs outside working day – requirement 4 hours (call centre, EFTPOS and ATMs are 24/7 operations), delivery 24 hours – gap 20 hours;
- business continuity event occurs outside working day – requirement system availability by 12 noon, delivery 8.00 A.M. the following morning – gap 20 hours (1 day).

Based on the RTO, it would appear that it takes 12 hours to transfer the banking system to the back-up system at the third-party provider. This delay would be caused by transferring staff and data to the third- party site and bringing up Mt Barney's system on the back-up computer. Furthermore, it appears that the batch jobs (this would include third-party debit and credit transfers from other institutions and cheque clearing facilities) run overnight take up to 12 hours to run and back-up prior to the system being available for the on-line banking system.

However, as the call centre, EFTPOS and ATMs are currently 24/7 operations, it appears that there is a second system in place to handle the banking business when the main system is down, and batch jobs are running. This may be a partition of the computer running a memorandum system comprising an 'end of business day' balance file and a transaction file that is brought up when the on-line system is brought down. Or it may be a standalone system normally used for the ATMs and EFTPOS that is updated from the main system in real time when the main system is on-line.

Actions that Mt Barney can take to reduce the current gaps include:

- reviewing the process of moving to the back-up site and establishing Mt Barney's systems to see if the transfer time can be reduced. This could include ensuring that someone at the back-up site had the passwords, etc. to bring up the Mt Barney system based on a telephone call so that it was ready and waiting when the Mt Barney staff arrived at the site;
- revising the overnight batch process to include more frequent check points so if there was a job failure the batch process would only have to revert to the previous checkpoint rather than start again from the beginning;
- if available, using the ATM system to support the critical business functions during the gap;
- implementing a 'hot site' or a 'second site' strategy for computer systems.

Chapter 5

Business Continuity, Emergency and Crisis Management

Introduction

Business continuity planning, disaster recovery, and crisis management are terms that are often used when considering the problems an organisation can face because of disruption to business; for example, industrial action, computer problems or a major power failure. These terms all refer to aspects of a wider process called business continuity management (BCM).

This chapter considers the importance of BCM, the relationship between BCM and enterprise risk management and the steps that need to be taken to implement a BCM process into an organisation.

Learning Outcomes

By the end of this chapter, you should be able to:

- explain the purpose of BCM;
- describe why organisations need to consider BCM, and explain some adverse outcomes of not having a BCM strategy;
- describe the causes and effects of business interruptions;
- describe how BCM fits into risk management;
- describe the steps organisations need to take to implement BCM.

Risk Treatment, 89–130

Published under exclusive licence by Emerald Publishing Limited
doi:10.1108/978-1-83662-306-920251012

What Is Business Continuity?

ISO 22301:2012 defines BCM as a:

> Holistic management process that identifies potential threats to an organization and the impacts to business operations those threats, if realized, might cause, and which provides a framework for building organizational resilience with the capability of an effective response that safeguards the interests of its key stakeholders, reputation, brand and value-creating activities.

The main purpose of BCM is to ensure that an organisation can respond to major disruptions that threaten its survival. BCM is also used increasingly to manage those disruptions that have a potential material effect on key objectives.

Key elements of BCM are:

- understanding the environment, the organisation operates in, including threats;
- determining which parts of the organisation would result in critical losses if threatened;
- quantifying the effect threats could have on organisational functions and processes;
- identifying and documenting the key infrastructure and resources that would enable the organisation to continue to operate despite interruption;
- structuring a response to threats that take into account these elements;
- ensuring key stakeholders are aware of the planned response.

Self-Help Question 5.1

You have been appointed to head the BCM unit of a medium-sized publicly listed manufacturing company. Which resources of the organisation are critical to its operation and require the development of business continuity plans (BCPs) or other risk management approaches? (You may base your response on an organisation where you have worked, or on one with which you are familiar.)

Answers to self-help questions are provided at the end of each section.

Benefits of BCM

Benefits of BCM include:

- assuring the future viability of the organisation despite interruptions to its processes;

- compliance with regulatory and governance requirements, as necessary;
- fulfilment of contractual requirements;
- reduced insurance costs;
- improved confidence in the organisation from suppliers, customers and staff;
- reduced threat to the organisation's reputation resulting from unforeseen risk events.

Implementing BCM ensures that stakeholder confidence in the organisation is maintained but there is no absolute guarantee that BCM will provide effective resilience against any disruption event. However, it is also true that in the majority of major disasters, organisations that lack robust risk management practices can be overwhelmed by the event. Resilience can be built into an organisation's major systems, processes and activities by the application of normal risk management techniques.

Business Interruption

Following any sort of material damage to a commercial property (for example, fire or stormwater) there may be additional loss due to the interruption to normal trading activities and a subsequent inability to meet ongoing business costs. This is known as business interruption (BI).

There are many causes of BI, both natural and non-natural (caused by human action).

The 2015 Global Claims Review, published by Allianz, lists the top 10 causes of BI losses as shown in the following table.

	Cause	**% of losses**
1	Fire and explosion	59%
2	Storm	6%
3	Machinery breakdown	5%
4	Faulty design/material/manufacturing	5%
5	Strike/riot/vandalism	4%
6	Cast loss (entertainment)	3%
7	Flood	3%
8	Collapse	3%
9	Human error/operating error	2%
10	Power interruption	2%

Numerous other events can also cause BI losses, and the likelihood of these occurring depends on the region. Other potential causes include natural disasters, such as tsunami, storm and earthquake (Italy's top cause of BI losses over the analysed period), collision, power interruption and cyber-attack.

This last cause, cyber-attack, is increasing in importance due to the current and increasing dependence on technology. Not only is the risk increasing but costs and significance are also on the rise. In fact, a survey conducted by Dimensional Research in 2015 found that 80% of respondents believed that losing digital data would have more of an effect on their business than losing buildings, vehicles or goods.

It can also be considered that negative public opinion is a key cause of BI. It usually arises because of poor risk management of previous events but can also drive future events that will require risk management and BCM.

Tianjin Explosion. On 12 August 2015, a fire and two subsequent explosions occurred at a chemical storage warehouse in Tianjin port, China. Over 170 people were killed (including 115 firefighters and police officers) and almost 800 were injured. The explosions also damaged property and disrupted numerous businesses. It has been estimated that the total loss from this incident could reach $6 billion. The cost includes the immediate physical damage as well as clean-up costs and business losses. Indeed, the incident caused numerous BI and contingent business interruption (CBI) losses (CBI is when a business suffers a loss because a supplier or customer has suffered a BI event).

Two years after the incident, its long-term effects were still to be fully realised, but it highlighted the value and necessity of effective risk management, as well as the potential magnitude of BI and CBI exposure in today's globalised and increasingly interconnected environment. The incident prompted a revision of all CBI covers and has led to a surge of interest in procurement risk management. Since this incident, many reinsurers have been insisting on a procurement risk analysis before providing cover, and many large organisations are conducting such analyses and even requiring their main suppliers to do the same.

'Quiet catastrophes'

However, causes of BI are not always obvious or significant, and don't always cause large losses. As pointed out by the Business Continuity Institute (BCI) (2005):

> whilst bombs, fires and floods capture the headlines, almost 90% of business-threatening incidents are, 'quiet catastrophes' which go unreported in the media but can have a devastating effect on an organisation's ability to function. Many of the causes are outside of an organisation's control and they are often at the mercy of the emergency services or suppliers who define the timescale of an interruption.

Research conducted by the Institute for Crisis Management in 2016 shows that the top 15 causes of organisational crisis are varied and mostly arise from routine events within the organisation, as shown in the following table.

	Cause	Percentage
1	Mismanagement	29.20%
2	Discrimination	20.61%
3	White collar crime	10.45%
4	Consumer activism	6.45%
5	Whistle-blower	6.23%
6	Workplace violence	5.10%
7	Cyber crime	4.95%
8	Class action lawsuits	3.71%
9	Executive dismissal	3.46%
10	Defects and recalls	2.99%
11	Environmental damage	2.51%
12	Hostile takeover	1.64%
13	Catastrophe	1.01%
14	Sexual harassment	0.48%
15	Other	0.42%

One thing that needs remembering at all times when dealing with possible causes of failure in business processes is the 'domino effect'. The immediate cause of most disasters is the occurrence of an 'active failure' such as human error, or a technological failure such as a warning system malfunction or the absence of a machinery guard. However, these events are usually preceded by a sequence of 'latent failures', which create the environment that allows the active failure to occur. In effect, these latent failures can be described as the root causes of the disaster, with the active failure as the 'source'.

Self-Help Question 5.2

BI can affect all organisational stakeholders.

In Self-Help Question 5.1, you determined the main sources of BI for a medium-sized publicly listed manufacturing company. Consider the same organisation you chose for that question and make a list of the major stakeholders that need to be considered in the BCM process.

Answers to self-help questions are provided at the end of each section.

The Relationship Between BCM and Risk Management

As mentioned earlier, the management of exceptional events or situations is one of the core missions of risk management and therefore the continuity of business activities is a major goal of risk management professionals. Preventing or limiting interruptions to business processes and activities is an integral part of any enterprise risk management plan.

When considering BI issues, management will identify the various risk events that could result in normal organisational activities being interrupted and will put in place various strategies to avoid, share or reduce those risks as mentioned in Chapter 4. This approach to BCM is similar to that adopted in the USA by the National Fire Protection Association Standard, *NFPA 1600:2005*, which has been accepted by the USA National Standards Institute as a national American Standard.

In the United Kingdom, the British Standards Institute has issued *BS 25999-1:2006 Business Continuity Management Code of Practice* based on the Business Continuity Institute's 'Good practice guidelines'.

Business continuity is clearly an approach that falls within the domain of risk management professionals; however, business continuity has developed a set of specific tools to reflect its narrower focus and specific methods that have led larger organisations to create a specific position for risk managers devoted to continuity: business continuity manager.

Nevertheless, business continuity is not a new discipline of management but an additional set of tools for risk managers to use to carry out their mission. In fact, integrating business continuity into the risk management approach has become essential in a strategic and dynamic approach to ERM.

The table shown below, adapted from the British Standard, illustrates how these toolkits are intrinsically interconnected and complement each other:

	Risk Management	**Business Continuity Management**
Key analytical method	Risk assessment	Business impact analysis
Key parameters	Impact, probability, velocity	Impact, probability, velocity, and delays
Type of incident	All types of events (widely different impacts)	Events causing significant business disruption impacts (identified in the risk management process)
Size of events	All risks in the range: low to high impact and low to high likelihood	Focuses on (but not restricted to) high consequence, low probability events

	Risk Management	Business Continuity Management
Scope	Focuses primarily on risks to all modes of operation	Focuses primarily on non-routine modes of operation. Survival is a major driver, but also included are disruptions with some material impact on the achievement of critical business objectives.
Intensity	All events, from gradual to sudden onset	Mostly sudden or rapid events (though response may also be appropriate if a creeping incident becomes severe)

Activity | Business continuity management resources

Upper management should decide on a specific methodology for all operational managers or risk owners to develop their own plans to ensure the continuity of the operations, activities and processes under their control. Each of the major scenarios or exposures should be covered by a specific plan and reviewed regularly to reflect the evolution in their internal and external control.

Upper management should put in place their own continuity plans to ensure the continuity of operations at headquarters and ensure the continuity of the decision process.

One area of common interest to all, which is strategic in scope, is the area of IT continuity and cyber security, as this is a source of total interruption and can result in a severe blow to reputation.

Excellent sources of information about BCM are ISO 22301:2012 *Societal security – Business continuity management systems – Requirements* and ISO 22313:2012 *Societal security – Business continuity management systems – Guidance*. These are available for purchase at www.iso.org.

There are also valuable resources available on the website of the Business Continuity Institute: www.thebci.org/index.php/resources.

Recovery Strategies

Strategies have to be selected to cover the three stages of BCM. These stages are the initial response to BI event – the emergency response; the process to get the core business activities and their dependencies available as soon as possible – the continuity phase; and the process to return the organisation to its 'business-as-usual' condition – the recovery phase. These stages generally overlap each other, and each stage has particular requirements.

The 'business as usual' state is often different from the system state prior to the disturbance, especially when the root cause analysis has been conducted efficiently, as the new usual must include the changes needed to avoid a repetition of the event.

The process is set out in the diagram below.

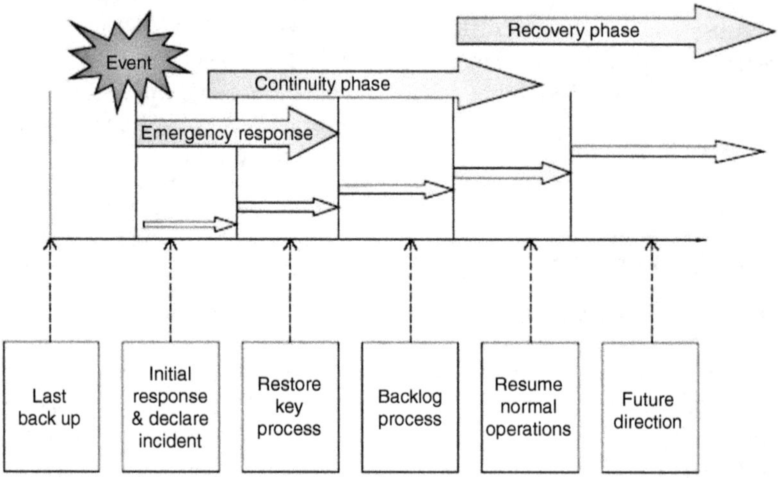

Emergency Response

The emergency response is the immediate reaction to the occurrence of a disturbance event. The strategy needs to ensure that people's lives, the organisation's reputation and property are not exposed to risks, or at least acknowledge the risks and have in place actions to reduce the level of resulting harm and ensure that the business does not collapse because of a lack of immediate response and leadership.

The strategies must satisfy local regulatory requirements; for example:

- emergency evacuation plans;
- workplace health and safety issues and reporting;
- assurance that the business is prepared to handle media scrutiny – e.g. the readiness of a spokesperson.

Continuity Phase

The main purpose of the continuity phase is to ensure the continuing operation of the organisation, at least at the minimum acceptable level agreed upon by the board during the BIA process (MTO and RTOs). Response strategies are concerned with getting the organisation's core business activities and their dependencies back into operation within the agreed timelines. These strategies have to ensure that the required facilities and resources are available in a manner, place and time that achieve these objectives.

Recovery Phase

The recovery phase is designed to return the organisation to its long-term sustainable capability. This may not be the same 'business as usual' state that existed prior to the event as a BI event may affect a function, activity or area of an organisation that cannot be recovered to its original state, for example because it was based on a unique asset that no longer exists or because the business opportunity has gone, perhaps because of brand reputation. Additionally, if a post-event root cause analysis has been conducted efficiently, as any organisation should, the new 'business-as-usual' state must include the changes needed to avoid a repetition of the event.

Recovery response strategies are about repairing and replacing facilities, infrastructure, supplies, personnel and so on, taking into account the long-term strategy of the organisation. Many of these strategies will be long-term in nature and do not have to be fully mapped out in advance, or are time- or event-specific and cannot be fully developed in advance. For example, in the event of a fire at an organisation's main premises, the extent of the damage incurred with dictate the strategy: repair and continue, demolish and rebuild, or a move to new premises. The strategy cannot be selected in advance. What can be planned for, though, is for a market watch to be set up so that the facilities manager is always aware of what space is on the market for lease and what properties are available for purchase so that, in the event of a fire, he knows where to start no matter what the organisation's needs are.

People and Resources

The people and other resources involved in these three phases of business continuity are not necessarily the same.

In the emergency phase, the organisation will need leadership from the top to handle the media and make urgent decisions. Other people involved in the emergency phase are internal and external emergency personnel and facilities experts to prevent the emergency situation from spreading, including fire-fighters and computer technicians.

In the continuity phase, the majority of the work will be carried out by predetermined specialist teams who will be responsible for making the systems and infrastructure available and business users who will be responsible for carrying out business activities.

In the recovery phase, which is certain to overlap the continuity phase, the teams are concerned with bringing the business back to full operational status. These teams will include external recovery resources for cleaning up after a fire and recovering critical documentation, etc., property personnel for organising new premises and external suppliers for replacement equipment. These personnel will have to work with and around the continuity teams.

Business Continuity Planning

Business continuity planning – also known as the management of disruption-related risk – is a critical component of any risk management program because it addresses a large number of high consequences, low likelihood risks.

A BCP is, in effect, a plan for controlling risk exposures with the sole objective of ensuring an organisation's survival in the event of a major disruption to business services. It seeks to mitigate the downside consequences of exposure to disruption-related risk as effectively as possible.

BCPs specifically address the management of disruptions that could significantly damage or even destroy the organisation. These plans provide a framework and resources to tackle any major unexpected event as it occurs, and they also help the organisation manage the subsequent recovery from an unexpected, catastrophic event.

A BCP should provide a framework in which an organisation's management may work in the abnormal conditions created by an event or incident which causes disruption to normal activities. This facilitates the management of consequences and leads them back towards organisational recovery.

Every organisation should prepare plans for preventing and coping with actual or potentially severe loss situations covering both salvage operations and plans for carrying on business following the occurrence of a major loss. Most organisations are likely to have more than one such plan, each addressing a specific group of similar risk scenarios, such as include:

- area type events – such as earthquakes and flooding;
- site-specific events – such as fire, bombings and explosions;
- organisation-specific events – such as product failure, fraud and damage to reputation.

The documentation of a BCP may include:

- a disaster recovery plan, including
  - loss prevention and control measures
  - an emergency plan
- a crisis management plan (CMP)
- contingency plans.

All of these plans should be well documented (with copies held off-site in secure locations) and should be tested and updated regularly to ensure they remain relevant to the current state and context of the organisation.

Using the BCP that is appropriate to the particular type of incident or event, the management should be able to marshal the organisation's skills, knowledge, manpower and other resources to resolve all of the problems created by the incident or event.

Disaster plan

The disaster plan is essentially preventative or, if these measures fail, it is the first line of defence. It should cover:

- loss prevention and control measures
- an emergency plan.

Loss prevention and control measures

This element is concerned with identifying and assessing all of the major hazards on an ongoing basis and implementing risk and loss control measures prior to the occurrence of any incident. Under normal conditions, loss prevention and control measures should be implemented as soon as the funds are available.

Emergency plan

This sets out in broad terms the management structures, procedures and resources that may be used to handle a major emergency whilst it is occurring and immediately afterwards until it is brought under control. The plan details measures to counter the immediate effects of the major loss incident such as saving lives and limiting damage to bring the situation under control as quickly as possible and protect reputation.

Crisis management plan

The CMP is complementary to the disaster plan and focuses on the communication, command and control organisation. For example, the plan describes who the decision makers are, where they would meet, how information would flow up to the decision makers and how decisions would flow down to operational personnel. The aim of the plan is to reduce the impact of the emergency by getting the business back into operation as quickly as possible. In this phase, regaining the confidence of the public, customers and employees is as important as repairing the physical damage; hence the importance of communication during this phase of the event. This is often called crisis communication.

There should also be recovery plans outlining how certain elements of a business can be brought back to full activity (for example, IT disaster recovery plans).

Contingency plans

Controlling risks invariably involves reducing the likelihood that a loss will occur or the consequences of any loss that may occur, or both. Neither outcome is ever likely to totally eliminate loss, nor is it certain that the control measures will always work as expected. Every organisation should therefore have in place **contingency plans**, which are plans that attempt to take into account all possible future events and outline potential responses – they can be thought of as 'Plan B' plans. These plans not only reinforce the control measures taken but, more importantly, act as a further means of limiting the consequences of loss as they enable organisations to adjust and adapt more quickly to unexpected circumstances.

Further Reading – Business Continuity Planning Resources

Various publications are available for guidance on business continuity.

- The Standards Australia handbooks HB 292:2006 *A Practitioners Guide to Business Continuity Management* and HB 293:2006 *An executive guide to business continuity management* outline standard business continuity practices and emerging practices in Australia, the US and the UK.
- *BCM Legislations, regulations & standards*, produced by the BCI, describe legislation, regulations and standards around the world. It is regularly updated (last updated February 2016).
- ISO/IEC 27031:2011 *Information technology – Security techniques – Guidelines for information and communication technology readiness for business continuity* focus on information and communication technology aspects of BCM.

Activity | Reviewing the BCP

Review the BCP for your organisation, or that of an organisation of which you are aware.

- *Verify that the plan contains all the elements included above as a 'typical structure'. If it doesn't, ascertain by discussion with relevant managers the reason for the difference and determine if the plan would be made stronger by the inclusion of the additional information.*
- *Does the plan give sufficient details regarding the author, revision, distribution list and so on to enable complete knowledge to be gained about the administration of the plan?*

BCP Contents

The contents of a BCP include the following.

- Part 1: Plan overview
- Part 2: Accountability, roles, responsibilities and authorities
- Part 3: Notification, escalation and activation
- Part 4: Command centre
- Part 5: Contacts
- Part 6: Checklists
- Part 7: Supporting information
- Part 8: Critical business activities – recovery action plan

- Part 9: Recovery resource profile
- Part 10: Recovery site location
- Part 11: Communication plans
- Part 12: Standard form templates
- Appendices

Part 1: Plan Overview

- Introduction – what is the plan and how is it structured?
- Purpose of the plan – what is the basic aim of the plan; what are the critical success factors that have to be achieved and what is the level of continuity capability that must be achieved?
- Scope – what business processes, systems, assets and disruption scenarios is the plan intended to cover, and what is not included?
- Objectives – what is meant to be achieved by the use of the plan?
- Assumptions – what are the basic assumptions on which the plan is based, including existence and use of resources?
- Plan ownership – who is responsible for the plan, its updating and its exercising?
- Event/Decision log – what records are to be kept and by whom in the event of the activation of the plan?
- Details of other BCPs that may relate to the plan – for example, a 'loss of computer systems plan' referenced in a 'loss of head office plan' where the computer centre is located within the head office premises.

Part 2: Accountability, Roles, Responsibilities and Authorities

- The emergency management team (EMT) may be chaired by the CEO and may include some of the organisation's senior executives. The purpose of the EMT is to manage emergencies of such magnitude that the strategic objectives, or even the survival of the organisation, are at stake to ensure the safety of staff and the public during a physical emergency and to activate the organisation's crisis management or BCPs as required.
- A BCP management team has a similar role to the EMT but for events other than those classified as an emergency. (One team might be called, for example, the loss of key building management team.) The BCP management team generally comprises senior management and specialist expert staff. The team should be led by an executive or senior manager who is capable of leading under conditions of extreme stress and capable of making good decisions based on high uncertainty. Senior managers do not necessarily have these skills and experience so many organisations employ specific crisis managers who have armed forces or emergency services leadership backgrounds for this role. The purpose of this team is to manage crisis situations, short of full-scale emergencies, for a specific continuity event or a core business activity, to their conclusion. Part of the role might involve coordination or oversight of the recovery/restoration process mentioned in an earlier section of this module.

As part of the risk-management team, the business continuity manager's role is to coordinate the efforts of the business continuity team (BCT) in resuming services following a disruption event and ensure that the crisis management team (and as necessary the EMT) is kept fully informed of actions being taken.

- The BCT comprises the business unit and support staff whose role is to ensure the continuity of the business functions in accordance with the BCP. The team will include all necessary persons to ensure that the BCP can be fully activated, including IT&T professionals, premises and services personnel, business unit personnel and HR staff.
- This part should include details of the membership of the teams and their nominated alternatives to carry out the role if they should not be available as required. The part also should include the specific duties of each of the teams, and as necessary individual team members, on the occurrence of a disruption event, the initial data that must be gathered and the initial decisions and actions to be taken.

Part 3: Notification, Escalation and Activation

- Details of the process for notifying the business continuity manager of a disruption event, the escalation of information to management, the BCPMT and the EMT and the relevant emergency management, crisis management and BCPs – preferably by, or at least including, the use of flowchart diagrams;
- Call out (call tree) cascade process including details of third-party service provider if required;

Part 4: Command Centre

- Location and contact details of BCM command centre/s, including map of BCM command centre location/s, transport logistics, car parking facilities, etc., if required;
- Details of the command centre resources, including relevant floor plans and IT&T and electrical cabling schematics;
- Details of access; etc. to the command centre, when it should be used and by whom

Part 5: Contacts

- Internal
- External
- Subject experts (who may be either internal or external resources);

Part 6: Checklists

- Details of relevant checklists and memory aids

Part 7: Supporting Information

- Health and safety including dealing with injuries and fatalities and the resultant staff welfare and counselling
- Media and public relations
- Emergency services liaison
- Finance
- Legal advice
- Suppliers (intra-organisation and outsourced providers)
- Insurance advisory – who to contact with what information
- Activation of specialist services
- Communications – e.g. staff and customer helplines;

Part 8: Critical Business Activities – recovery Action Plan

- Schedule of critical business activities and their interdependencies or support activities, including their maximum tolerable outage (MTO) and recovery time objective (RTO), that is, maximum acceptable downtime;
- Details of regulatory and/or contractual requirements in respect of the core business activities and their interdependencies or support activities;
- The recovery action plan to achieve the recovery time and recovery point objectives of the core business activities and their interdependencies or support activities;
- Diagrammatic recovery action plan to show the tasks required, the order in which they should be completed, and the estimated time taken to complete, for example, a Gantt chart setting out full details of the process;

Part 9: Recovery Resource Profile

- Personnel required, numbers, skills, etc. or else specific roles
- Infrastructure required – e.g. standard workstations; i.e. desk, chair, telephone and PC, office equipment and specialist equipment
- IT&T requirements including systems, computer equipment, software applications, technology connectivity, telecommunications, telecommunications links, and backed-up data
- Vital documents and records both technology and paper-based and appropriate supplies of stationery
- Recovery site location requirements – e.g. disabled person access.

Part 10: Recovery Site Location. This part applies no matter if the recovery site is supplied within the organisation or by a third-party supplier.

- Activation process – preferably as a flowchart diagram
- Recovery site (work area) floor plan layout

- Location of recovery site including a map of location and details of travel requirements/logistics including public transport, car parking facilities, etc. if necessary
- Details for relocation of staff (including transport and accommodation)
- Miscellaneous information such as security, mail arrangements, etc.

Part 11: Communication Plans

- Details of communication plans to be implemented following activation of the BCP.
- Maintain an up-to-date data bank with the information that communicators will need.

Part 12: Standard Form Templates

- Meeting agendas
- Internal briefings
- Decision and action log
- Task list status report
- Telephone message
- Action or task worksheet.

Appendices

- Contracts and service level agreements
- Information that needs continual updating – staff lists, contact lists, relocation site floor plans, etc.

Self-Help Question 5.3

Develop a generic notification, escalation and activation section for a BCP.

Answers to self-help questions are provided at the end of each section.

Testing and Training Programmes

BCPs need to be tested before they are fully implemented. Testing is also commonly known as exercising and has two main objectives. It is used:

- to enable continual improvement of the organisation's BCPs to ensure the recovery/restoration of its core business activities and their dependencies occurs within the set objectives;

- to evaluate and enable the continual improvement of the organisation's BCM competence and capability.

Developing an organisation's BCM skills and capability is achieved through a structured and consistent testing programme. To be successful, a testing program should begin simply and escalate gradually. It is also important that only the resources that will be available during an actual business continuity event are engaged during the test. However, if the test involves using, or could affect, live organisation systems, experts in these systems must be available to resolve and rectify issues if something goes wrong in the test or if unexpected matters arise that are outside the knowledge and skills of the testing team.

Adopting and applying a structured and systematic approach to the development and implementation of a testing program will promote a greater understanding of the BCM process for all individuals.

According to the Business Continuity Institute, testing an organisation's BCPs will:

- identify areas for improvement or missing information;
- highlight assumptions that need to be questioned;
- provide information and instil confidence in test participants;
- develop team work among participants;
- raise awareness of business continuity throughout the organisation;
- analyse the effectiveness and timeliness of restoration procedures (depending on whether or not this is tested as part of the recovery stage).

Approaches to Testing Programmes

Armit and Marvell, in their paper, 'Maintaining and exercising business continuity plans', state:

> There is always a drive to large-scale multiplatform, multi-user tests but in most cases this is inappropriate in the early stages of the planning cycle. In fact best practice has shown that to improve plans and work towards successful testing, a three-year cycle should be adopted. Tests in the early years are probably misnamed and can lead to trepidation; the word test conjures up exams and success or failure criteria, which is not the aim. A better name might be a training exercise or workshop. The aim in the first two years of a programme is to prove the procedures and plans and educate those involved in their roles and responsibilities. To assist in this, exercises should build up in a structured manner. It may be a cliché but don't run before you can walk.

This table below shows a progression and potential combinations of tests that would satisfy the requirements of Armit and Marvell.

Type	Process	Participants
Desk check/ desktop review	Review and challenge the contents of the plan	• Author of plan • Independent checker
Walkthrough plan and/or infrastructure	Extended desk check to view interaction and the roles of participants	• Author of plan • Main participants
Simulation	Incorporates associated plans: • Business • Site/buildings • Communication • Public relations • IT disaster recovery BCM resource recovery suppliers	• Facilitator • Main participants • Observers • Co-ordinators
Functions	Moves to and recreates one or a number of business functions at an alternative pre-planned site	• Employees and staff in specific business areas • Facilitator • Co-ordinators • Observers • BC resource recovery providers
Full plan	Close down of the entire site/ building and relocation of work	• Staff required for recovery activities included in the BCP • Facilitator • Co-ordinators • Observers • BC resource recovery providers

Adapted from: Elliot, Swartz and Herbane, 1999, p. 84.

The Standards Australia/Standards New Zealand Handbook HB 292:2006 *A practitioners guide to business continuity management* recognises six progressive test types. These are:

- desktop review (sometimes known as plan audits)
- desktop walkthrough
- desktop scenario exercise
- call-out and notification communications exercise
- recovery exercise
- live scenario exercise (sometimes known as 'large scale testing').

Desktop review

A desktop review is a physical review of the documentation to ensure that the plan is accurate, complete, comprehensive, simple to read and understand, and structured in a logical manner. This review will probably be carried out by the BCP co-ordinator or business continuity manager, the BCP owner and those staff or other persons who will use the plan following a business continuity event.

Desktop walkthrough

A desktop walkthrough is a guided presentation, generally by the relevant BCP co-ordinator or owner, to those personnel with allocated responsibilities within the plan. The presentation will include discussion of the contents of the plan, the circumstances under which the plan would be activated, and how the plan would be expected to be used if activated. This walkthrough enables the relevant personnel to understand their roles within the plan and challenge assumptions, procedures and so on based on their own knowledge. This will assist in getting the personnel engaged with the BCP.

Desktop scenario exercise

A desktop scenario exercise is similar to the walkthrough but uses hypothetical scenarios to examine the assumptions made in the plan. A variant of this test is to extend the hypothetical scenarios to include role playing for one or more scenarios.

Call-out and notification communications exercise

A call-out and notification communications exercise involves activation of the relevant call-out trees and contacting the personnel required in the case of a disruption event. This test will verify the currency of the contact details held in respect of the plan and the assumptions made about contacting personnel, especially out of hours and on weekends. It will also bring home to the persons contacted, and those who have to contact other personnel, the reality of what will happen if a plan is activated.

Recovery exercise

A recovery exercise is a test of an individual or a small number of key elements of a plan in isolation from the remainder of the plan's functions. This is conducted by closing down or removing or restricting access to the elements of the system or infrastructure being tested. This process, which can be carried on until all of the plan's elements are tested, ensures the viability of the plan and the recovery capability of each component part, without the high risk and cost of testing all of the plan's elements at one time. The more elements of a plan that are tested together, the higher the likelihood that one of the recovery strategies will fail and probably prevent the completion of the total test, resulting in increased costs for no or little benefit. The call-out and notification communications and recovery exercises are parts of what is commonly known as component testing.

Armit and Marvell list the following examples of component testing:

- An (out-of-hours) telephone test to prove the capability of the cascades in place and ensure all key team members can be contacted in a timely manner.
- An audit of off-site data with random testing to prove the currency and validity of the data to the business.
- Recovery of individual's specific technologies to prove in isolation that technological procedures are accurate.
- Execution of identified business 'workarounds' to prove the business can operate without technology or in a reduced capacity.
- An invocation of recovery contracts to ensure the contracts in place are adequate to requirements.

It is recommended that each of the plan's elements be tested as part of component testing to ensure that a gradual build-up to a future complete test is undertaken. By following this approach, organisations will be assured that all personnel and subcomponent areas are aware of their roles and responsibilities before a full test is undertaken.

Live scenario exercise

A live scenario exercise is the ultimate level of testing involving testing the complete plan or even for a number of overlapping or complementary plans. For example, a test of the continuity plan for the loss of the head office of an organisation might also invoke plans for the loss of IT systems and a call centre or specialised department housed in the head office.

Caution also must be exercised when conducting a live scenario exercise that the findings of the exercise, on which the executive and the board will rely as to the ability of the organisation to meet its business recovery objectives, are representative of business as usual. For example, it cannot be assumed that because a bank satisfactorily booted up its disaster recovery system and linked to the branches for trading on a Saturday morning when only four branches were open and transactions were limited that the recovery system will be able to cope with a 'normal business day's' transactions being input from the whole of the branch network and administrative staff.

It is critical that BCP testing is also subject to stress testing to ensure that it can satisfy the BCP and recovery objectives. If this is not possible, because of the nature of the organisation's business, then the persons who rely on the findings and results must be made fully aware of the limitations of the test and the risks and possible consequences associated with these. If the BCP test is not conducted under full stress conditions, testing all of the BCP functions, it should be referred to as a component exercise.

While extensive testing will ensure that the interdependencies between the various plans are satisfactory and that the plans are robust, a test of this nature will require extensive planning and will be expensive in terms of resources and management time to stage. A test on this scale will also greatly increase the risk of the test affecting the organisation's major business objectives. The benefits must be carefully balanced with the costs and risks of conducting the test.

Full-scale tests are often carried out over weekends or other periods when the normal business of the organisation is not being conducted. If this is the case, the planning needs to take account of any anomalies that may occur as a result of the timing (for example, transport facilities may not be readily available for staff over a public holiday), and sufficient leeway must be built into the testing plan to ensure that systems can be properly reset and their production status confirmed in sufficient time prior to normal work recommencing.

Tests of this nature are very difficult to conduct in many businesses today because of the prevalence of continuous (24/7) operations. In these cases, tests are often planned as part of a regular maintenance program to ensure that the business is not unduly affected. For example, in a financial institution with mirrored computer sites where there is a regular swap between sites for equipment maintenance, the maintenance swap can be used as a test for a loss of IT systems BCP.

Undertaking Scenario Exercises

Developing scenarios of how business continuity events could arise and are likely to play out is an excellent way of testing an organisation's BCPs. There is a growing trend to use a team approach involving the main actors to develop the scenario rather than baffle the team with an unexpected scenario (see last paragraph on role playing). To use this technique the organisation should:

- choose highly critical continuity events or issues only;
- develop continuity event scenarios with a plot or storyline around those events or issues;
- role-play the potential event and the activation of the BCP.

Choose critical issue scenarios – as scenario planning is time-consuming, it should only be used for issues that are really critical to the organisation. For example, situations where if the organisation did not respond correctly the consequences could be disastrous.

In the case of business continuity, these issues are likely to be those that involve a major IT systems problem, major damage to the organisation's physical assets or would result in loss of life. Although the likelihood of the event occurring may be low, the consequences would be very severe.

Develop scenario plots – a storyline or plot needs to be developed for each scenario, setting out the conditions and circumstances that may give rise to:

- the continuity event;
- the hypotheses relating to the event that need to be tested.

The plots themselves will be simple – the purpose of the scenario exercise is to test the ability of the relevant continuity teams to use the emergency and BCPs to manage the event and continue the business in the prescribed manner.

Role-play the scenario – the scenario should then be played out, from identifying a disruption event, through the notification and escalation of the information, to the activation of the relevant emergency, business continuity and communication teams and plans. If external professionals (for example, media and emergency services personnel) can be involved in the scenario enactment, this will increase the realism of the exercise.

Role-playing a scenario also brings out the real-time issues related to a potential continuity event without having to go through the real-time consequences. It will ensure that all persons with roles in the scenario, including the BCP management team, the EMT and the communications management team understand what is required of them in the case that the plan is activated. This helps members of the various management teams prepare for a possible event in less stressful conditions than an actual event and highlights weaknesses in either the preparations of the organisation and its plans or the skills of the team.

Effectiveness of BCP Testing

The higher the level of testing and the more components of a plan tested, the higher the level of assurance of the plan's overall viability that is gained. However, these benefits must be weighed against the disruption and costs of conducting the tests and the increased risk of the organisation's continuity being affected by testing the plan.

The trade-off between cost and benefit is illustrated in the following figure:

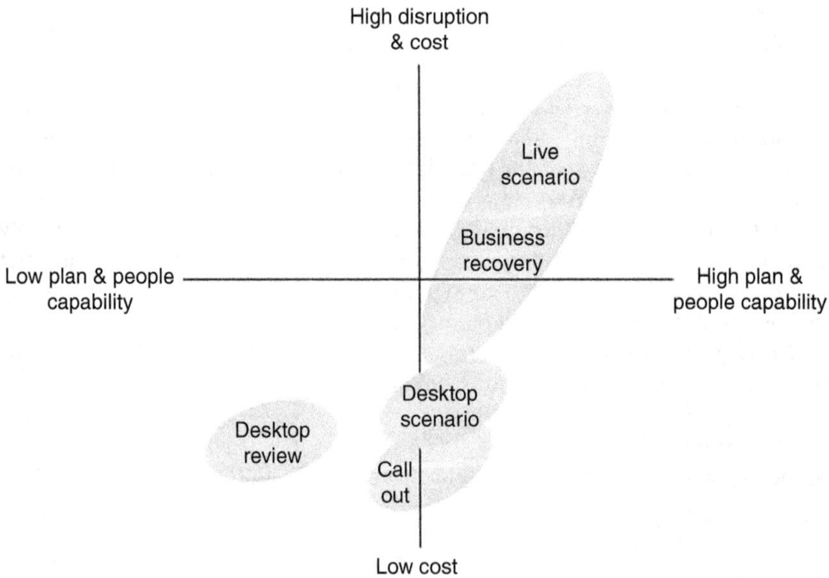

The Standards Australia/Standards New Zealand Handbook HB 292:2006 *A Practitioners Guide to Business Continuity Management* sets out the following considerations that should be addressed to ensure effectiveness when testing BCPs:

- The test is capable of highlighting issues that will verify plans are practical, feasible and up to date.
- Participation in the test can promote increased familiarity of the plans for those individuals with responsibilities under the plans.
- The test will provide appropriate assurance that key individuals understand their roles and responsibilities during a disruption.
- The test will be able to confirm that resource requirements and key contacts are appropriate to the task at hand and are current.
- The practical issues regarding implementing and managing alternate workarounds will be examined during the test.
- Staff will be appropriately and adequately rehearsed in the activation and implementation of plans.
- Outputs from the test will support continuing improvement and maintenance of the plans.
- Scenarios should be based on events that have occurred or would have occurred if proper risk management mitigation had not been in place, either to the organisation or to other organisations either within the same industry or same geographical area, that could feasibly happen to the organisation.

Case Study – BCP Component Exercising: Call-Out Communication

In two organisations, recent testing started with proving the call-out communication cascades. These are simple tests to organise, very cost-effective and are the perfect way to raise awareness of business continuity and how it affects individuals.

This test aimed to prove that within three hours of an incident being identified out of hours, key messages could be passed to every member of staff. The primary organisation used in this example employed 1,500 staff within the scope of the test.

The test specified that every member of staff contacted would complete a log, pass on and record a specific message and answer four questions. Log-keeping is essential in all incidents for many reasons and encouraging staff to keep logs during simple tests ensures that more complex, stressful events will be logged adequately. The message passing was considered important to help to ensure that staff logged key events accurately and could transmit this information to others.

The questions were:

- Do you have your plan at home?
- What version is it?
- Do you have a company laptop?
- If yes, is the laptop at home?

The first two are standard questions that allow the control team to understand how effective their distribution of plans has been and to identify if staff have them to hand. The last two questions were specific to this organisation. Many business areas had insisted that they had company laptops and as such planning was not essential as they would have the information on their laptop and would not be impacted.

A single call was made to the initial 'out-of-hours' contact. He was then responsible for contacting the initial crisis management team and subsequently triggering cascades across the organisation. Each member of staff contacted was instructed to call into a central area to allow the flow of the test to be monitored by the BCP management team. This element had been introduced after an earlier test that, having been left to run alone, had missed out significant large areas of the business. As the organisation was still trying to educate not test, there was more value to the organisation in triggering these areas independently and logging the event than there was in leaving them to fail. After three hours, the test finished.

The results showed 672 people, or 45% of the workforce, were contacted directly within three hours, and that over 90% of staff who had company laptops had left them at work. Whilst the contact figure does not look significantly high, there was no single area of the business that had not been contacted and, for a first event, this was deemed a success; when retested 12 months later, more than 1,000 people were contacted.

Self-Help Question 5.4

With regard to the facts and results set out in the above case study, describe the benefits you think that the organisation gained by conducting this BCP component test.

Answers to self-help questions are provided at the end of each section.

BCP Testing Plans

Prior to any testing of a BCP, a structured plan should be developed by the BCP owner with the assistance of the business continuity manager and the relevant business and technical experts.

Comprehensive planning is critical in ensuring a properly structured and appropriate BCP test. The major questions/issues to be addressed in the planning stage include:

- What is the objective of the test, and how will we know if this objective is achieved?
- What could go wrong during the test, and how could we either prevent this or mitigate the consequences?
- If something does go wrong, how will we know and what could we do to rectify the matter?
- Under what circumstances would the test be cancelled or aborted?
- Are any pre-tests required and can this testing be scheduled?

Most of these issues can be best addressed using brainstorming techniques with appropriate systems experts and business users. The outcomes from these planning sessions are used to populate the BCP.

As with all plans, the BCP test plan should contain details of the author and date of creation; have a section to show amendments; have an approval section for signature by the managers of the business functions involved in the test together and the team leaders and technical experts responsible for ensuring the safe testing of the plan; and include a list of personnel to whom the plan has been distributed.

The contents of the draft plan should be used to carry out briefings of all personnel, both internal and external, who may be affected by the BCP test. This includes staff and management in the areas subject to the test, functions dependent upon the activities being tested and senior management. All relevant feedback should be incorporated into the final BCP test plan.

The plan must be accepted and approved by relevant senior management, systems experts and so on. It must be ensured that these personnel are fully aware of the test's assumptions and risks.

BCP Exercise Plan Contents

1. Name of plan – test plan unique name
2. Date of test – when is the test to take place and over what period?
3. Type of test – desktop review, live scenario, etc.
4. Test scenario – what is being tested?
   For example, a loss of a call centre with relocation to backup site.

5. Objective – what is to be achieved?
   For example, demonstrate that call centre functions can be operated from backup premises within MTO and RTO criteria.
6. Scope of test – what is going to be tested and what is not?
   For example, that call centre systems are available at the backup site but not that staff can be transported from the call centre to the backup site.
7. Resource requirements – systems, infrastructure, personnel, services, supplies and records
8. Roles and responsibilities – who is responsible for what in the test?
9. Risk matrix – what risks might arise as a result of the test (for example corruption of live customer data), what mitigation measures are in place to reduce the risk to an acceptable limit and what process is in place to rectify any problems?
10. Go/no-go scenarios – what are the issues that need to be considered before the test can be authorised to begin?
    For example, do communications experts need to be on standby to ensure correct communications links are opened?
11. Early termination scenarios – under what circumstances would the test be brought to a premature close?
    For example, corruption of live data or an actual interruption event? Success criteria – how is the success of the exercise to be defined?
    For example, live systems made available for call centre activities in back-up locations.

Training

To ensure the test runs smoothly, all personnel who will be involved must be thoroughly briefed before the test begins on their roles and responsibilities. They should be told what the organisation is trying to achieve and why the test is important. They must also be made aware of the risk events that could occur during the test, how to recognise them and what to do and who to tell if one occurs.

All personnel involved must keep a detailed log of what they did and any anomalies that arose and how they were dealt with. The logs need not include every transaction but must list the process being carried out, when it started, total number of transactions processed, and time of completion. Logs are useful for debriefing reviews and reports.

Although the test is intended to be run under emergency conditions, the welfare of involved staff must be taken into consideration. If the test location is not the staff's usual work location they need to be advised of the local amenities and facilities, emergency rules, for example fire exits, and issues such as catering.

When conducting BCP testing, it is important that one or more independent observers are present to record any matters that arise during the overall test that would not have been logged by an individual team. For example, intervention by a systems expert to resolve an issue that the user could not resolve, or environmental conditions such as temperature fluctuations. One of these observers should be, or represent, the business continuity manager. User or technical managers may also be observers – although not involved directly in the test, their observations may help improve the BCP.

When the test is complete, a debriefing session should be held immediately, generally by the business continuity manager, to discuss the issues that arose and ways of improving either the test or the BCP. The findings from the debriefing together with the logs should be used to prepare a comprehensive report on the test and its outcomes for senior management.

Awareness

It is important to develop a BCM culture within an organisation. Successfully doing so primarily depends on BCM becoming an integral part of the organisation's strategic and day-to-day management philosophy rather than an 'add-on'.

Effective risk management depends, in part, on the behaviour of individuals within an organisation, and a significant number of business continuity events can be traced to unthinking behaviours or to thinking that does not take into account the reality of the context. Poorly designed operations, systems and working conditions can all encourage behaviours that might lead to accidents, errors or wilful sabotage; however, such behaviours are not inevitable. An organisation's attitudes and values regarding effective working are important factors that influence the approach to work, and ultimately to an organisation's continuity. It is insufficient to provide good systems and procedures if the culture is not conducive to error-free working.

Embedding a BCM Culture

Culture has been defined as consisting of shared values (what is important) and beliefs (how things work) that interact with an organisation's structure and control systems to produce behavioural norms (the way we do things around here).

A poor organisational culture is likely to lead to weaknesses due to underperformance at the person–work interface – often due to poor training or communication. It can encourage an atmosphere of non-compliance with good operating practices and tends not to encourage staff to take action to remedy problems that could result in continuity issues.

A BCM culture change is not achieved quickly and plans to improve the culture of an organisation must take into account the existing culture, which would have evolved over an extended period. A culture change programme is also very unlikely to succeed unless there is a commitment to change at the highest management levels. Attempts to change culture too quickly may result in resistance to change.

An important aspect of plans to develop a values-driven BCM culture is 'organisational learning' – the process of involving personnel who learn to change their ways of thinking and acting as a result of shared experience and addressing shared problems. Mutual trust and confidence between management and the workforce are necessary to develop a strong BCM culture, and it is vital that managers at all levels of the organisation accept that business continuity is a line management responsibility.

Components of a BCM Culture

A BCM culture does not exist in isolation within an organisation, it is part of the risk management culture. Furthermore, it is influenced by organisational culture and is a composite of components, as set out in the figure below. Before it can be said that a BCM culture exists, all these components must be in place and be working effectively.

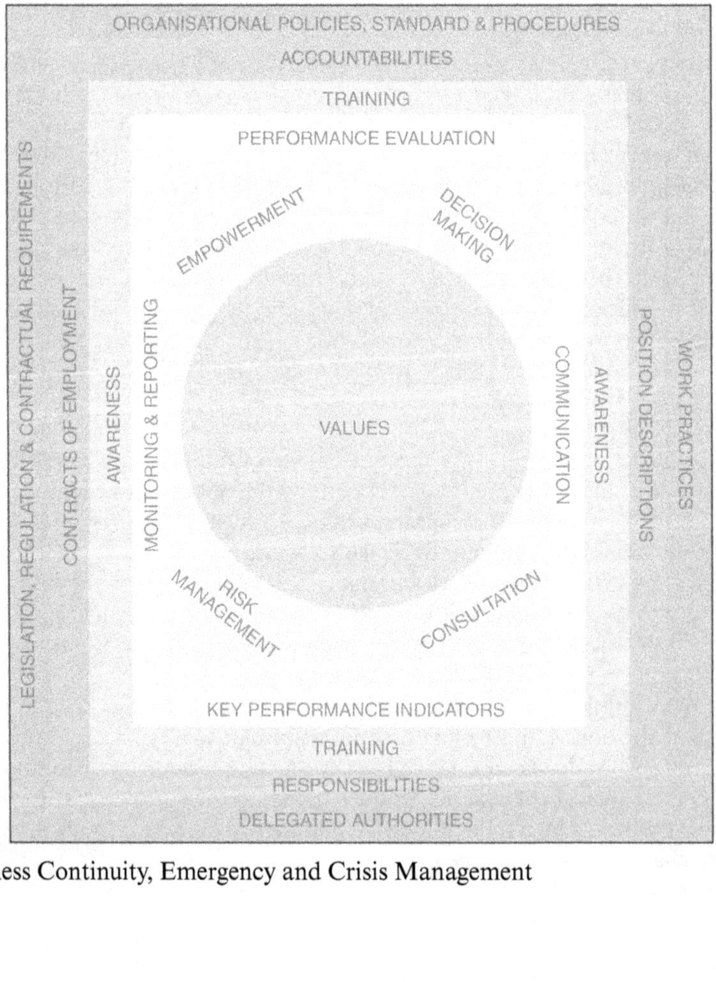

Business Continuity, Emergency and Crisis Management

These components can be summarised as the external and organisational structure, individuals' accountabilities and responsibilities, training and awareness, feedback loops, the working environment, and the values of the organisation and its people.

The characteristics and requirements of these components are as follows.

External and Organisational Structure. This component sets the context of the required culture by reference to the regulatory and third-party contractual environment, the desired work practices and group policies, standards and procedures, including the formalised delegated authorities of personnel. It creates the framework in which all the other components operate.

Accountabilities and Responsibilities. This component concentrates on the individual employee. It defines the employee's role, responsibilities and accountabilities, and individual authorities. Accountability implies acceptance of the responsibility for any decision or course of action adopted, the consequences thereof, and a commitment to resolving any issues that arise as a result.

Training and Awareness. A BCM culture is the same as an informed culture. An informed culture is one in which the members of the organisation understand the risks of their operations and are alert to the many ways in which the system's defences can be breached or bypassed. This understanding comes from the awareness of continuity operating requirements and tools, techniques and practices used to manage these requirements gained through training and relevant specialist communication.

Feedback Loops. Feedback loops are an integral component of a BCM and risk management culture. These loops ensure that performance is monitored and reported and is used to reinforce the BCM culture of the organisation. Communication in this context is the two-way communication up and down the organisation about lessons learned and the reinforcement and renewal of the culture based on these lessons. When properly delivered, positive feedback is likely to bring about significant improvements in compliance with BCM requirements.

Working Environment. This component addresses the day-to-day working environment. That is, the hazard identification, risk assessment and risk mitigation; the consultation with the people involved in carrying out the tasks to ensure that they understand the risks and have input in the risk mitigation strategies; the normal decision-making process to agree the level of risk mitigation; and the empowerment to ensure that all employees have the authority to insist on proper business continuity practices (for example, ensuring that all potential purchases of new hardware take into account the BCM implications of the implementation of that hardware into the organisation).

Values. The Oxford Dictionary defines values as 'the principles or moral standards of a person or social group; the generally accepted or personally held judgement of what is valuable or important in life'. In the context of a BCM culture, values include the organisation's standards and attitudes to business continuity as well as the standards and attitudes of individual managers and workers.

Values are the glue that holds all of the other components together inside the framework. When decisions have to be made within the context of the framework (for example, they are legal, authorised and educated), they are made with reference to the values. If the values are universally held within the organisation, then decisions made in accordance with these values will be acceptable to all interested parties. Having a set of values to which the whole organisation subscribes gives a truly valuable base for making decisions in a time of extreme uncertainty.

Communication and Crisis Management Programmes

Larry Smith, president of the Kentucky-based Institute for Crisis Management in the US defines a crisis as:

> [...] a significant business disruption which stimulates extensive news media coverage. The resulting public scrutiny will affect the organisation's normal operations and also could have political, legal, financial, and governmental impact on its business.

Mitroff, Pearson and Harrington refer to a crisis across a broad range of areas:

> A crisis can affect the very existence of an organisation, a major product line, a business unit, or the like. A crisis can also damage an organisation's financial performance. A crisis can also cause the death of or harm the well-being of consumers, employees, the surrounding community and the environment itself. Finally, a crisis can destroy the public's basic trust or belief in an organisation, its reputation and its image.

Goemans states that there are four characteristics defining crisis:

1. A crisis constitutes a series of events rather than the management of a single event.
2. A crisis may be caused by a disaster, although not necessarily a physical disaster.
3. A crisis has a diffuse origin making it difficult for decision-makers to gain a macro view of events.
4. It is unclear what action needs to be taken.

It can be seen from these definitions that the main difference between a crisis and a normal business continuity event is that a crisis goes to the heart of the survival of the organisation, involves the interest of a wider audience than just the organisation's employees and customers, is of great interest to the media, and which has to be managed without necessarily knowing the full facts of the situation, see Chapter 4.

An emergency does not necessarily generate a crisis, but it can escalate into a crisis. For example, a small fire in a plant would be classified as an emergency. If that fire were to spread, engulfing a building containing toxic chemicals and resulting in a deadly explosion and spreading gas cloud, it would be considered a crisis.

In addition to crises caused by fires, explosions, accidents and product recalls, Campbell, in *Crisis Control: Preventing and Managing Corporate Crises*, notes eleven business situations that may result in an organisational crisis:

- business scandal
- senior executive resignation or termination
- government investigation
- bankruptcy
- lay-offs
- hostile takeover
- loss of vital information
- major reorganisation or merger
- regulatory changes
- abrupt market changes
- criticism of corporate governance.

Often emergency events become crises because the organisation does not take the required steps to either avoid the initial emergency incident, even though they had sufficient knowledge and warning, or else are slow to realise the full consequences of the incident and hence are slow in reacting and limiting the damage.

Managing a Crisis

There are three key points in managing a crisis. Firstly, upper management must understand how the incident can affect an organisation and its goals and how the crisis can hurt the organisation. Secondly, upper management must be able to identify the persons and groups that control the public opinion of the organisation and the crisis incident, with special attention to social media. Finally, management has to understand how best to react to and communicate with those groups, or how to be able to by-pass them and control public opinion directly.

As previously noted, one of the main distinguishing features between an emergency and a crisis is the interest of the media in the event. The media and other special-purpose interest groups, for example Greenpeace and local community groups, are generally the persons who control the public opinion of the organisation. Taking control of, and managing the crisis communication, is, therefore, critical to the successful management and resolution of a crisis.

The media, besides being a major communications stakeholder in its own right, is also an essential channel for delivering the organisation's desired messages to the other important organisation stakeholders. Every effort should be made to facilitate communication with the media, including social media.

Crisis Communication and the Media

In a report on the disastrous Union Carbide explosion in Bhopal, India in 1984, the management consulting firm of Arthur D Little noted:

> In the immediate aftermath of a large-magnitude incident, both non-technical and technically-trained reporters converge on the site, looking for quick 'answers' to the question of what caused the event. Most reporters are responsible, restrained, and unbiased in their reporting. However, a fringe group usually appears on-site that is more interested in developing causation theories, which seem to have great public appeal, regardless of their veracity.

An organisation dealing with a crisis that can or does affect a wider audience must expect this type of media attention and must learn to deal with it appropriately, and nowadays pay a special attention to social media.

Do	**Don't**
Take your time	Lie, guess or speculate
Think before you answer	Get upset or angry with the reporter
Keep to your own area and level of expertise	Let yourself be stressed by the situation or the reporter
Say if you don't know, cannot or may not answer the question	Use expert language/jargon
Stick to the facts	Discuss confidential information
Assume that everything is 'on the record'	Use the expression 'no comment'
Be firm, fair and honest	Talk about things outside your area of expertise

The Swedish Emergency Management Agency has issued the following simple but effective and essential rules to consider when talking to the media:

Douglas Hearle, a senior consultant in the field of crisis communication has similar advice and has developed a series of what he calls the 'F- words' to ensure that the crisis communication is effective. These words are as follows.

- **Fast** – be the first to bring the crisis situation to the attention of the organisation's stakeholders.
- **Fully** – provide as much detail as possible.

- **Factual** – ensure that you tell the truth and deal only with facts.
- **Frank** – be honest in all communications with the organisation's stakeholders.
- **Forthright** – don't deny the existence of the crisis. Being involved in a crisis is not an admittance of guilt.
- **Focus** – ensure that the organisation's communication's message is focussed and consistent.
- **Facility** – provide the media with facilities to assist them to do their job.
- **Feedback** – communication is a two-way process, look for feedback and listen to what is being said.
- **Feeling** – make sure that the organisation and the people in it have empathy for and show compassion to any victims of the crisis incident.

No matter what you do you will never be able to control all of the communication with the media. Crises by definition arise when least expected and they can generally be relied on to happen at the most inconvenient time, at least for the organisation concerned. As Campbell says:

> It is amazing how many night watchmen become corporate spokespersons when a disaster occurs on the night-time watch at large industrial plants. Equally, it comes as no surprise how few night watchmen are trained to face a barrage of questions from media, neighbours, environmentalists and others following a negative event. This night watchman is often the only person available for comment in the first 30 minutes of a site disaster after hours.

As part of planning for a crisis, an organisation should create a crisis management team and allocate specific tasks to specific team members. One of these tasks will be to act as a spokesperson in the event of a crisis. However, in the event of a crisis, what has often noted is that senior management pre-empts the crisis management team and is individually willing to speak to the media as experts in their own area of the organisation. Similarly, the CEO or board chairman, if not appointed as the organisation's spokesperson, will often assume the role of spokesperson even if they have not been trained for the task.

Board chairmen, CEOs and senior management are not, as a rule, used to having their decisions and pronouncements questioned. Reporters on the other hand are trained to question in detail any matter addressed to them, and expect to have their questions answered. The result can be an abrasive media representative and a defensive or even hostile organisation spokesperson. This does not make for positive communication by the organisation and may easily result in adverse media coverage detrimental to the organisation's reputation or reduce the organisation's ability to manage the crisis.

All persons who are given the responsibility to act as spokespersons for an organisation while managing a crisis must be given sound training in dealing with the media and other possible anti-organisation stakeholder groups such as environmentalists and local community activist groups as part of the preparation for a crisis. Trying to do this training when the crisis has commenced is far too late.

Crisis Management Team

The selection of appropriate personnel as members of the crisis management team is critical (or as we have been referring to it in this module, the EMT). Each crisis an organisation faces is likely to be different and will require a specifically tailored response, but a number of functions and activities are common to all crises. Managing a crisis is likely to be complex and demanding; critical decisions are likely to be made without the benefit of the full facts to support the decisions; and the decisions will need to be made fast and probably under stressful conditions. People who are perfectly capable of managing the day-to-day activities and functions of an organisation, although they are hard-working, decisive and innovative managers, may not necessarily have the personality and experience to manage the same functions or activities in a crisis situation.

Members of a crisis management team (or an EMT) are therefore chosen for their skills and abilities at managing people and functions while under stress and having the ability to make good decisions under conditions of uncertainty. These people are not necessarily all members of the senior management team – indeed it is likely that a number of the team members will come from middle management. Some people may be specifically employed in roles to enable them to take control of emergencies and crises – for example, people with training and experience in the armed forces or emergency services.

Campbell recommends that the crisis management team comprises a team leader, who may be the organisation's CEO, although this is not mandatory, and team members to be responsible for the following roles:

- corporate affairs and media
- human resources and family
- emergency services and security
- operations
- command centre and call-out
- administration and commercial services
- recovery.

The responsibilities of these team members are as follows:

- **Team leader** – confirmation of the crisis status, co-ordinating the team, liaising with the EMT (if the EMT is a separate team), allocating resources, setting priorities and selecting and briefing the crisis spokesperson.
- **Corporate affairs and media** – creating communications, media management, briefing the crisis spokesperson and monitoring communications feedback, including blog manager and social media.
- **Human resources and family** – welfare, rehabilitation, counselling and management of staff and staff family communication.
- **Emergency and security** – liaison with emergency services, site and personnel security, external assistance and evacuation as necessary.
- **Operations** – liaison with managers of ongoing organisation operations.

- **Command centre and call-out** – alerting and call-out of team, command centre set-up and command centre operations.
- **Administration and commercial services** – legal, insurance and financial issues;
- **Recovery** – activating recovery and restoration plans.

As with any other continuity management team, there needs to be a fully trained alternative for each member of the team, including the team leader, who can step into the position if the primary team member is not available.

In their 1995 paper 'Defining competencies and establishing team training requirements', J Cannon-Bowers, S Tannenbaum, E Salas and C Volpe identified the following characteristics, requirements and key dimensions for an effective team:

- **Characteristics** – individual task proficiency; clear, concise communication; collective orientation; and shared goal and mission.
- **Requirements** – shared understanding of the task; shared understanding of other members' responsibilities; team leadership; collective efficacy (aware of each other's needs); and self-monitoring.
- **Key dimensions** – adaptability; shared situational awareness; performance monitoring and feedback; leadership/team management; interpersonal relations; coordination; communication; and decision making.

Although the organisation's CEO may not, in fact, be the main spokesperson for the crisis management team it is essential that he or she is involved in and seen to be involved in leading the management of the crisis. The media will want to know the CEO's thoughts on the crisis and what he or she intends to do. Other important organisation stakeholders, especially the owners or investors and the regulators will expect the CEO to advise them directly, if not personally, of what steps the organisation is taking to resolve the crisis. The CEO is the public face of the organisation and is the person that the public relies on to inform them what is happening.

Campbell provides a CEO action list setting out the matters a CEO needs to consider in the face of a major crisis. These matters are as follows.

- The primary role is to provide corporate direction on resolving the problem and to minimise the impact on employees, the corporate reputation, the community and share value.
- Immediately, it is important to confirm the real situation. Getting accurate facts is sometimes difficult when the pressure is mounting; however, analysing the facts in order to identify response actions has to be a key objective in the early stages.
- Two streams of action are needed: one stream to manage the crisis response and one stream to manage the daily business. Life goes on, and although a crisis can stop an organisation in its tracks, business resumption is essential and part of the immediate recovery process.

- Take into consideration at all times the corporate position. Confirm a consistent message strategy and make sure that one spokesperson is giving a clear message right across all stakeholder audiences.
- Confirm how the crisis is affecting the company's audiences. Research can be very important here, and employing research to monitor attitudes to the response can be invaluable on the road to recovery.
- Be prepared to lose business and market share initially to gain maximum results in your response.
- Take the initiative. Be prepared to report truthfully. Show the stakeholders what you are doing and why you are doing it. Emphasise and use language the community understands. Clarify information rather than promise results.
- Do not let lawyers slow down the crisis agenda. Take good legal advice but avoid being gagged on disclosure.
- Do not lose control of yourself or your temper. Overreaction can cause confusion in the response process and a lack of confidence in the company. There will be dramatic changes in information and they have to be dealt with responsibly.
- Keep a close eye on your competitors. They will use your crisis time as an opportunity.
- Get on top of your financial audience before they are led by business analysts, academics and financial journalists. Help the financial analysts, the banks and your insurers understand that you are on top of the issues and controlling market vulnerabilities.

Enlist industry and government support. Make sure your industry and the government understand the seriousness of your problem and do all they can to support your recovery, using the best means available.

Most of all think ahead. Use lateral thinking to interpret both unintended consequences and how the business may finish up. Direct your recovery team to start building bridges and repairing reputation.

Crisis Management Plans

The purpose of a CMP has been defined by the Business Continuity Institute as 'a documented framework to enable an organisation to manage any crisis event regardless of cause (including those where no business continuity response is appropriate such as a threat to reputation'.

The outcomes of a CMP include the following:

- a clearly defined and documented plan to support the organisation's crisis management team during a crisis event;
- clearly defined crisis management roles, accountability, responsibility and authority;
- prompt tactical decisions made at the crisis location;
- prevention or at least minimisation of the impact of a crisis event by localising the response;

- maintenance of public, stakeholder, market and regulatory confidence and trust;
- maximisation of the organisation's reputation and brand image;
- compliance with legal and regulatory requirements.

Campbell lists the following benefits of having a CMP in place:

- increased awareness of exposure to crises;
- understanding of the full range of issues likely to be encountered;
- a plan specifically configured to an organisation's operations;
- improved crisis communication between management, employees, media, government, suppliers, and customers;
- employees that better understand their roles and responsibilities, their strengths and weaknesses, and their part in the bigger picture;
- enhanced corporate governance, management control and an improved reputation with external opinion makers such as government, bankers, financial analysts and industry peers.

He goes on to say that the ultimate benefit of a crisis plan is the capability given to managers and staff to retain effective control of any situation as a direct result of their own planning and training. This ensures that employees and third parties, assets and earnings, the environment and corporate reputation remain as safe and secure as possible.

The key steps in developing a CMP include the following:

- appoint an executive owner for the CMP;
- define the objectives and scope of the plan;
- develop and approve a CMP development process and programme;
- create a crisis management planning team to develop the plan;
- agree the responsibilities of the crisis management team and their relationship; with other plan teams;
- decide the structure, format, components and content of the plan;
- determine the strategies, such as alternative locations, on which the plan is based;
- gather information to populate the plan;
- nominate individuals to fulfil roles within the plan;
- draft the plan;
- circulate the draft of the plan for consultation and review;
- gather feedback from the consultation;
- amend plan as appropriate;
- agree and validate the plan, for example by using it in a test;
- repeat process for the crisis communications plan (if separate);
- agree a programme of ongoing exercising and maintenance of the plan to ensure it remains current.

The contents of a CMP will depend on the nature and complexity and on the products and services of the organisation and on the likely matters that can cause a crisis for the organisation. Like all continuity plans the CMP should be modular in design so individual sections can be given to personnel on a need-to-know basis.

The contents of a CMP would include the following:

- **Plan overview** – including introduction, purpose of plan, scope, objectives, assumptions and owner. This section should include information and flow-charts of the crisis management process.
- **Roles and accountabilities** – owner, crisis management team, crisis management team and crisis manager.
- **Escalation and activation** – details of the process for escalation of crisis events and plan activation procedures. This section should include diagrams to show the escalation and activation processes.
- **Crisis management personnel** – membership of crisis management team and crisis management team and alternatives, including the crisis manager.
- **Command centre** – location and contact details of command centre and alternative command centre including maps, travel directions, etc. as necessary. This section should also contain details of the facilities contained within the command centre.
- **Contacts** – details of staff, emergency services, suppliers, regulators media and so on.
- **Other information** – escalation procedures for invoking BCPs, emergency plans etc.; task checklists, form templates, etc.; locations of first aid facilities, hospitals, etc.; and legal and regulatory compliance requirements.

The roles of the key players include:

- **Owner** – take overall charge of the CMP, appoint the members of and chair the crisis management team, appoint the crisis manager and take overall responsibility for management of any crisis.
- **Crisis management team** – provide strategic direction for the management of any crisis including agreeing the priorities of allocation of scarce resources as required.

In most organisations, the EMT will share its membership with the crisis management team.

- **Crisis manager** – recommend members of the crisis management team for endorsement by the crisis management team and take ownership for the implementation of the team's strategies and decisions.
- **Crisis management team** – provide an effective fit-for-purpose operational crisis management capability to implement the team's strategies and decisions.

The CMP owner is responsible for ensuring that the CMP is maintained on a current basis at all times. The plan should be reviewed at regular intervals and at least annually as well as when there is a change in the organisation structure, processes, goods, services, facilities or strategies.

As noted above, an excellent way to agree and validate a CMP is to use it as a test to manage a hypothetical crisis situation. To do this the organisation should choose a highly critical risk event and develop a plot or storyline around those events or issues. As this process can be time consuming, it should only be used for those issues which are really critical to the organisation – the ones where if you don't get it right, the outcomes could prove to be disastrous. For example, the scenario might either involve a total product recall or else the total loss of the organisation's head office. Although the likelihood may be low, the consequences would be catastrophic.

Storylines should be developed by a management team that consists of people who have a thorough understanding of the organisation's activities and the context in which the organisation relates to its external stakeholders. The team should include imaginative people with marketing, public relations, customer relations, safety and security and financial skills and, where possible, should include people who can 'think outside the box'.

The storylines should be broken down into sections and additional scripts devised around the various strategy alternatives developed. The crisis management team is then convened and facilitated through role playing the 'management' of the scenario. If external professionals (for example, media and emergency services personnel) can be involved in the scenario enactment, this will increase the realism of the test.

Role playing a scenario also brings out the real-time issues related to a potential risk event or crisis, without having to go through the real-time consequences. This helps members of the crisis management team prepare for a possible crisis and highlights weaknesses in either the preparations of the organisation or the skills of the team.

Summary

Please keep the following points from this chapter in mind:

- The main purpose of BCM is to ensure that an organisation can respond to major disruptions that threaten its survival.
- Implementing BCM ensures that stakeholder confidence in the organisation is maintained. Organisations that lack robust risk management practices can be overwhelmed by a disruption event.
- Resilience can be built into an organisation's major systems, processes and activities by the application of normal risk management techniques.
- Following any sort of material damage to a commercial property, there may be additional loss due to the interruption to normal trading activities and a subsequent inability to meet ongoing business costs. This is known as BI.

- Recovery strategies have to be selected to cover the three stages of BCM. These stages generally overlap each other and each stage has particular requirements. The stages are:
  - the emergency response
  - the continuity phase
  - the recovery phase.
- A BCP is a plan for controlling risk exposures with the sole objective of ensuring an organisation's survival in the event of a major disruption to business services. It seeks to mitigate the downside consequences of exposure to disruption-related risk as effectively as possible.
- BCPs need to be tested before they are fully implemented. Testing is also commonly known as exercising. Common types of test are:
  - desktop review (sometimes known as plan audits)
  - desktop walkthrough
  - desktop scenario exercise
  - call-out and notification communications exercise
  - recovery exercise
  - live scenario exercise (sometimes known as 'large scale testing').
- It is important to develop a BCM culture within an organisation. Successfully doing so primarily means BCM becomes an integral part of the organisation's strategic and day-to-day management philosophy rather than an 'add-on'.
- The main difference between a crisis and a normal business continuity event is that a crisis goes to the heart of the organisation's survival, involves the interest of a wide audience, is of great interest to the media, and has to be managed without necessarily knowing the full facts of the situation.

Answers to Self-Help Questions

Self-help question 5.1

- The major business continuity vulnerabilities in an organisation will generally arise from the following.
- IT and Telecommunications systems. These systems can affect the organisation's record keeping and processing – e.g. accounting, purchases, sales or stock recording, automated manufacturing control systems, logistics systems (such as ensuring that materials are supplied in time for manufacturing, or goods are available at the dispatch point when needed).
- Infrastructure, especially buildings and plant and equipment. These resources are especially vulnerable to external forces such as utilities, lack of spare parts/replacements for faulty equipment, weather, fire and flood.

→

- Personnel. This covers the resignation/death of key staff, industrial disputes and accidents to personnel.
- Loss of records, both manual (hard copy) and computerised records.
- These areas may be considered to be critical to your operation and require the development of BCPs.

Self-help question 5.2

The major stakeholders in an organisation are likely to be:

- management and staff, including labour organisations
- directors
- shareholders, including analysts and advisors
- major debt providers (may be banks or third party lenders such as debenture holders)
- the media
- major suppliers and customers
- regulators, including the Stock Exchange.

Depending on what the organisation is manufacturing and the residue from manufacturing activities, further stakeholders may include the local community, local government authorities and special interest groups such as Greenpeace.

Self-help question 5.3

The notification, escalation and activation section of a BCP can best be developed diagrammatically, as illustrated below. This makes the process easy to follow and highlights the major escalation and decision-making points. For a specific BCP, the diagram could include the data to be provided to each team in order for it to make its decisions, the decisions to be made and the criteria against which the decisions should be judged; for example, to MAO and RTOs.

Self-help question 5.4

Armit and Marvell advised that the benefits from this exercise were many. As people across the business were contacted in their homes this brought business continuity out of the project phase and into their lives. The next day at work over 45% of employees talked about business continuity and challenged their management as to what it all meant; there could be no quicker or more efficient way to raise the awareness of business continuity other than a real incident. Business managers now took a real interest in their cascades and ensured that everyone was included. The cascades

→

→

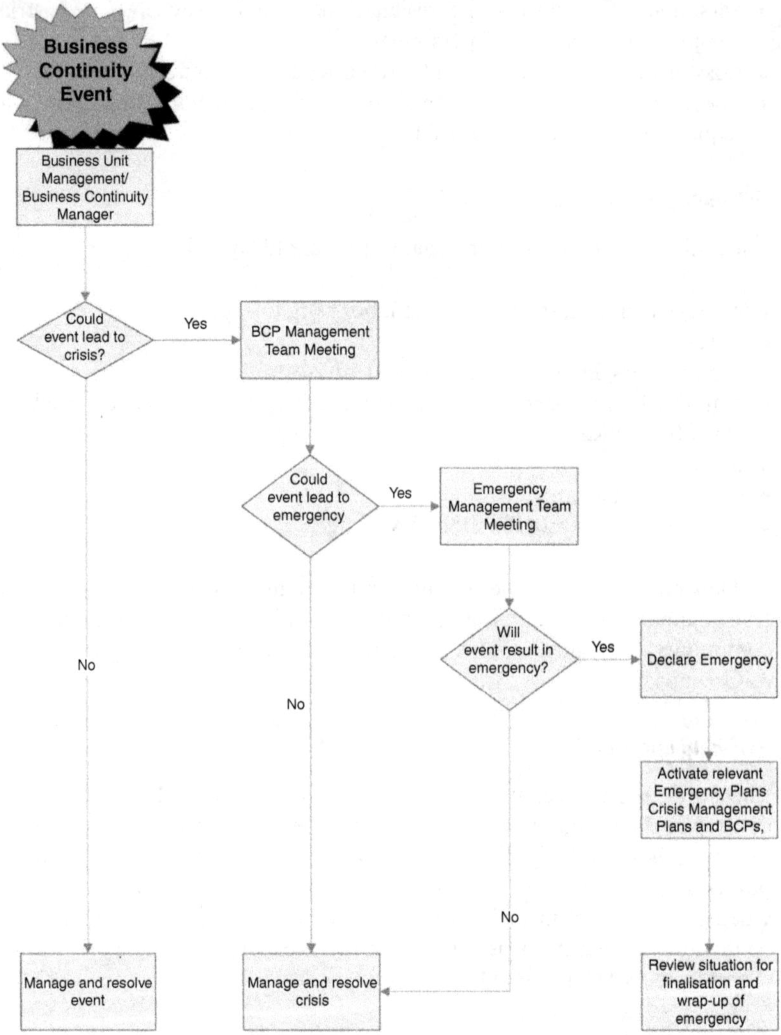

Business Continuity Event Diagram

were revised as people recognised that making over five phone calls was impractical. Ownership for maintenance was accepted and taken away from the central area into the units affected and plans were amended to show that reliance on laptops was flawed.

Chapter 6

General/Financial Risk-Related Controls

Introduction

Controls are processes that are designed to help organisations limit their losses. The risk management process helps determine which controls need to be implemented, and how. An organisation's board is central to the effective deployment of internal controls, as it has the power and global vision to ensure controls are implemented, that they are enacted with integrity and that appropriate supporting committees are established. Audit and risk committees are two key types of control, and these committees are responsible for a number of vital internal processes that can protect an organisation from certain financial risk events.

Without effective and reliable controls, an organisation becomes liable for a number of risks that can not only damage its reputation but threaten its survival.

This chapter will explore financial controls: what they are, how they should be implemented and who has responsibility for the different actions involved.

Learning Outcomes

By the end of this chapter, you should be able to:

- describe the difference between control types;
- explain who is responsible for implementing risk controls;
- describe the difference between audit and risk committees and what role each plays;
- identify the applicable standards;
- define a gatekeeper and understand that role.

Risk Treatment, 131–147

Published under exclusive licence by Emerald Publishing Limited
doi:10.1108/978-1-83662-306-920251014

Control Set-Up

The concept of control is widely used in management circles and may be misunderstood and therefore needs to be clarified. First of all, there are several types of controls that might be considered, as follows:

- **Operational controls** – these aim to measure and ensure the effectiveness and efficiency of operations conducted in the organisation.
- **Financial controls** – these aim to provide reliability of financial reporting/financial impact.
- **Compliance** – these provide assurance that operations and decisions within the organisation comply with all applicable laws and regulations.

Here we are focusing on financial controls. They are central to managing any organisation effectively and need to be within the scope of the risk management efforts in any organisation, in close cooperation with the internal auditors. To the extent that they are done well, they can contribute to an organisation's ability to safeguard its assets, use its resources economically and efficiently, and produce accurate and reliable financial information. Reliable information is essential to developing a complete and accurate picture of financial performance and guiding decisions regarding the future.

Responsibilities

The board has overall responsibility for a company's internal control framework and, as such, is responsible for ensuring that proper internal controls are implemented and monitored.

While management is responsible for implementing internal controls and processes, the directors retain individual responsibility for ensuring that significant risks are not only identified but that there are management controls in place to manage the risks. This requires the board to have an understanding of the organisation's risk profile as well as the organisation's risk appetite. Then management and the board must ensure that the risk management systems are working effectively and that the information produced is sound and reliable enough for the CEO, CFO and board to confidently sign-off that the organisation's financial reports give a true and fair statement of the organisation's financial condition.

The board is required to use its expertise to determine the integrity of the material provided to it by management and can be assisted by various professional experts in this process. Financial and accounting matters should receive dedicated attention from the audit committee, which engages the services of external auditors to carry out independent investigations into the company's affairs on its behalf. Over the years there have been several high-profile court cases that focused on the role of auditors who were engaged to test the effectiveness of the controls implemented by the company. When considering the duties and responsibilities of auditors, the Courts also considered the role of the board in establishing effective controls within the company. A leading case in this area is known as the AWA Case (*AWA Ltd* v *Daniels* (1992) 10 ACLC 933 at 985).

Case Study – AWA Case

In 1985, AWA Ltd appointed a single person to manage its new foreign exchange operations (FX). The manager worked alone, basically unsupervised, and engaged in fraudulent activities. This type of investment was new to AWA and for a while the manager was so successful that the foreign exchange operation looked like it would become 'the largest dollar-generating department' in the company. This success was short term, however, and in order to conceal mounting losses the manager made unauthorised borrowings from a number of banks on behalf of AWA. These borrowings went unknown until 1987, at which time it was revealed that AWA was suffering losses of nearly A$50 million.

From 1985 to 1987, auditing procedures were undertaken at AWA that failed to either note or report the discrepancies in the records. Some of the record-keeping discrepancies the records were not entered into the record book after 30 June 1986, and were not in chronological order and contract notes were not in sequence. The auditors did not cross-check all records and did not alert upper management to the lack of records, nor did they conduct a more in-depth review when the discrepancies were uncovered.

AWA sued its auditors for failing to detect the fraudulent activities, failing to advise the board of the internal control weaknesses discovered by the audit process in September 1986 and again in March 1987, and for signing the misleading profit confirmation letter following its interim audit of December 1986.

AWA admitted that its internal controls (in relation to the foreign exchange dealings and account-keeping) were deficient but claimed that the loss was caused by the auditor's failure to draw attention to those deficiencies and to note the problems in its reports to the board. AWA claimed that the auditors were responsible for detecting and reporting deficiencies or inadequacies in the company's systems. The auditors denied any breach of duty to AWA, and claimed contributory negligence on the part of the company and management.

The Court held in favour of AWA and made various statements in relation to the responsibilities of auditors and the responsibilities of the directors. The court did find that 20% of the fault lay with AWA and its management. While it has become a leading case for the obligations of accountants, various statements were also made in relation to the obligations of the CEO and the directors, pointing to a responsibility to ensure that adequate controls were in place and to actively monitor to ensure that the corporate governance systems were adequate and effective.

> [...] [I]gnorance is no longer necessarily a defence to proceedings brought against a director. In some respects, at least, the director must inform himself or herself about the

> affairs of the company ... That duty involves becoming familiar with the business of the company and how it is run and ensuring that the board has available means to audit the management of the company so that it can satisfy itself that the company is being properly run. (Daniels v Anderson [1995] 16 ACSR 607 at 664)

Justice Rogers found that it was necessary first to determine what the roles and responsibilities of the board and management were. Rogers J took the view that the board's role was generally to set the corporate goals and to provide oversight and review of the implementation of those corporate goals. In doing this, the directors were entitled to rely on the managers to carry out the day-to-day control of the corporation's business affairs and to:

> [...] go carefully through relevant financial and other information of the corporation and draw to the board's attention any matter requiring the board's consideration. (Daniels v Anderson [1995] 16 ACSR 607 at 664)

The directors were also entitled to rely on the skill, judgement and advice of properly appointed auditors, so that, in the absence of any reason for suspecting differently, the directors were entitled to rely on the information and advice of the management without verification.

Over the progress of the case, there was no dispute over the alleged gross negligence of the senior management, whose lack of proper records and internal controls showed inexperience while their lack of care in relation to the foreign exchange contracts meant that the matters were not brought to the attention of the board. For this reason, AWA was found 20% negligent in relation to the claim and the auditors 80% responsible.

Self-Help Question 6.1

Consider the examples of AWA and list three governance-related processes that the relevant board failed to implement and that contributed to the significant losses incurred by the respective businesses.

Answers to self-help questions are provided at the end of each section.

Ethical Culture Must Be Taken into Account

Business culture varies across organisations and it is important to understand how an organisation's culture affects its risk management efforts. Understanding what values are important among the leaders of the organisation may provide insight into the willingness of organisational leaders to take certain risks. While most organisations have a set of defined business values, sometimes management's actions and decisions may not reflect those stated values.

Recognising when those differences potentially exist and calling attention to them may be risk management's most important contribution. Challenging decisions from an ethical lens may be something that risk managers might want to consider. Of course, doing so, may represent a significant personal risk for risk management leaders if there is little support and endorsement from those in key governance roles, such as the board of directors.

The Role of the Audit and Risk Committees

The board is responsible for establishing an audit committee and/or a risk committee and defining the roles in a charter of terms of reference (see table below).

These committees should comprise a mix of genders to benefit from a wider diversity of ideas and opinions and avoid group thinking phenomenon.

As several committees may be involved in the evaluation of risks it is important that the board explains the delegated duties and responsibilities to each committee. The board should consider how the committees shall report to the board. If there is more than one committee, a clear definition of roles and responsibilities is important to ensure sufficient information is passed to all involved and to avoid duplication and misunderstandings. Co-operation between the audit committee and the risk committee is also crucial to ensure a common risk management approach.

The Audit Committee

The audit committee has a particular role: acting independently of executive management to ensure that the interests of the shareholders are properly protected in relation to risk management, internal control and financial reporting.

There is a need for a clear overview of the organisation's risk and control framework, which will allow the audit committee to monitor and evaluate the effectiveness of the company's internal controls, risk management and reporting. One of the biggest risks the audit committee faces today is the risk of not seeing the threats in front of them until they are at hand.

Management is under an obligation to ensure the audit committee is kept properly informed and should take the initiative to furnish accurate and appropriate information to the committee. The internal auditor, who tends to be a staff member and independent of the risk manager, should be regularly invited to the meetings of the audit committee to bring independent assurance to the table.

The audit committee assists the board to fulfil its corporate governance responsibilities by:

- having a good understanding of the organisation's structure, controls and types of transactions as well as the business model and its associated risks;
- maintaining free and open communication with external auditors, internal auditors, groups that are part of the second line of defence and internal managers;
- having the power and authority to investigate any matter based on full access to organisational records, operations and people.

The Risk Committee

The new and broader view of risk and the need for improved risk management after the financial crisis has resulted in boards considering the need to create risk committees. The main purpose of the risk committee is to assist the board in ensuring that the company has an effective risk management process, which includes the management of the key risks the company is facing and the follow up of risk appetite, risk tolerance, risk framework and risk strategy.

In some organisations, based on their tasks, size, complexity and maturity, risk profile and risk culture, there is a preference not to establish a separate risk committee but to organise a joint audit and risk committee. In large organisations with complex operations or in specific businesses, there may be good reasons for creating a dedicated risk committee.

European banks are required to organise separate audit and risk committees (see Capital Requirement Directive CRD IV). Basel III is the global regulatory standard on capital adequacy and liquidity for the banking sector. Developed by the Basel Committee on Banking Supervision (composed of organisations with direct banking supervisory authority and central banks), Basel III is officially defined as 'a comprehensive set of reform measures to strengthen the regulation, supervision and risk management of the banking sector'.

The Basel III accords were released in December 2010 as a response to the global financial crisis of 2008. Compared with Basel II, Basel III aims to improve resilience to financial and economic shocks of the banking sector. It introduces stricter requirements to strengthen bank capital requirements, notably through a decreased leverage ratio and a higher bank liquidity ratio.

Basel III is built on the three pillars of the Basel II framework, which was released in June 2004. Pillar 1 relates to capital requirements (quality, leverage ratio etc.), Pillar 2 involves governance and risk management and Pillar 3 includes transparency and disclosure requirements. Solvency II, the regulatory framework for insurance companies in the European Union, was also modelled upon the Basel II three-pillar structure.

For more information, visit the dedicated section for Basel III on the Bank for International Settlement (BIS) website: www.bis.org/bcbs/basel3.htm

In non-financial organisations, the risk committee may be organised at the executive level, sometimes reporting to the audit committee and sometimes chaired by the CFO. Regardless of the organisation, it is important that non-financial risks are well managed and reported comprehensively to the board.

The need to create a separate risk committee may arise from:

- the requirements of the relevant regulator/s;
- the alignment between risk management and strategy;
- the need for more detailed oversight of the risk management infrastructure (people, process, infrastructure);
- the complexity of the major/critical risks to be assessed.

Risk committee members must be knowledgeable about risk governance and business activities to be able to challenge the board or management decisions. The chief risk officer (CRO) or the director or head of risk management should participate in the meetings of the risk committee. The members of the risk committee should be independent and include independent board members (for example non-executive board members), as is also the case for audit committees.

The below table shows possible responsibilities for each committee.

Note: Some organisations do not have a risk committee and responsibilities assigned to each committee depend on individual organisations.

Responsibilities of the Audit and Risk Committees

	Responsibilities	Risk Committee	Audit Committee
1	**Review risk management systems**		
a	To recommend to the board the framework and system to manage risks	X	
b	To discuss the organisation's risk tolerance, risk appetite and strategy with management and the CRO and give an opinion on acceptability of the proposed levels of risk to the board	X	
c	To be informed by management, including the CRO, of any changes in conditions, circumstances or new opportunities that could affect the allocation of risk appetite to the different risk categories and provide advice to the board	X	
d	To oversee the conduct and review the results of enterprise-wide risk assessment, like proposed strategic acquisitions and disposals	X	X Relevant to be able to challenge financial reporting

(*Continued*)

(Continued)

	Responsibilities	Risk Committee	Audit Committee
e	To assess and evaluate the risk profile in light of the activities concerning risk appetite, risk development and risk aggregation and provide advice to the board	X	
f	To help coordinate activities of the various standing committees for risk oversight	X	X
g	To initiate and monitor special investigations into areas of corporate risk and break-downs in internal control	X	X
h	To review the nature and level of insurance coverage	X	
i	To engage management, including the CRO, in promoting a positive risk culture	X	
j	To monitor the effectiveness of risk management functions throughout the undertaking and ensure that infrastructure, resources and systems are in place for risk management and are adequate to maintain a satisfactory level of risk management discipline	X	X
k	To monitor the independence of risk management functions throughout the organisation	X	X
2	**CRO or equivalent head of risk management**		
a	To advise the board about the appointment of the CRO/head of risk management and, when and if appropriate, the replacement of the CRO and ensure that the function gets the necessary means to operate	X	
b	To assess the performance of the framework and procedures in place	X	X Relevant for monitoring of internal control and financial reporting
c	To organise regular communication with the CRO, who is also permanently invited to the risk committee meetings	X	

	Responsibilities	Risk Committee	Audit Committee
3	**External audit**		
a	To review the external auditor's reporting		X
b	To exchange with the audit committee on the risks identified in the financial reporting process (including sustainability reports) and their impact		X
4	**Relationship and coordination**		
a	To understand how the organisation's internal audit work plan is aligned with the risks that have been identified and with risk governance (and risk management) information needs (to be undertaken in coordination with the audit/risk committee)	X	X
b	To exchange with the audit/risk committee on the risks identified by internal auditors, their impact and recommendations	X	X
c	To identify areas where assurance is required, and to ensure that appropriate assurance is received and that this informs and updates the organisation's risk profile	X	X
5	**Annual reports**		
a	Report annually on the effectiveness and efficiency of risk management in the organisation	X	X
6	**Annual reviews**		
a	Review annually the performance and terms of reference of the committee in order to determine whether it is functioning effectively by reference to best practices	X	X
7	**Oversee the integrity of the financial reporting process and financial reports**		
a	To recommend that the board approve the financial statements and reports after the review process with management and external auditors has been completed		X
b	To review any significant financial reporting issues and report to the board		X

(*Continued*)

(Continued)

	Responsibilities	Risk Committee	Audit Committee
8	**Review the efficiency of internal control and risk management systems**		
a	To review the adequacy and effectiveness of:		
	– the organisation's policies and procedures to assess, monitor and manage financial and non-financial business risks	X	X
	– internal control systems	X	X
	– legal and ethical compliance programs		X
b	To regularly meet with management, the external auditors, the internal auditors and other assurance functions to discuss issues and concerns warranting committee attention, including but not limited to their assessment of the effectiveness of the internal controls and risk management systems and the process for improvement	X	X
c	To receive reports from the support functions	X	X
9	**Review and appraise the audit activities: independence, objectivity and effectiveness of the audit process**		
a	To make recommendations to the board for the appointment and replacement of the external auditors		X
b	To comment on the annual report regarding the statutory auditor's provision of non-audit services		X
10	**Supervise the internal audit function**		
a	To recommend to the board the appointment or dismissal of the chief audit executive		X
b	To review the scope of the internal audit plan, including the work program and the quality control procedures, and to approve the internal charter		X
c	To assess the performance, independence and objectivity of the internal audit function		X

Case Study – WorldCom Inc

Internal auditors have also been known to uncover large frauds as part of their work. It was an internal auditor from WorldCom who first discovered that senior executives had tried to conceal growing losses that would impact on the company's share price.

In 2002, Cynthia Cooper was Vice-President of Internal Audit at WorldCom, which was then a major global communications provider operating in more than 65 countries and providing data transmission and internet services for business. During an audit in May 2002, Ms Cooper discovered that WorldCom had engaged in an accounting scheme to manipulate its earnings and thereby maintain its share price. The company had been classifying operating costs as capital expenditure, which meant that its profits were consequently inflated.

In carrying out her internal audit role, Cooper uncovered approximately US$3.8 billion of the fraud in June 2002 during a routine examination of capital expenditures and alerted the company's new auditors, KPMG (who had replaced Arthur Andersen, WorldCom's external auditors at the time of the fraud). Cooper took her findings to the Audit Committee of WorldCom's Board in June 2002. The WorldCom Board fired its CFO, Scott Sullivan, and revealed to the investing public and government regulators that from 1999, and continuing through to May 2002, the company – under the direction of Scott Sullivan (CFO), David Myers (Controller) and Buford 'Buddy' Yates (Director of General Accounting) – had used fraudulent accounting methods to mask its declining financial condition, thereby painting a false picture of financial growth and profitability to prop up the price of WorldCom's stock.

The company's audit committee and board were notified of the fraud and acted swiftly: Sullivan was fired, Myers resigned, Arthur Andersen withdrew its audit opinion for 2001, and the US Securities and Exchange Commission (SEC) launched an investigation into these matters on 26 June 2002.

The fraud was accomplished primarily in two ways:

- under-reporting 'line costs' (interconnection expenses with other telecommunications companies) by capitalising those costs on the balance sheet rather than properly expensing them; and
- inflating revenues with bogus accounting entries from 'corporate unallocated revenue accounts'.

WorldCom's Chapter 11 filing was the largest bankruptcy filing in American history. Investors lost US$200 billion as a direct result of the bankruptcy. By the end of 2003, it was estimated that the company's total assets had been inflated by around US$11 billion.

The failure of WorldCom's CFO to advise their external auditors of the line cost transfers and the lack of consultation with the auditors about the accounting treatment of the transfers highlights the importance of a strong internal audit function as part of the corporate governance framework.

The Role of Corporate Gatekeepers

The term **corporate gatekeeper** was first used by Reinier H. Kraakman in his series of articles on gatekeeper liability (1986). His articles considered the role of parties who had the ability to force corporate wrongdoers to cease their wrongful conduct by withholding their professional services and support. He referred to the specialised services that this group could withhold as the 'gate' and to the specialists as the 'gatekeepers'.

Gatekeepers are individuals who have access to information about the company, often perform a monitoring role, and have a professional reputational risk associated with condoning corporate misconduct. This group includes independent professionals who act as intermediaries for the company, providing verification or certification services to investors (Coffee 2004), including auditors and analysts.

Certification services provided by professional gatekeepers that are relevant to a company's governance include:

- independent auditors verifying company financial statements;
- debt rating agencies evaluating company creditworthiness;
- securities analysts assessing the company's business and financial prospects compared with those of its competitors.

Professional gatekeepers are also called 'reputational intermediaries' because they assess or vouch for the corporate client's own statements about itself or a specific transaction (Coffee 2002). This should be part of the mission of economic intelligence and blog managers using powerful search engines, in-house or outsourced for smaller organisations, and monitored by the risk-management function.

The failure of Enron (and other large corporate failures) has caused commentators such as John C. Coffee Jr to question why the professional gatekeepers fail in their primary role. Coffee has speculated that one of the reasons for these failures was the dominance of the Big 5 audit firms (as they were then) and the erosion of auditor independence during the late 1990s when the Big 5 started cross-selling consulting services.

During this time, the auditing function was treated as a portal of entry into a lucrative client, rather than as the main service being provided. Before then, the provision of consulting services to audit clients was not a frequent event but, by 2002, audit firms were, in some cases, receiving up to three times the amount of income from clients for consulting services than they were for audit services.

The specific role of an external auditor is to provide an independent review and verification of the financial statements prepared by management for presentation to the board. The board relies on the services provided by professional gatekeepers but, in particular, it relies on the external auditor fulfilling the professional gatekeeper role in an accurate and independent manner.

Coffee and others have commented that the strategy of using the audit function as a loss leader for other consulting services adds additional problems to an already conflicted situation created by auditors being paid by the client for 'independent' reports.

Put simply, reputational capital is not an asset that professional services firms will inevitably hoard and protect. Logically, as legal exposure to liability declines and as benefits of acquiescence to a client's demands increase, gatekeeper failure should correspondingly increase – as it did in the 1990s. Market bubbles can also explain gatekeeper failure (and this perspective probably works better in the case of the securities analysts, who faced little liability in the past) because, in an environment of euphoria, investors do not rely on gatekeepers; hence, gatekeepers have less leverage with respect to their clients.

The importance of the professional gatekeepers in the success or failure of companies is an area that has not received the degree of attention that might be expected. However, studies of significant organisational failure highlight the role of fraud and financial mismanagement rather than external factors such as terrorism, climate change or natural disasters, thereby emphasising the importance of implementing effective financial controls.

Company	Loss Amount	Date	Description
Enron	US$74 billion	2001	Numerous crimes were committed by Enron executives, including misrepresenting earnings, embezzlement and illegal market manipulations. The company went bankrupt (the largest bankruptcy in US history at the time) and the top executives were tried for fraud.
Bernie Madoff	US$65 billion	2008	The largest Ponzi scheme ever, Madoff's scheme involved investment fraud and theft ran from the 1990s to 2008 when it was finally exposed.
Lehman Brothers	US$130 billion	2008	Lehman invested huge sum of money in the mortgage market, and therefore suffered in the market downturn. It was the largest bankruptcy in history and a catalyst to the global financial crisis.

Company	Loss Amount	Date	Description
Société Générale	€4.9 billion	2008	A rogue trader conducted a number of false trades on European index futures. The trader closed the trades before the internal control timeframes were triggered, thus avoiding detection.
Morgan Stanley	US$9 billion	2008	A single trader betted against the US real estate bubble using credit default swaps.
Aracruz	BRL $4.62 billion	2008	The company invested heavily in foreign exchange options, believing in the strength of the Brazilian real, just before the currency lost value.
MF Global	US$41 billion	2011	MF Global betted on European sovereign debt in an attempt to diversity the business. The strategy ended in bankruptcy.
UBS	CHF 1.9 billion	2011	Unauthorised trading disguised as forward-settling ETF cash positions resulted in a huge loss for the Swiss bank.
JPMorgan Chase	US$2 billion	2012	JPMorgan Chase engaged in credit default swaps that contributed to the global financial crisis and market manipulation.

The main responsibility for preventing fraud within a company lies with the board, which is responsible for overseeing management to ensure that effective controls are in place. However, given the role played by managers and employees of organisations that have suffered financial scandals, it is not surprising that the International Standard for Auditing 200 (ISA 200) requires the auditor, as a professional gatekeeper, to:

> […] maintain an attitude of professional scepticism recognising the possibility that a material misstatement due to fraud could exist, notwithstanding the auditor's past experience with the entity about the honesty and integrity of management and those charged with governance. (Hoffman 2002)

In ISA 200, auditors are alerted to look for fraudulent financial reporting being accomplished by management over-riding the controls that otherwise appear to be operating effectively. Some techniques used by management to over-ride controls implemented by the board and management include:

- recording fictitious journal entries to manipulate operating results;
- inappropriately adjusting assumptions and judgements used to estimate account balances;

- omitting, advancing or delaying recognition in financial statements of events and transactions occurring during the reporting period;
- concealing or not disclosing facts that could impact the figures in the financial statements;
- engaging in complex transactions that are structured to misrepresent the financial position or by altering financial performance records related to significant and unusual transactions.

The Role of the External Auditor

The external auditor is the professional gatekeeper engaged to ensure full and accurate disclosure of the company's financial position, through the independent verification of the company's financial reporting.

The external auditor is required to report to shareholders on the organisation's balance sheet and profit and loss account (income statement). These documents must be submitted to shareholders in a General Meeting and are required to carry a statement of the auditor's opinion that:

- the financial statements are properly drawn up in accordance with relevant regulations and legislation to give a true and fair view of the state of the organisation and its results;
- the financial statements are properly drawn up in accordance with applicable accounting standards.

In addition, the auditor is required to form an opinion as to whether:

- all the required information and explanations were obtained;
- proper accounting records and other records (including registers) have been kept;
- returns received from branch offices of the company are adequate;
- the procedures and methods used by the chief entity (holding company) and its controlled entities (subsidiaries) in arriving at the amounts taken into any consolidated financial statements were appropriate as to the circumstances of the consolidation.

The audit report is required to note any deficiency, failure or shortcoming relevant to the matters noted above.

In order to carry out the audit function, at all times the auditor requires access to the accounting and other records of the company and the right to obtain from the officers of the company such information and explanations as are required for the audit.

Activity | International standards

Nearly all European countries require the use of the International Financial Reporting Standards (IFRS) and several of them use (or are committed to using) the International Standards on Accounting (ICAs).

Visit www.ifrs.org and www.iaasb.org to view each of the Standards and to read why they are important. You can also view which countries have committed to using them.

Activity | Local associations tools

Although there are some international standards, countries still have their own nationally applicable frameworks and legislation that may give rise to risk treatment tools specific to that country.

- *What other forms of risk treatment are used in your country?*
- *Are there any forms of risk treatment that differ from the international standards? How do they differ and why?*

Summary

Please keep the following points from this chapter in mind:

- There are several types of controls:
  - operational controls
  - financial controls
  - compliance
- Financial controls are central to managing any organisation effectively, and need to be within the scope of the risk-management efforts in any organisation.
- An organisation's board has overall responsibility for a company's internal control framework and is responsible for ensuring that proper internal controls are implemented and monitored.
- The board is required to use its expertise to determine the integrity of the material provided to it by management and can be assisted by various professional experts in this process.
- The board is responsible for establishing an audit committee and/or a risk committee and defining the roles in a charter of terms of reference
- Co-operation between the audit and risk committees is crucial to ensure a common risk management approach.
- The audit committee acts independently of executive management to ensure that the interests of the shareholders are properly protected in relation to risk management, internal control and financial reporting.

- The risk committee assists the board in ensuring that the company has an effective risk management process, including managing key risks and following up on risk appetite, risk tolerance, risk framework and risk strategy.
- Basel III is the global regulatory standard on capital adequacy and liquidity for the banking sector and requires financial institutions to implement separate audit and risk committees.
- In non-financial organisations, the risk committee may be organised at the executive level, sometimes reporting to the audit committee and sometimes chaired by the CFO.
- Gatekeepers are individuals who have access to information about the organisation, often perform a monitoring role, and have a professional reputational risk associated with condoning corporate misconduct.
- Professional gatekeepers are also called 'reputational intermediaries' because they assess or vouch for the corporate client's own statements about itself or a specific transaction.
- The external auditor is the professional gatekeeper engaged to ensure full and accurate disclosure of the company's financial position, through the independent verification of the company's financial reporting.

Answers to Self-Help Questions

Self-help question 6.1

The board failed to:

1. establish the delegation of authority and its limits in relation to the foreign exchange business;
2. understand the nature of the new business and the risks associated with it;
3. implement processes to ensure that the manager was acting as they intended.

Chapter 7

Risk Financing Techniques

Introduction

While strategic risk management is still not standard practice in many organisations, many large global organisations have discovered the numerous benefits of enterprise risk management (managing risks in a holistic fashion).

The core risk management mission must always be kept in mind: It is not simply to eliminate risk but to make sure that only risks that provide a good return are retained by the organisation, optimising risk taking.

Risk financing is the process of funding the negative financial consequences of risk (threats). It includes funding the actual cost of risk events, such as small frequent losses, and the potential costs of much larger but infrequent losses. Risk financing techniques include retention and transfer, such as insurance contracts.

Risk financing is the part of the risk treatment process where risks are to be transferred, shared or retained. For example, buying insurance is transferring the financial consequences of a risk event with an insurance company, there is some element of sharing if there are deductibles and/or limits. Retention (sometimes called self-insurance) is preparing to internally fund the financial consequences of a risk that the organisation decided to retain.

The origin of the funds when financing risks, whether they come from within or without the organisation, has been for a long time the only key to distinguishing between retention and transfer; however risk management professionals now also consider who bears the financial uncertainty brought by the risk.

Risk Treatment, 149–174

Published under exclusive licence by Emerald Publishing Limited
doi:10.1108/978-1-83662-306-920251016

Learning Outcomes

By the end of this chapter, you should be able to:

- describe risk retention;
- describe risk transfer;
- describe the risk financing process;
- identify how best to finance a risk;
- define the burden of risk;
- differentiate between the treasury and insurance functions of an organisation;
- explain the importance of risk financing and reviewing, monitoring and documenting the process.

Risk Financing

All organisations face risk events that may have an impact on their financial position. Ultimately, if funds from other sources cannot be found to finance the cost of risk events that have occurred, the suppliers of equity to the organisation bear the ultimate risk. A strategy for meeting such a potential financial impact is risk financing. The following example illustrates risk financing.

Case study – Acron Chemicals

Acron Chemicals has designed a new process for manufacturing polystyrene foam that is used in a range of different applications from car seats to life jackets. The new process involves a toxic gas that is stored under pressure and is heavier than air. It presents a substantial risk to humans if they are exposed to it.

In deciding whether or not to implement the new method of manufacturing, Acron needs to consider the potential financial impacts of a toxic gas leak and whether or not it can afford to take on the risk.

Acron conducts a risk assessment on the basis of retro-fitting their existing urban facility and estimates that a major gas leak could result in 20 deaths and 1,000 injured, with perhaps 10 of those injured never making a full recovery. The financial cost of compensating victims of such an event is estimated at € 200 million.

The risk financing decision that Acron faces is how to fund this potential risk event. Their options are:

1. Retain the full € 200 million. This means, if the event were to happen, Acron would need to source € 200 million from operating profit, cash reserves and/or available lines of credit from its bankers.

2. Retain only a small deductible and share the remainder of the exposure with its insurer.
3. Retain a portion of the loss through a significant deductible, such as € 5 million, and share the remainder of the exposure with its insurer.

In order to make this decision, Acron needs to consider several issues.

- Can Acron fund a € 200 million loss and stay in business?
- How certain is Acron that the loss would not exceed € 200 million? What is the possibility of human injury or property damage exceeding this amount?
- What is the cost of insurance with a low deductible?
- What is the cost of insurance with a high deductible (e.g. € 5 million)?
- What opportunities may have to be foregone if Acron self-funds a potential € 200 million loss?
- What opportunities may have to be foregone if Acron self-funds a potential € 5 million loss?
- What would the impact on Acron's reputation be and could that affect Acron's ability to win future contracts?

Acron's risk manager and chief financial officer (CFO) meet to discuss these issues and determine the following:

- With a recent average operating profit of € 200 million per annum, current cash reserves of € 20 million and a banking facility of € 100 million that has not been used, Acron could finance such a risk event itself, even after the € 50 million cost of retro-fitting of the plant to the new manufacturing process.
- The risk manager feels that the € 200 million estimate of the potential loss to Acron is as accurate as could be, taking into account current engineering and scientific information regarding the number of deaths and injuries. He cannot, however, forecast how the judiciary may view such an event in the future and set out compensation for victims. In his view, the cost cannot be calculated.
- Acron's insurance broker has obtained estimates of the cost of public liability insurance as being € 3,000,000 with a deductible of € 100,000, at least until the plant operates safely for a number of years. The broker suggests that there would be no more than a 20 per cent discount for a € 5 million deductible.
- The CFO and risk manager agree that taking on the risk of a € 200 million event would mean that Acron could make no other investments until the new manufacturing process had reaped substantial rewards.
- The CFO indicates that tying up € 5 million capital could be managed as the budget for the retro fit was calculated and sales and expenses had met annual forecasts.

The CFO and risk manager decide to advise the CEO and Board that, subject to a feasibility study, the public liability risk associated with the new manufacturing process should be financed by purchasing insurance above a substantial deductible. They believe that the company would be much better placed to take advantage of market opportunities and/or fund unexpected challenges to their competitiveness in the chemical industry if the company is not burdened with the unknown financial risk from the new manufacturing process.

The CFO and risk manager also believe that a good financial case could be mounted to divert capital to the higher deductible. The funding could be generated using operational funding, given the sound profits being achieved, or through a structured retention arrangement using a captive insurance company.

The CFO and risk manager of Acron Chemicals had a clearly identified risk event that they knew needed to be financed if it occurred. They followed a process of identifying:

- the potential scale of the risk;
- several options for dealing with it;
- the issues that needed to be considered, such as the opportunity cost of their capital. That is, if capital is used to fund risk, what other business opportunities are foregone because there is not enough capital to fund items such as new plants and machinery.

This demonstrates that risk financing is a process that forms part of the risk treatment process. It includes the process of identifying how a risk might best be financed using retention and/or risk sharing.

Risk financing is generally much more complicated than the Acron example might indicate – this organisation would face much broader risk financing issues. For example, in addition to Acron's public liability risk, it would face a large number of other insurable and non-insurable risks, all of which would need to be financed to prevent the organisation from experiencing a risk event crisis. An example of a non-insurable risk is the possibility of a major increase in the price of raw materials; Acron would need to be financially prepared for such eventualities.

Generally, an organisation finances day-to-day business risks using operational profit and cash flow or through the use of cash reserves. In the case of an increase in raw material cost, Acron may try to increase product prices. However, if the market for its product would not allow this, it would need to finance the occurrence of this risk event by operating at a decreased profit. If the increase in raw material cost were so great that it eliminated all profit, Acron would have to start using its cash reserves unless another arrangement, such as a bank loan, could be arranged.

Risk Financing and Risk Management

Risk management involves the entire process of thinking about an organisation, defining success, understanding risks (threats and opportunities) and then managing these factors to help reach organisational goals. Risk financing falls under the 'Treat risks' phase of the risk management process, as shown in the figure below, and involves considering options for paying off the financial consequences of risks.

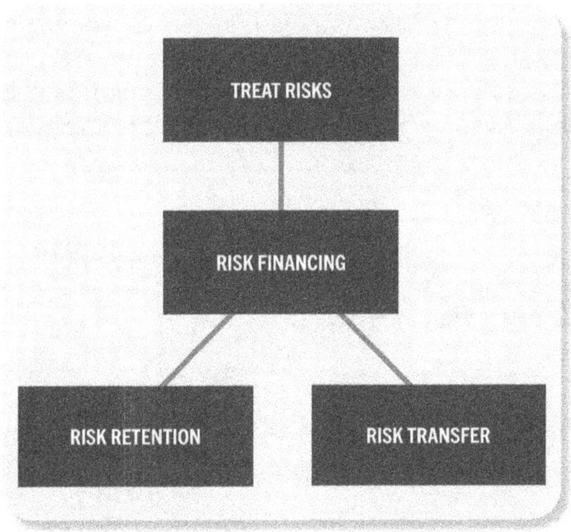

In order to gain a better understanding of the role risk financing plays in the overall management of risk, it is advantageous to understand the concept of the 'burden of risk'.

The burden of risk is the psychological strain felt when the potential consequences of risk are identified but have not been experienced. This means that the potential impact is uncertain, which can lead to stress. Because some risks can never be fully avoided or eliminated, organisations always bear some burden of risk.

Vaughan and Vaughan identify the following aspects of the burden of risk.

- The greatest burden in connection with risk is that some losses will actually occur. This is primarily why individuals attempt to avoid risk or alleviate its impact.
- The uncertainty as to whether the loss will occur requires the prudent individual to prepare for its possible occurrence – e.g. through accumulating cash reserves or buying insurance.
- The accumulation of cash reserves has its own burden in that it represents an inability to use the cash reserves for other activities. Accumulating and retaining cash reserves to cover future risk events prevents other opportunities from being realised.
- The uncertainty connected with risk usually produces a feeling of frustration and mental unrest.

When risks are financial, organisations will implement risk financing by:

- transferring risk for financing through a contract (partner or insurer);
- sharing risks with others – e.g. buying insurance with deductibles and limits
- putting in place a plan for financing retained risk – e.g. diverting funds to an account specifically to cope with risks occurring.

Not all organisations are affected in the same way by the burden of risk. A risk-taking organisation will act differently to a risk-avoiding organisation. For example, a risk-taking organisation may take on larger debts because the CEO is confident of future success. A risk-avoiding organisation will take on smaller debts because the CEO may be more cautious about future expansion or success.

Self-Help Question 7.1

Consider the burden of risk that an owner and head baker of a small bakery business might operate under. Identify at least five risks that would have significant financial consequences if they occurred.

Answers to self-help questions are provided at the end of each section.

Why Is Risk Financing Important?

Risk financing is an essential part of the risk treatment process. Failing to treat or finance risks adequately can lead to the complete collapse of an organisation.

Block 1 listed a number of organisations that failed to effectively manage risks. The table below lists the financial impacts of those failures.

Company	Event Description	Effect
Japan Meteorological Agency	Tsunami and nuclear power plant meltdown	US$309 billion • property damage • clean-up costs • compensation
Toyota	Product recall due to faulty brakes	No published costs as of July 2017; however, the 2009 and 2010 recalls cost up to $3.2 billion • repairs • lost sales • fines
BP/Transocean	Marine oil spill	US$61.6 billion • fines • settlements • medical costs • clean-up costs • property damage

Company	Event Description	Effect
Volkswagen	Falsified reporting of excessive emissions levels	US$18 billion • fines • settlements • buybacks • compensation
Samsung	Manufacturing defect causing explosions	US$5.3 billion • recalls • compensation • (Plus US$17 billion of lost revenue)

These organisations managed to survive major financial impacts. Many others do not. Risk financing may not prevent an organisation from failing after a major crisis, but an organisation is more likely to survive with a risk financing strategy than without one.

The Risk Financing Process

Risk financing forms one part of the overall risk treatment process; it specifically relates to the funding of potentially large financial losses over a limited period of time thus reducing the potential that a loss will generate an operationally significant loss of cash. Such losses can occur in one event or can accumulate quickly over a series of events, either of which can have a major effect on the organisation's ability to function.

The funding of risks with a large financial impact is a central focus for all organisations and can be managed in large organisations by separate treasury and insurance functions. The treasury function manages financial risks such as the movement in interest rates and foreign exchange rates, while the insurance function, generally combined with the risk management function in many organisations, manages the purchasing of traditional insurance products such as fire policies and general liability policies.

A generally accepted process for risk financing has evolved for both the treasury function of organisations and for the insurance function. In both cases, senior executives are involved in establishing risk financing strategies; consequently, risk financing as part of the organisation's finance strategy usually does not suffer from a lack of management commitment. However, when insurance pricing is relatively cheap, or where it is a very large and diverse organisation, Chief Executive Officers and organisational boards of directors tend to leave much of the decision-making to the Chief Financial Officer. This can lead to a lack of understanding of the implications of risk financing strategies across the senior executive team and consequently across the organisation. The challenge for risk management professionals is to ensure the risk financing strategy is appropriate for the overall risk profile of the organisation and well understood by the senior executive team.

The risk financing process occurs in unison with the risk treatment process.

During the identification of risk treatment options, some risks are considered for retention of their financial impacts for later self-insurance or for risk sharing.

Activity | Treasury management

Treasury management (or treasury operations) usually refers to management of an enterprise's cash and short-term financing, i.e. holdings in, and trading in, government and corporate bonds, currencies, financial futures, options and derivatives, payment systems, and the associated risk financing activities.

Research the use of the term 'Treasury' or 'Treasurer' by searching the internet for 'Treasury Management'.

Steps in the Risk Financing Process

The risk financing process consists of the following steps:

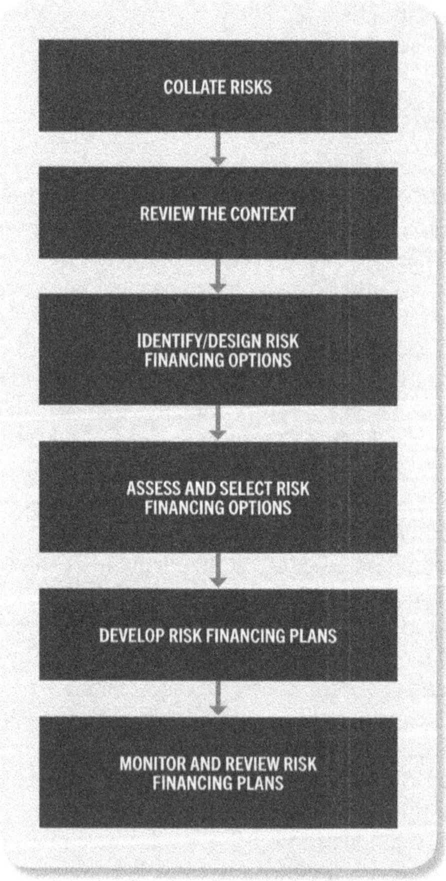

Collate Risks

Risks that need collating include those identified during the risk treatment phase as having significant elements of residual financial impact.

During the risk treatment phase of the risk management process, many risks will be reduced to a low level because of the identification and implementation of risk treatments. Some risks may still have the potential to cause a financial loss to the organisation because further risk treatment is either impractical or the expense would exceed the cost of insurance or a financial hedge product.

Because insurance and treasury programs are usually annual strategies, the majority of risks requiring financing are already identified. It is essential for the risk manager to review an organisation's risk profile to identify new or emerging risks that need to be included in the risk financing strategy. Collated risks should be categorised into:

- business or non-insurable risks
- insurable risks
- treasury risks.

The likelihood and consequences of these risks should be carried over from the risk assessment phase because this is vital knowledge for making decisions regarding risk financing strategies. In some cases, the consequences may be considered 'major' or 'catastrophic', based on inherent knowledge such as the financial loss due to a fire that destroys a manufacturing facility. In some cases, it may be necessary to expand the work completed in the risk assessment phase so that the potential financial effect is fully appreciated for each key risk prior to developing risk financing strategies.

Review the Context

At the beginning of the risk management process, organisations establish criteria that outline which risks are acceptable as part of establishing the overall context for risk management across the organisation. These are related to the organisation's risk appetite and risk tolerance (see Blocks 1 and 3). The risk criteria will almost always include a financial category with levels of financial impact that range from insignificant to catastrophic.

During the development of the risk financing component of the finance strategy, these levels need to be reviewed to ensure the risk manager understands how much financial risk the organisation can tolerate. In other words, the original context set by the organisation for the acceptance of financial risk needs to be reviewed so that there are clear objectives that need to be met for the risk financing strategy. For example, if a moderate financial consequence is considered to be €100,000 and exposures above this amount can only be carried with very low levels of likelihood of occurrence, the risk financing strategy will need to ensure that risk sharing with insurers and other third parties is put into place for exposures in excess of €100,000.

Sometimes an organisation will choose to set lower levels at which risk sharing takes place, particularly for insurable risks, because of the potential for stakeholders to perceive management has made poor decisions. For example, a company could choose only to buy insurance above €5 million because a review has shown the cost relative to the likelihood of a major insurable event was prohibitive and the company could afford to absorb €5 million. However, when management considers how external stakeholders would view a €5 million reduction in profit if an event did occur, they may choose to buy the extra insurance.

The point here is that decisions are not made on the numbers alone, there are issues like stakeholder perceptions and management risk appetite that will influence the decision.

Lastly, as the cost of risk financing varies over time, an organisation's risk appetite needs to be periodically reviewed. For example, insurance costs are changeable and when prices are high, an organisation may need to consider carrying a higher than normal risk retention.

Identify/Design Risk Financing Options

Once risks needing financing have been identified and the risk appetite of the organisation is established, risk financing options can be identified and designed.

At this stage, the treasury, insurance and operations areas of an organisation may establish separate risk financing options and implement them as individual risk financing strategies. This technique can work successfully as long as the overall risk financing strategy is co-ordinated at a central point, perhaps by the Chief Financial Officer (CFO). It is essential that proposed changes to any of the strategies are reviewed to ensure the organisation does not unwittingly take on more risk than it is prepared to retain. Consider the following example.

Suppose that, in setting the risk financing strategy, the treasury function chose a risk retention level of €1 million, the insurance function chose a risk retention level of €€500,000, and the operations area established budget contingencies of €500,000. These decisions were all accepted by the Board as they were within the overall appetite for financial risk of €3 million.

Sometime later, due to the volatility of commodity markets caused by instability in the Middle East, the treasury function and CFO determined that hedging is becoming prohibitively expensive at lower protection levels and hence decided to retain risk up to €2 million. The CFO knows that this keeps the overall risk retention strategy under the €3 million established by the Board.

A short time later, the Head of Operations is provided with an opportunity to bring forward maintenance on a vital piece of equipment because of a forced shutdown. He commits to spend his entire budget contingency (€500,000) in the coming month.

Immediately, the organisation is exposed to a €500,000 financial impact for which there is no strategy for funding. If the organisation was risk averse when setting up the €3 million risk retention level, there may be easy access to funds if needed. If not, there may not be this access.

Another point to make is that the same outcome could occur even if the risk financing strategy was co-ordinated at one point; however, the difference is that the risk would have been taken with full knowledge of the potential consequences and there would be no surprise if they did occur.

Risk financing is mainly concerned with retained and shared financial risk. In most cases, there will be a combination of the two; for example, when purchasing conventional insurance as a risk financing strategy, an organisation needs to determine how much to self-insure (that is, the excess or deductible) and how much to share with the insurer.

For some risks that an organisation decides to retain, a risk financing plan will be required; for example, for establishing provision accounts or contingent debt facilities.

The identify/design stage of the risk financing process is the stage where different options need to be found and planned in sufficient detail to permit them to be assessed.

Identifying Risk Financing Options

Identifying risk financing options means finding and describing potential methods for financing risk events if they eventuate.

Action	Result
Risk	Loss of sole manufacturing facility due to fire.
Consequence	Complete loss of facility and all sales until the plant is rebuilt.
Options	• Rebuild from operating cash flow – not possible as cash flow will cease because no more sales can be made • Rebuild from cash reserves – viable if sufficient cash is available • Rebuild from insurance with excess funded from reserves • Rebuild using debt (draw down on existing line of credit or call on contingent line of credit) • Rebuild using cash injected from equity holders or call on contingent equity

As the manufacturing facility is the sole source of sales and, hence, operating cash flow, the first option identified above is not viable. The other options are viable depending on the financial strength of the company and the opinion lenders or main equity holders have of the organisation. For example, for the organisation to obtain debt or equity, the providers of that debt or equity will need to feel comfortable that their loan or investment will be repaid.

Details on how such options are designed are covered later in this module. For the moment, understand that when identifying risk financing options, even options that may not be initially obvious, or those which may appear too costly should be included for evaluation.

Self-Help Question 7.2

Consider the risk financing options of new equity, which is a cash injection into an organisation to pay for the financial cost of a risk event occurring.

How would this option vary between a publicly listed organisation and a local council?

Answers to self-help questions are provided at the end of each section.

Assess and Select Risk Financing Options

Similar to the risk treatment process, the evaluation phase of the risk financing process is about balancing cost versus benefit decision-making. The decisions about options for risk financing are easier than for those involving other kinds of risk treatment because the cost-benefit analysis involves dollar amounts and has fewer intangibles. However, the cost-benefit analysis is rarely simple due to finance issues such as the cost of capital, equity versus debt, the time value of money and the opportunity cost of capital.

The 'assess and select' stage of the risk financing process evaluates selected options against risk financing objectives. In selecting the most appropriate risk financing options, the following key questions need to be addressed.

- For a risk-sharing option, is the cost reasonable or would it be more cost-effective to retain the risk?
- If the cost is not reasonable for any of the identified risk-sharing options, can we afford to retain more risk or will the risk have to be shared at the unreasonable cost?
- For an unconventional treasury or insurance solution, do we have the skills or access to advisers needed to implement the strategy?
- For risk retention strategies do we have the skills or access to advisers needed to implement the strategy?

Answering some of the above questions requires consideration of the organisational culture and overall appetite for retaining, versus sharing, risk.

Consider the situation of Zandu in the case study below, which explores some of these issues.

Case Study – Zandu

Zandu is a franchise operating in small premises in shopping malls. As tenants, they are only responsible for the contents of their premises, not the potential damage to the building they are located in.

The management team has considered the risk of fire at each franchise store and considers the risk very low, with the cost to refit one store being approximately € 250,000. They are planning to have more than 50 stores nationally and they have identified the following options for financing the risk of fire.

1. Fund from the cash flow of the business – that is, if one or two stores were to burn down, the profits from the remaining stores would be used to refit the stores.
2. Fund from cash reserves – hold € 500,000 in funds to cover a worst-case scenario where two stores burnt down in one year.
3. Arrange € 500,000 line of credit from a bank.
4. Pre-agree € 500,000 equity injection from franchisees at € 10,000 per franchise store.
5. Buy insurance with € 1,000 deductible for each store.

For each of these options, the typical annual cost may be as follows.

1. Zero – however, for a fire or two, each franchisee and the franchisor would make less profit in the year of the fire/s. For example, if a fire were likely, they would need to consider the cost of paying for one store every couple of years. Fortunately, such fires are in fact reasonably rare and they would not expect a fire at a store more than perhaps once in a decade.
2. If € 500,000 were to be held in reserve, there would be an opportunity cost because holding this reserve would prevent two other stores from being fitted out. Say the return on a € 500,000 investment in two stores was 20% (€ 100,000) and the cash could earn 7% (€ 35,000) in a savings account, the opportunity cost per annum from holding € 500,000 in reserve instead of opening two new stores would be € 65,000 (€ 100,000 – € 35,000).
3. Arranging a € 500,000 line of credit from a bank will cost around € 5,000 per annum. This cost needs to be balanced against the possible risk event of a store burning down at the cost of € 250,000 or the even less likely event of two stores burning down at a cost of € 500,000.
4. Pre-arranging an € 500,000 equity injection from franchisees is similar to option 2 except that each franchisee must hold cash ready to inject and this would present opportunity costs for each franchisee.
5. A typical insurance policy may cost € 1,500 for fire only.

Franchisees may choose different options depending on their level of risk appetite – for example, some may want certainty around their annual profit in the event of a store burning down and would want to buy insurance; some may be willing to repay a loan but not to take the risk of having to pay straightaway if a fire occurred; and some may be prepared to take the risk by not having a risk financing strategy and hoping a fire does not occur.

Non-Financial Influences

When evaluating risk financing options, non-financial influences need to be taken into account. For example, in deciding whether to retain or share risk with an insurer, management needs to consider whether they would benefit from having an insurance company involved in managing claims and whether the benefits would outweigh any additional costs. Another example is that management would need to consider the drain on resources in enforcing a contingent equity arrangement after a risk event that triggered the pre-arranged contract. Often it is simply easier to insure, because contingent equity arrangements require detailed drafting of unique contracts to arrange for an injection of cash in exchange for some level of ownership of the organisation after a specified risk event. Finally, there might be an impact on the rating for listed companies as rating agencies tend to assess an insurance contract as a potential asset (see IFRS Phase 2). Irrespective of which option looks the best financially, all options should be considered for the more intangible costs and benefits.

Self-Help Question 7.3

List some of the potential intangible benefits of the following risk financing strategies:

- purchasing a foreign exchange hedge contract;
- purchasing fire insurance for a large, complex facility;
- purchasing a motor fleet insurance policy.

Answers to self-help questions are provided at the end of each section.

Develop Risk Financing Plans

Risk financing plans are needed to implement risk financing strategies. Developing risk financing plans requires including an appropriate level of detail so that it is clear what has to be achieved, by whom and by when. Each plan or group of plans should include documented processes for monitoring and review, which we will now discuss.

Monitor and Review Risk Financing Plans

The risk financing process needs to be monitored and reviewed to make sure it remains relevant to the needs of an organisation. A difference between risk financing plans and risk treatment/reduction plans is that risk financing plans usually involve third-party advisers and counter-parties such as banks or insurers involved in risk sharing, whereas risk treatment plans involve just the organisation.

Employees responsible for reporting to senior management about the monitoring of risk financing strategies need to ensure that they have timely access to outsourced risk financing information.

Self-Help Question 7.4

Identify three main characteristics of the risk financing process that differentiates it from the broader risk treatment process.

Answers to self-help questions are provided at the end of each section.

Risk Financing Strategies

An organisation's risk financing strategy outlines how its approach to financing risks is aligned to its business aims. A risk financing strategy also has to make effective and efficient use of an organisation's capital and available insurance markets.

Strategic risk financing involves the following:

- understanding the risks an organisation faces;
- using analytical tools to predict the potential cost of those risks;
- applying business goals and strategies to determine how to use insurance and other sources of capital to finance those risks.

Risk financing strategies need to be documented so that the decision-making process that leads to the identification of the preferred strategy is transparent. Along with budgets and timelines, the strategic plans should include clearly defined roles, including the roles played by external advisers such as the organisation's insurance broker.

Risk financing strategies require a diligent monitoring and review regime, as the success of the strategy is fundamental to ensuring the ongoing survival of the organisation. For example, the financial circumstances of the organisation can change quickly, as can the financial circumstances of counter-parties with whom risks are being shared.

The following case study explores some of these issues.

Case Study – Top Deck Advisory

Top Deck Advisory is an external audit corporation that has a large market share of the top 500 companies in Europe. The primary insurer of their professional indemnity policy is Networked Insurance, an insurance company approved by its local supervising agency.

Because of the numerous law suits against audit firms in the past 20 years, insurance is expensive and Top Deck carries a large excess relative to its earning potential. The firm has been comfortable with such a large excess because of its profitability and because it keeps partners focused on auditing organisations appropriately.

Mid-year, 20% of the partners of Top Deck resign and moved to another organisation. Despite 'non-compete' clauses in their contracts, which do not allow them to audit existing clients for 12 months, the walk-out puts a strain on Top Deck's business and immediately eats into profitability because clients cannot be properly serviced until new people are hired.

The managing partner becomes aware that some of the partners who resigned had been inattentive to their audit management as their focus changed to their impending resignation. Top Deck now has concerns about the potential for professional liability claims.

Two months later, a major rating agency downgraded Networked Insurance from A- to BBB+ for its claims-paying ability. Top Deck is now in a position where it has less profit, heightened possibility of claims and a less stable lead insurer, which could lead to non-payment of a claim. Top Deck now needs to take some action on its risk financing strategy.

Some options Top Deck will need to consider include the following:

- Reduce costs such as management bonuses to boost reserves in the event of unfunded losses, and help manage the damage to reputation a number of claims could have on the firm by investing in client relationships and media advertising.
- Work with their insurance advisers to immediately replace Networked as their primary insurer or, at the very least, introduce additional insurers into the program to reduce their dependency on Networked. If possible, Top Deck would want the new insurer/s to cover claims arising from past business activity for at least the past year.
- Work with their insurance advisers to find an alternative risk financing product that would cover already notified claims in the event that Networked could not meet its obligations at some time in the future.

Implement, Monitor and Review Risk Financing Strategies

Once risk financing strategies have been implemented, it is essential that the strategy is monitored and reviewed. There are two reasons why monitoring and reviewing of strategies are necessary:

- the financial circumstances of an organisation can change quickly;
- an organisation's insurance portfolio can be complex.

The case study about Top Deck showed how the financial circumstances of an organisation can change quickly. Organisations need to constantly review both internal and external changes to ensure that the risk management strategy is aligned with the organisation's needs.

Typically, the insurance portfolio of a large organisation consists of a number of insurance policies. Each has its own uniquely worded policy, combinations of lead and co-insurers, different deductibles, different renewal dates, and each one is of differing importance for diverse reasons.

Organisational operations take place within this context of possible changing financial circumstances and insurance portfolio complexity.

The treasury function is maintaining or closing hedging contracts from decisions made weeks, months or even years ago, while preparing to implement new strategies. Operational managers are setting their budgets and working on new strategies to improve profitability and cash flows. The more complex the organisation, the more challenging it is for the risk financing strategy to be implemented cohesively and without unfunded surprise losses.

The risk financing strategy should be well co-ordinated both internally and externally with service providers. Contracts should be in place to hold external providers accountable for both the amount and quality of risk sharing polices (quality in this context refers to the credit worthiness of counterparties such as banks and insurers and the quality of contract or policy wording).

For example, an insurer that has a financial strength rating of AAA may provide an insurance policy that covers core business activities but excludes some of the non-core activities of the insured. On the other hand, another insurer may provide a higher quality policy wording giving broader coverage but may not have the same ratings or be locally placed with a weaker insurer, outside of developed countries. Clearly it is better to have most claims paid than run the risk of not having a major claim paid because the insurer becomes insolvent.

Risk financing strategies need to be quickly implemented so that managers can focus on monitoring the changing business needs and circumstances of the risk sharing arrangements in place.

Types of Risk Financing Strategies

There are two main categories of risk financing:

- risk retention
- risk transfer.

These two categories overlap; for example, when an organisation purchases insurance. As most policies have a deductible, which is the amount an organisation must pay towards a claim before its insurance begins to pay, the organisation is sharing the risk with the insurer and retaining the deductible; these arrangements are also called hybrids as they combine elements of retention and elements of transfer.

Within each category there are a number of risk financing options.

Risk Retention

Risk retention involves making an informed, conscious decision to accept the effects of exposure to a particular risk. Organisations usually decide to accept a risk exposure after fully considering its likelihood and consequence.

Risk retention is the most common form of risk treatment when:

- severity is extremely low

or

- the likelihood of the risk event is considered exceptionally remote.

EXAMPLE

Building Insurance Policy

Many building insurance policies exclude nuclear explosion cover. An organisation in Italy would most likely not choose to discontinue operations because of this exposure as the likelihood is very low; however, it could be an issue for French, Swiss or British organisations, depending on their distance from the nearest nuclear power plant.

Organisations cannot (or should not from an economical perspective) eliminate all risks. Even if the organisation attempts to adopt all the previously listed control measures, there is a point where the organisation is powerless to eliminate or further reduce risk exposures or their effects either because they cannot or the costs exceed the benefit.

Organisations may also decide to accept risk exposures integral to their business operations, always bearing in mind that there may be some level of unplanned risk retention.

EXAMPLE

Ministry of Transport

The Ministry of Transport must accept certain risks because the only way to avoid them completely would be to not provide its services. As a compromise, the Ministry of Transport chooses to control these risks to the extent that is practically and commercially possible and bear the residual risk.

Planned Risk Retention

Planned risk retention involves an organisation:

- making a conscious decision to retain an identified risk exposure;
- implementing financial arrangements to cover any losses that may occur.

Even if a major loss occurs, planned risk retention can ensure the profitability and survival of an organisation if the organisation properly manages, budgets and finances risk retention.

Unplanned Risk Retention

An organisation unconsciously accepts and retains a risk exposure in instances when it has not identified a risk exposure. This unidentified risk exposure means the organisation has to directly bear the unidentified risk exposure/s and any losses/associated costs.

Unplanned risk acceptance, which can be the result of poor risk management processes, can affect the stability (or survival) of an organisation if a major unplanned risk event occurs. However, it may be the case that the identified and analysed exposure is deemed too low to warrant a specific treatment and left to ad-hoc treatment should it occur, or even be included in maintenance expenses (when the potential cumulative financial impact in a year for example is below a given threshold; for example for a car park of 1,000 cars treat glass break as an unidentified line of the maintenance budget).

Choice of Retention Levels[1]

At this stage, the professional reader confronted with a real-life situation must be asking one crucial question: 'What is the right level of retention for my organisation?' The answer is simple, indeed simplistic, it can be disappointing but there is no way around it: The ideal retention level is the level with which the board is comfortable.

This is a reminder that the final choice in risk financing is in the hands of top management; it is their safety that is at stake, theirs and their organisation's.

There are, however, a few guidelines:

- Whatever is the 'ideal' level chosen, it will apply only to the 'conscious' retention, i.e. the retention linked to 'identified' exposures. It is advisable to have some leeway, a margin for those exposures that have not been identified. Losses will happen some day and they will have to be financed out of current cash flows (or the postponement of an investment project, like some Japanese firms did for development in Europe, frozen to help rebuild the key facilities destroyed by the Kobe earthquake in 1995).
- Non-voluntary, or compulsory, retention must be considered first (those for which there is no known or available transfer mechanism).
- Then an appropriate level of retention must take into account all the basic financial balances and the objectives of the firm:

[1]The content on this page reproduced from Condamin, L, Louisot, J and Naïm, P 2006, *Risk quantification: Management, diagnosis and hedging*, John Wiley & Sons Ltd, West Sussex, pp. 222–223.

- cash-flow
- liquid assets, acid test, quick ratio, etc.
- stockholders (or stock market) reaction of a lessening growth pattern
- stockholders (or stock market) reaction to a decrease in the profit per share (the dividend per share).

In the real world, it is rare that a firm will adopt a retention level in excess of 5% to 10% of its annual profit. This is not an accepted norm, rather a founding based on factual evidence.

One last reminder, risk financing is always based on the final assumption that, should the survival of the firm be at stake, financing the losses will take precedence over any other consideration. All funds available will be channelled to close the breach in the hull.

As mentioned earlier, this is the reason why in the wake of the Kobe earthquake several Japanese firms, with no pre-financing plans for earthquake in an area deemed safer than others in Japan, froze all investments abroad, and especially in Europe, to fund the rebuilding of vital interests in Japan. In the same fashion, Union Carbide had to reduce its worldwide activities and shrink to a much smaller operation to preserve its existence. The sale of subsidiaries was the likely consequence of the process of indemnification of the victims of Bhopal but did preserve the 'core business'.

Activity | Treasury management

- *Reflect on the previously described risk financing options.*
- *Consider how they apply to either your organisation or a client's organisation.*

It may help to consider the following questions:

- *Are there some risk exposures the organisation should avoid or has made a conscious decision to avoid?*
- *What methods of risk control does the organisation use to reduce the likelihood of occurrence and the consequences of risk?*
- *What significant risk exposures does the organisation accept/retain? Why?*

Risk Transfer

Many of life's undertakings involve the risk of harm or loss. By taking out an insurance policy, a person (or group) can **transfer** the financial consequences of this risk to the insurance company in exchange for a monetary payment (a premium).

The insurance policy protects insureds from unforeseen events (for example, robbery and fire). This protection also allows insureds to take risks they would not be able to afford without insurance (for example, buying a house).

The principle of insurance is that the losses of the few are borne by the contributions of the many.

When establishing risk transfer arrangements, there are a number of key issues that the risk manager and CFO should consider. These issues are relevant regardless of whether the arrangement is with the capital or the insurance markets. These considerations are as follows.

- Don't risk more than the organisation can afford to lose. If the hedge or insurance cost seems expensive or unjust, don't automatically retain more of the risk. If need be, revisit the organisation's risk retention decision. Don't gamble the organisation's future if a way can be found to fund the expense.
- Don't buy too much, too little, or too much and too little at the same time. As Vaughan and Vaughan (2008, p. 61) point out, without a sound knowledge of the risks of the organisation and the extent of the risk sharing protection available, organisations can easily buy protection well beyond what is required in one area, while leaving gaping holes in the protection program in others. Another trap involving buying too much and too little at the same time is buying insurance with a low deductible but with an insufficient upper limit on the policy.

This means buying cover for more frequent losses that should be financed directly by the organisation and gambling that the really big event will never occur.

- Advice should be sought before hedging or buying insurance. When obtaining advice there are two issues the risk manager and the CFO need to consider. The first is the need to resist the temptation to outsource the decision-making process almost entirely, and the second is the potential for a conflict of interest for advisers.
- Outsourcing decision-making – Vaughan and Vaughan outline that a potential problem with outsourcing decision-making to an insurance broker (2008, p. 61) is that a broker may try to protect an organisation from all risks and therefore encourage the purchase of more insurance rather than less. A similar situation exists when buying hedge contracts: the majority of organisations seek advice about hedge contracts from their banker, and bankers do not like to see clients exposed to risk if reasonably priced hedge contracts are available. However, what may be reasonable to the banker might not be reasonable to the organisation's senior executives.
- Conflicts of interest – a major problem for organisations seeking advice on hedge and insurance programs is the potential for their advisers to have a conflict of interest. Whether a conflict of interest arises depends on how the adviser is remunerated. For example, if an organisation's banker is asked about whether or not it should hedge and to what level, there is potential for the banker to recommend to hedge or to purchase a larger or more conservative contract because their bank earns income from a hedge contract.

  - Insurance brokers may receive commissions from insurers, although they are paid by the insured in the premium, and this may lead a broker to advise the purchase of one insurance policy over another because of the level of their commission. This may also lead to a broker recommending the purchase of policies with lower deductibles and higher limits, as the more premiums collected, the higher the commission for the insurance broker.

  - There is a growing trend for organisations to pay a fee to insurance brokers to ensure the broker does not receive any further commissions. This helps address any conflict of interest regarding remuneration to the broker and, as long as the broker has negotiated a large enough fee to make their business of providing advice worthwhile, the service from the broker should be satisfactory.
  - Organisations should be aware that it is difficult to be sure that an insurance broker is not receiving additional commission. In recent years there has been significant litigation in the US and Europe against insurance brokers for receiving contingent commissions from insurers. This is when insurers pay a broker additional premium based on the overall volume of business the broker places with the insurer. The litigation commenced because authorities believed these commissions created an inherent conflict of interest for insurance brokers. Brokers were forced to change their business models to adjust how they were remunerated.

- Credit quality – purchasing an insurance policy does not guarantee payment if the insurer is not able to pay. Counter-party risk is the risk that the bank or insurer with which an organisation has a hedge or insurance contract cannot pay.

To assist organisations in making decisions about counter-party risk, there are rating agencies that provide financial strength ratings of insurers and other financial institutions. These include AM Best, Fitch, Moody's, and Standard and Poor's. These agencies study the financials and business environments of the organisations they are rating and also interview senior executives concerning the accounts, operating results and future business strategy and outlook. The rating agencies then assess the financial strength of the organisations. Using a rating agency's advice can prevent an organisation from exposing itself to counter-party risk.

In addition to the rating agencies, large international insurance brokers have internal teams that assess the financial strength of insurers and establish approved insurer lists. International insurance brokers will issue directions to their broking personnel if a particular insurer should not be asked to quote business because of a weak financial position. If a client wants to deal with an insurer that is not approved, the broker will usually ask the client to sign a document indicating they are doing so at their own risk.

It is common for large organisations to further reduce counter-party risk by using more than one counter-party for the same transaction. In banking, these are referred to as syndicates. In insurance, this is called co-insurance; each insurer is called a co-insurer, and there is usually a leading insurer in charge of the daily processing of the contract. If one bank or insurer cannot pay, an organisation can pursue the other banks or insurers.

Activity | Standard and Poor's financial strength ratings

Visit www.standardandpoors.com. From the left-hand menu, select 'Ratings Definitions', then use the drop-down table of contents menu to select 'E Insurer financial strength ratings'. Read this section, paying close attention to the differences between rating levels.

What is the role of the rating?

Ineffective Management of Risk Transfer

Organisations cannot entirely transfer risk exposures other than by perhaps a sale agreement and, even then, some contingent liability may remain. When an organisation shares its risk exposure (either wholly or in part) with another party, it actually acquires a new risk as the organisation to which it has transferred the risk exposure may not manage the exposure properly. In essence, the nature of the risk exposure has only changed (rather than been removed).

EXAMPLE

Call Centre

Outsourcing of a function such as a call centre is a good example of an organisation acquiring new risks. While the risks relating to the operational aspects of running a call centre may fall with the provider, the risks relating to poor performance of the call centre (such as damage to reputation) remain with the organisation outsourcing the service.

Risk Implications

The following is a list of possible risk implications arising from an ineffective transfer of risk:

- the indirect consequences of the loss on the reputation of the organisation (for example, a subcontracted call centre designed to reduce operational delivery risk could damage a company's reputation indirectly if the call centre does a really poor job dealing with its customers);
- the financial capacity of the other party to pay for the loss;
- the impact of legislation (for example, trade practices and workplace health and safety laws);
- protection for a criminal offence (for example, breaching fair trading laws which cannot be contractually transferred).

Additional Risk Financing Products

In addition to insurance, there is a range of risk financing products available to many organisations. These are generally referred to as hedging products (hedging means to undertake one investment to protect against the potential loss in another investment). Hedging products include foreign exchange, interest rate and exchange traded commodities. For example, an airline may be concerned about the price of fuel increasing for pre-booked flights. The airline could enter into a commodity hedge by buying a futures contract for the commodity aviation fuel. This would lock in the price of fuel at the time flights were booked, even if the price of fuel had significantly increased. Airlines are always pre-selling seats and are continually buying futures contracts on a weekly or monthly basis.

In the case of Acron Chemicals, if a major raw material were natural gas, Acron Chemicals could protect against the movement in the price of natural gas by purchasing a commodity futures contract that would allow them to buy gas at a set price in the future. If the price increased, Acron would be protected by a guaranteed price for their raw material needs. There is still a risk involved in purchasing a futures contract, as Acron may need more gas than they purchased futures contracts for, or the party supplying the futures contract may become insolvent and be unable to honour the contract.

Summary

Please keep the following points from this chapter in mind:

- Risk treatment is a planning process during which organisations devise ways of addressing identified risks to help ensure their business objectives are met or exceeded.
- Risk financing is the process of funding the financial consequences of risk.
- The risk financing process involves the following steps:

  - collate the risks identified during the risk treatment process as having residual financial risk
  - review the context of the established risks to identify the risk financing strategy
  - identify/design risk financing options
  - assess and select risk financing options
  - develop risk financing plans
  - monitor and review risk financing plans.

- There are two main categories of risk financing:

  - risk retention
  - risk transfer.

- Risk managers need to be innovative in developing a range of treatment options. The risk manager needs to be aware that the most appropriate risk treatment is not always the most obvious.

- The funding of risks with a large financial impact is a central focus for all organisations and can be managed in large organisations by separate treasury and insurance functions. The complexity of these functions means that management need to ensure the organisation has the appropriate skills both internally and externally to implement appropriate risk treatment and finance strategies.
- Once planned, the risk treatment and financing processes need to be closely monitored because of the ever-changing nature of modern organisations and the importance of successful implementation of key risk mitigation strategies.
- Failure to act or failure to monitor and review the effectiveness of risk treatments may result in very serious known risks catastrophically affecting an organisation. Effective implementation is also vital, as without it, the organisation can have an unfunded cataclysmic loss.

Answers to Self-Help Questions

Self-help question 7.1

Risks with significant financial consequences for the owner of the small bakery could include any of the following:

- fire or gas explosion;
- loss of natural gas to heat the ovens;
- injury, causing incapacity and resulting in business interruption;
- injury to an employee and the need to pay compensation;
- injury to a member of the public and the need to pay compensation – e.g. slip/trip/fall or food poisoning;
- damage to surrounding property from a fire on the bakery premises;
- a competing bakery opening an outlet near to this bakery and selling product at reduced prices.

Self-help question 7.2

For a publicly-listed company, an injection of equity is complex and takes considerable time. A prospectus for the issue of new shares has to be prepared and issued and then investors need to 'subscribe' to the issue of shares.

A local council can either raise rates charged to its constituents or it can turn to the state government for additional funds.

Both organisations would need to follow a set process, and both would take some time. The company's future is left to the market to decide, whereas the functions performed by local council will always be performed by this council or another one if it was absorbed because the state government did not rescue it.

→

→

Self-help question 7.3

Some of the potential intangible benefits are:

- For a foreign exchange hedge contract – advice from the advising banking institution on the bank economists' view of the likely movement of exchange rates over the period of interest.
- For fire insurance for a large, complex facility – access to the insurance company's experience of managing fire risks in large complex facilities.
- For a motor fleet insurance policy – access to the insurer's risk management training facilities to improve driver skills, plus access to the insurer's data on the key causes of accidents for the type of motor fleet insured.

Self-help question 7.4

The main differences between the risk financing process and the risk treatment process include the following:

- Risk financing is focused on financial impact and there are long established processes for fulfilling the treasury and insurance functions in large organisations; whereas risk treatment is much broader and less defined.
- Risk financing strategies usually involve large amounts of risk sharing with third parties such as banks and insurers; whereas in the broader area of risk treatment, risk sharing is only one component.
- Risk financing has developed specialists in areas of insurance and treasury management and there is a large adviser pool from which to source skills and knowledge; whereas, in risk treatment, there is often a need to be innovative and to rely on internal staff to be resourceful enough to manage risks that are particular to the organisation.

Chapter 8

Insurance Sector

Introduction

As explored in the previous topic, insurance is a key risk financing technique. It is used by all organisations (albeit to different extents) because it is a cost-effective way of ensuring financial survival in the case of sizeable risk events.

Because of its centrality, it is important for all risk managers to understand the basics of the industry. This topic will explore the insurance market, the different players and their roles and the interactions between parties. It will also explore the two main options for insurance policies and the instances in which one could be more beneficial than the other.

Learning Outcomes

By the end of this topic, you should be able to:

- define the major participants in the insurance market;
- explain the role insurance plays in risk financing;
- describe the differences between traditional and claims history-based programmes.

Insurance Market

Major Participants

The major participants in the insurance market are:

- insurers
- insurance intermediaries/agents
- customers (policyholders).

Risk Treatment, 175–181

Published under exclusive licence by Emerald Publishing Limited
doi:10.1108/978-1-83662-306-920251019

The following diagram provides a summary of these participants and their roles.

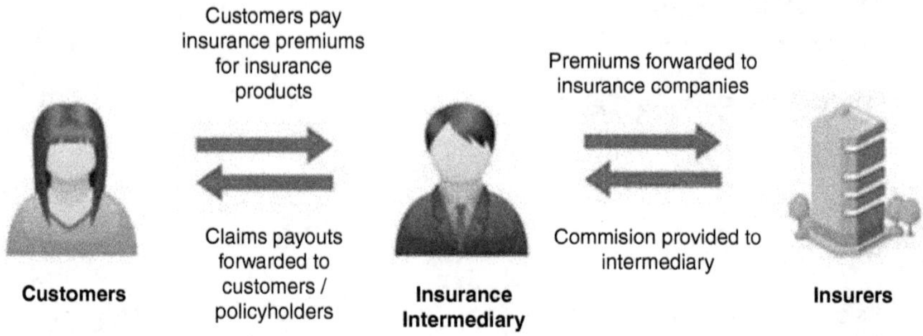

Roles in the Insurance Industry

Insurers

Insurers issue financial products in the form of insurance policies and are responsible for providing cover to purchasing policyholders. Various legislation and regulations bind insurers in the way they issue and maintain policies.

Insurance Intermediaries

Insurance intermediaries are financial intermediaries as they sell policies on the insurer's behalf and collect money from the insured to forward to the insurer.

The primary role of insurance intermediaries is to arrange the distribution and purchase of insurance products. Insurance intermediaries may operate under their own licence or as an authorised representative.

Key intermediaries include:

- brokers
- strategic alliance partners (banks)
- dealers
- agents.

Other Intermediaries

Intermediaries for insurance companies are not always insurance brokers or individual authorised representatives. Banks and other financial institutions act as intermediaries for insurance companies when they offer insurance coverage to their own clients for:

- mortgage and loan protection
- consumer credit protection
- cover for personal property
- personal accident and sickness insurance.

Customers

Customers are the lifeblood of all businesses. A business's response to customers has an ongoing effect on the customer's attitude towards the organisation. It is important, therefore, that businesses get it right from the first time they make contact.

Financial intermediaries tend to refer to their customers as **clients** rather than customers.

Distribution

As the insurance market has become more complex over time, so have the ways of getting insurance products to customers. The two main sources from which customers can obtain insurance are through:

- insurers – via call centres or the internet (for example)
- insurance intermediaries.

Call Centres

Call centres, which are mainly used for personal lines insurance, offer a number of advantages to an insurer:

- ability to retain direct control over the business being written (when insurance intermediaries are used to distribute products, a measure of control is lost);
- ability to meet the market need to deal directly with insurers;
- Saving administration costs by centralising all customer service functions into one specialised unit.

Note: Representatives selling insurance in an insurer's call centre act as representatives of the insurer. The insurer is therefore liable for the financial services these representatives provide.

Insurance Intermediaries

Rather than researching and making decisions on their own, some customers prefer to receive advice from a qualified/authorised insurance salesperson. Typically, insurance intermediaries come in two basic forms:

- agents
- brokers.

In general, **agents** work for, represent and are accountable to the insurer while brokers work for, represent and are accountable to the client.

Remuneration

Advisers, agents and brokers receive remuneration from insurers in the form of a commission based on a percentage of premiums paid by customers. In addition to commissions received from insurers, many brokers also charge their customers on a fee-for-service basis and are obligated to be transparent on their total remuneration.

Where brokers charge fees, it could be argued that this is unreasonable as they already receive commission from the insurer. A fee-for-service broker does not claim a commission and may request that an insurer's premium quote not include commission or brokerage.

Agents

Agents are insurance intermediaries who act on behalf of the insurer when arranging insurance cover for customers. They are responsible for ensuring they assess and meet their customers' financial needs when arranging insurance products.

Generally, insurers and brokers are fully responsible for the actions of their agents. They are liable if their agents breach the legislation.

Insurers and brokers are also responsible for:

- providing their agents with the necessary training;
- the actions of their agents (unless the agent specifically tells the customer they are acting outside the terms of their authority from the insurer).

Insurance Brokers

Insurance brokers are intermediaries who act under their own licence. Brokers ensure they assess and meet their clients' needs with the appropriate insurance products. Brokers are usually legally deemed to act on behalf of clients rather than insurers.

In general, insurers are not responsible for brokers' actions (depending on the relevant country's legislation). In certain circumstances, brokers can act on behalf of the insurer (under what is referred to as a binder) rather than the client to arrange insurance covers.

The code of insurance requires insurance brokers to take out professional indemnity insurance to cover their liability to their retail clients for negligence.

Purchasing Insurance Covers[1]

Purchasing insurance covers is the most common contractual risk transfer mechanism for risk financing. Although insurers perform a number of

---

[1]The content on this page reproduced from Condamin, L, Louisot, J and Naïm, P 2006, *Risk quantification: Management, diagnosis and hedging*, John Wiley & Sons Ltd, West Sussex, p. 220.

functions, compensating claims remain at the core of the insurer's role in the economic cycle.

It is worth remembering here a few common sense rules to be applied to anyone purchasing insurance covers:

- cover only those risks for which there is a real exposure;
- carefully read the definition of the insured perils;
- describe carefully and accurately the risk to be insured (answer with precision and honesty all questions asked by the underwriter);
- read carefully all exclusions (it can provide useful information as to the risks really incurred);
- regularly open to competition – open or clause bids (but always keep in mind long-term relationship, especially with long tail covers like product liability or professional indemnity);
- contract only with insurance company of good standing (solvency ratio, financial rating, etc.);
- evaluate the balance losses/premium on your contracts for the insurer;
- always use a professional competent insurance intermediary.

One common rule is that, over the long term, insurance covers are always more expensive than retention. The services provided by both the intermediary and the insurer must be paid and the stockholders get a return on their investment, the capital on which the insurance company capacity is built. However, retention limits are often low for any given organisation and the purchase of insurance is a necessity.

Claims History-Based Premiums[2]

So far, we have referred only to insurance programmes, often labelled 'traditional', that is, where premium conditions are fixed before the period of cover is started with no revision clause based on experience. If such a clause exists, the insured will bear part of the uncertainties and they are considered hybrid techniques, or truly shared risk financing techniques.

All the conditions and precautions relative to creating a captive or joining a pool may well discourage even some large businesses that may still wish to benefit from their loss control efforts. For such candidates, there exists an option that should be considered: insurance contract with premium adjusted to reflect the claims history experienced during the life of the contract.

As soon as an organisation has a dependable loss experience history over several years, it can choose a higher level of deductible, even an annual stop-loss that

[2]The content on this page reproduced from Condamin, L, Louisot, J and Naïm, P 2006, *Risk quantification: Management, diagnosis and hedging*, John Wiley & Sons Ltd, West Sussex, p. 222.

it will be able to finance internally. Henceforth, it can negotiate with its insurers a cover that will be in effect a surplus line, even if all claims, hence those below the stop-loss limit, are handled by the insurer. The cover can then stabilise the premium around the long-term annual average with a small variation for exceptional losses.

Only the premium for exceptional losses belongs to the insurer. The provisional 'premium' should be reviewed every three to five years to respond to the trend in losses experienced over the period. The insured then takes part in the profit or losses as reflected in the annual accounts for the programme. The period chosen allows for some offsetting of the yearly variation to stabilise the cost of risk element for the insured.

With this approach, it is clear that we are close to a retention mechanism manage by a third party and whereby the insurer is compensated for services in the bottom layer and receives a risk premium only for the excess line. However, the bottom line, like an SIR (self-insured retention) can be subject to different treatments. In the ultimate case, the insurer only receives a fee for his handling of the SIR and takes no risk in it. In other programmes, even the risk for this first line may be shared between insured and insurer in varying degrees.

The definition above is more a conceptual framework than an actual programme. It can be used to explain a number of different risk financing products offered on the market, from full retro plans to limited profit-sharing plans. However, it is really put to use only in cases of relatively high-frequency exposures. The list would never be up to date as brokers and consultants are always eager to create new forms to be included in sophisticated plans among other 'financing alternatives'.

Activity | Insurance useful resources

A solid knowledge of the insurance products and services and of the market mechanisms is an essential component of any risk manager's core knowledge. Some useful resources for advancing insurance knowledge are:

- Insurance Europe: www.insuranceeurope.eu
  - IE's video, 'The benefits of insurance': www.youtube.com/watch?v=ehvKU5wM0a8
- European Commission: https://ec.europa.eu/info/index
- News channels, e.g.
  - www.ft.com
  - www.telegraph.co.uk
  - www.insurancebusinessmag.com/uk/

See also the references and resources sections at the end of each block for more.

Summary

Please keep the following points from this topic in mind:

- The major participants in the insurance market are:
  - insurers
  - insurance intermediaries/authorised representatives
  - customers (policyholders).
- Two main sources from which customers can obtain insurance include:
  - insurers – via call centres or the internet (for example)
  - insurance intermediaries.
- Purchasing insurance covers is the most common contractual risk transfer mechanism for risk financing. Although insurers perform a number of functions, compensating claims remain at the core of the insurer's role in the economic cycle.
- Traditional insurance programmes have their premium conditions fixed before the period of cover is started with no revision clause based on experience. If such a clause exists, the programme is considered a hybrid technique, as the insured bears part of the uncertainties.
- Another option for an insurance contract is one where the premium is adjusted to reflect the claims history experienced during the life of the contract. This results in a cover that is in effect a surplus line.

Chapter 9

Insurance

Introduction

The previous chapter described the basic structure of the insurance sector, including two main ways of purchasing coverage and the roles involved.

It is also important for a risk manager to understand the different categories of covers that are available, especially those that relate to businesses. Each category of product serves a different purpose, and in most cases a portfolio/programme consisting of several policies will be required. A keen understanding of the distinction between policies and an ability to interpret different insurers' policies are key skills for risk managers.

This chapter will explore the different categories of products available, including property and liability covers, and will describe each in detail (except for domestic policies: these aren't designed for business, therefore are beyond the scope of this block). It will also explain what is meant by 'statutory classes'.

Also outlined are the contractual obligations connected to insurance policies and the parties to them, how limits are set and key terms and documents that will be encountered when reviewing products.

Learning Outcomes

By the end of this chapter, you should be able to:

- describe the different categories of product;
- identify which products are essential to different organisations and why;
- recognise statutory classes;
- explain why limits are in place and the implications of occurrence vs aggregate limits;
- define common insurance terms.

Risk Treatment, 183–205

Published under exclusive licence by Emerald Publishing Limited
doi:10.1108/978-1-83662-306-920251020

Types of Insurance Cover

Insurance products can be categorised as risk or investment products. Life insurance companies offer both investment and risk products whilst general insurers only offer risk products.

The Collins English dictionary defines risk as 'the possibility of incurring misfortune or loss'. Therefore, a risk insurance policy is one that provides cover against the financial consequences of incurring a misfortune or loss – which may or may not happen.

There are many kinds of general insurance products that can be categorised in several ways. The most common categories are:

- domestic
- commercial
- liability
- statutory
- marine.

Domestic Policies

These are policies designed to cover the property of an individual. They are also commonly referred to as **personal lines** insurance, because they cover personal property and/or wellbeing. Domestic policies include:

- home buildings and home contents
- motor vehicle
- travel
- personal accident and illness
- consumer credit
- pleasurecraft.

Commercial Policies/Commercial Lines

This is a broad classification, which includes:

- industrial special risks
- business pack
- machinery breakdown
- construction
- commercial motor
- electronic equipment.

Commercial lines (or business) insurance is designed to protect both small-to-medium size enterprises (SME) and large business corporations.

The two most common commercial insurance products are business packs and ISR policies.

Industrial Special Risks (ISR)

An ISR policy, also known as an industrial multirisks policy, is a policy generally used for large commercial organisations. Most insurers will have a minimum value of assets they require the insured to have before they will offer an ISR policy. The policy is divided into two sections. The first section provides cover for most of the organisation's physical assets – such as buildings, stock and plant and machinery. The second section provides business interruption cover – which is cover for loss of gross profit after a major loss such as a fire. Covers such as burglary, money, glass and accidental damage are included, usually with a sublimit. Public and products liability cover is not included.

An ISR policy is similar to an accidental damage home policy, in that it covers any event that is not excluded. The policy will be tailored to suit the needs of the individual insured organisation, rather than being an 'off the shelf' product.

An ISR policy will have a 'limit of liability' rather than a sum insured. The limit of liability is the maximum the insurer will be required to pay for any one loss at any one location (as the companies who need an ISR policy will usually have several operating locations). The policy will also have sublimits (lower than the policy limit), which apply to areas of cover such as burglary, money and accidental damage.

Business Insurance

Also known as business pack and business combined insurance, this is a bundled policy for smaller commercial organisations. It has several sections, which vary according to the insurer, but generally include:

- fire and related perils (often referred to as the 'property' section)
- business interruption
- burglary and theft
- money (theft of money)
- fidelity guarantee (theft by employees)
- glass
- accidental damage
- public and products liability
- machinery breakdown
- electronic equipment.

It is technically possible to purchase separate policies for these sections. However, with the exception of public and products liability, most insurers now offer only a bundled product.

Machinery Breakdown

This type of policy covers the cost of repairs to specified commercial machinery. However, normal wear and tear is excluded. The breakdown must be the result of an unexpected and unforeseen event. Machinery breakdown policies can also be extended to include a business interruption component for businesses that are heavily reliant on one or two key pieces of machinery.

Construction

These policies are also known as Construction all risks and Erection all risks. 'All risks' policies mean that all risks are covered, as opposed to 'defined [or named] perils' policies, which only cover risks that are specified in the policy documentation (e.g. business insurance policies). 'All risks policies' are also known as 'open perils' or 'special perils' policies.

A construction policy covers a building while it is being built. It has three sections:

- a material damage section covering the physical assets
- a business interruption section
- a public liability section.

In some countries, there is a particular type of construction insurance known as decennial insurance. In France, this is a mandatory insurance that contractors (builders, architects, etc.) must take out that holds them liable for building collapse for 10 years after the project is completed. This is a different type of policy from the one described above.

Commercial Motor

The cover provided by a commercial motor policy is essentially the same as that provided by a private motor vehicle policy. The difference arises in the items that are covered. These can range from sedans used by a business, to refrigerated vans, prime movers, trailers, and any other type of commercial vehicle. For larger fleets, it is common for the insured to provide a list of vehicles at the start of the policy period and another at the end, and the premium is based on these schedules. The policy covers all vehicles owned or operated by the insured, and the insured does not have to advise of each vehicle change as it occurs during the policy period.

Other Commercial Policies

Other commercial policies include:

- aviation
- pluvius (rainfall affected cover)
- crop
- electronic equipment.

Liability Policies

There are several types of liability policies. These include:

- public liability
- products liability
- professional indemnity
- directors and officers liability
- employment practices.

Public Liability

Public liability insurance covers an insured business against third-party claims for personal injury or property damage incurred while on the insured's 'premises'. The 'premises' is noted in the policy schedule and is usually shown as 'anywhere in [country]'. There is no cover provided when a third party suffers a financial loss only without any personal injury or property damage.

Product Liability

Product liability is the term applied to the legal responsibility of a manufacturer, distributor, wholesaler, retailer or supplier of a product to the purchaser, user or consumer, for personal injury or property damage caused by the product.

The term 'product' includes all types of articles or goods intended for personal, domestic or business use. Generally, product liability will be included with public liability. A policy covering both sections will be issued rather than a standalone product liability policy.

Professional Indemnity

Professional indemnity is a form of insurance offered to individuals, firms or companies practising a profession. It protects against a civil liability arising in the practise of their profession. This might be an act or omission by a principal of the business, an employee or, in some cases, a third party for whom the business has a responsibility to its principal or client. Insurance brokers are required by law to have a professional indemnity policy in place.

Medical malpractice insurance, which covers medical practitioners for professional negligence claims, is another form of professional indemnity.

Directors and Officers Liability

A directors and officers liability policy provides indemnity against wrongful acts by directors or officers of an organisation. The policy provides indemnity for civil liability, and most policies provide legal expenses cover for criminal proceedings.

Sums Insured for Liability Policies

All liability policies have a limit of liability rather than a sum insured but the way in which the limit is applied will vary according to the type of liability policy in question. For example, under a public liability policy, the limit will apply to any one occurrence, but for products liability, the limit will apply to any one occurrence and in the aggregate for any one policy period – that is, cover for all products liability claims lodged in any one policy period will be limited to the policy limit, irrespective of the number of claims, with sublimits for bodily injury, material damages, and financial damages.

Other Liability Policies

Other types of liability policies include:

- product guarantee
- product recall
- employment practices.

Statutory Classes

This term refers to types of insurance that are required by law and therefore compulsory if an organisation fits into one of the categories specified in the legislation.

Common statutory classes are workers' compensation and third-party bodily injury insurance (for motor vehicles).

Marine

Marine insurance offers a range of policies, including covers for:

- ships and other sea-going vessels;
- pleasurecraft and commercial craft on inland lakes and waterways;
- marine cargo – where a substantial part of the journey is a marine venture; this can include a portion of the journey that is via air or land;
- goods in transit where the cargo is transported via air or land;
- marine liabilities.

Conditions and Exclusions

Conditions and exclusions are part of all insurance products. They are set out in the policy document.

The policy conditions section sets out what policyholders must do (or not do) if they are to make a successful claim. Some typical conditions in a travel policy include:

- premium must be paid before the journey commences;
- all theft must be reported to police before a claim can be made.

The exclusions section sets out those things that the policy does not cover.

Again, using the travel policy as our example, typical exclusions may include:

- a loss resulting from a criminal or dishonest act by the insured or by a person with whom the insured is in collusion;
- any claim for additional expenses or fees arising from errors or omissions in the insured's booking arrangements and failure to obtain relevant visa or passport documents.

It is important for risk managers to be aware of the conditions and exclusions attached to insurance policies.

Limit Setting on Insurance Contracts

Indemnity limits are the largest total amount the insurance company will pay for covered losses. Many policies have multiple limits: a certain amount per person, another amount per accident, and sometimes an aggregate limit on all losses paid during one policy year or any other period for which the contract cover applies (policies generally last a year but can cover several years, e.g. finite insurance, or occasionally less than a year). Although these limits may apply in principle to all classes of insurance contracts, they are of limited impact in the case of direct damages to property and equipment cover, consequential damages, loss of revenues and loss of profit, even if some consideration can be given to a contractual limit of indemnity in any given event.

Ultimately, liability cover of all kinds is more likely to create specific issues for risk management professionals when applied to public liability, products liability and employers liability, and even more acutely when dealing with professional indemnity insurance. This is why professional indemnity limits should be set according to a specified process.

Employers and public liability insurance usually limit their liability in respect of damages and claimant's costs arising from any one occurrence, with no limit for the period of the policy. This means that the indemnity limit applies separately to each claim that is made under the policy. However, all claims arising from the same occurrence would be regarded by insurers as one claim.

Products liability and professional indemnity are usually arranged with either an **each and every** claims basis or an annual aggregate limit with no per occurrence limit. An aggregate limit means that the indemnity limit would apply as one single amount for all claims made in each period of insurance.

EXAMPLE

Indemnity Limits

What is important in this example is not so much the financial numbers, which must be adapted to each organisation, but the structure whereby product liability and professional indemnity typically have aggregate annual limits that may raise the question of whether to purchase additional cover if the annual limit is reached before the end of the cover period.

An employers' or public liability policy would normally have its indemnity limit defined as:

- € 10,000,000 any one accident / unlimited during the period of insurance.

A products liability or professional indemnity policy may appear as:

- € 5,000,000 any one accident / unlimited during the period of insurance

or

- € 5,000,000 any one accident and in the aggregate during the period of the insurance.

Why Have an Aggregate Limit for the Policy Period?

An **aggregate** limit is applied so that insurers can cap the maximum amount they may have to pay in claims during a policy period.

This is very common on products liability insurance where insurers could be otherwise open themselves up to unlimited liability for a faulty product. There is no way to quantify how much claims could cost, so this helps to restrict what the maximum loss may be.

Statutory classes, such as employers or automobile liability, cannot be restricted as this could mean that a valid claim that is covered by statute would not be covered.

The risk management professional will always have to consider how much insurance is needed and how to set limits that make legal and economic sense for the organisation. Intermediaries, like brokers, can provide professional advice on the type and amount of insurance coverage organisations should have to meet their individual needs and to comply with the laws of their country.

Insurance Terms and Documents

There are many terms used in the general insurance industry that have specific meanings.

Claim Form

A claim form is a document that clients complete when they wish to make a claim. The form asks for all the usual information that insurers need to determine whether a loss is claimable under a policy.

Deductible/Excess

This is the portion of any claim that the client retains and there are several types: fixed deductible, proportional, reached, cumulative, etc.

Endorsement

To endorse a policy means to make a change to the policy. This could involve a variety of changes, such as sums insured, items covered, location and so on. The process of changing a policy, and the document that details the change(s), are both referred to as an endorsement.

Insured

The 'insured' refers to persons or companies who are covered under a policy and thereby transfer risks to the insurer.

Insurer

The insurer is the company that accepts the risk from the insured, in return for a premium.

Policy Schedule

The policy schedule is prepared by the insurer or the broker. It details all of the information specific to that particular policy, such as:

- the policy number
- insured's name and address
- risk address of the property
- the period of insurance
- sums insured and deductibles
- details of which sections of the policy have been purchased
- any exclusions or conditions imposed specifically on this client.

Policy Wording

This is the document, often in a booklet form, which outlines the extent of the cover provided, the conditions and exclusions, and any optional extensions. It is often a pre-printed standard document. The policy schedule is attached to a policy wording, and together they form the policy document.

Premium

The premium is the amount that insurers believe equitably represents the exposure to loss of that particular risk when compared with all other risks in the same category.

Proposal Form

This is a document drafted by an insurer, which clients complete when they wish to take out insurance coverage. The proposal asks for information that the insurer will need in order to decide whether or not to insure the client and on what terms. It forms the basis of the insurance contract.

Underwriting/Underwriter

Underwriting is the process an insurance company undertakes to decide whether or not to take on a particular risk, and what terms and conditions they will require. Technically, an underwriter is a person (or people) in an insurance company who carries out this task, although the term is also used to refer to the insurance company itself.

Material Contractual Obligations

Insurance Policies or Contracts

An insurance policy is a legally binding contract between the insurance company and the policyholder. The policy details the insurer's and insured's rights, responsibilities and obligations.

An insurance policy:

- describes the scope of cover (what is covered and for how much);
- explains in what situations the insurer will pay compensation;
- states how much the insurer charges for its premiums;
- provides details on how to make a claim;
- explains the conditions of the cover/s.

In most forms of insurance today, a policy document refers to a generic legal document that details the terms and conditions of the policy. It often consists of a pre-printed booklet containing:

- generic policy wording;
- a tailored section addressing risk-specific information;

- a product disclosure statement (PDS) including the insurer's disclosure obligations;
- notification on the procedure customers should follow if they need to claim under the policy.

Sections in a properly constructed policy document typically include:

- title
- preamble
- agreement
- basis of settlement
- definitions
- schedule
- exclusions
- conditions
- additional benefits
- endorsements.

Title

The title indicates the type of policy concerned and the name and address of the insurer.

Preamble

The preamble (sometimes called a **recital**) makes reference to:

- the proposal or information the customer provided;
- the importance of this information to the insurer;
- the insurer's promise to provide the cover set out in the selected sections;
- if the premium has been (or will be) paid;
- the specified period of insurance;
- if cover will be provided for loss, damage and liability occurring during the period of insurance upon the happening of certain events;
- if cover is subject to the provisions of the policy.

Agreement

The articulation of the contractual agreement (more formally known as the **operative clauses or insuring clauses**) refers to:

- the obligations of the insurer (for example, the circumstances under which the insurer's promise to the customer will be activated);
- the events to be insured;
- any limits set upon the insurer's liability.

Statements made as a part of the operative clause (which sets limits on the insurer's liability) are subtly different from exclusions (addressed shortly). If a limitation is included as part of the agreement itself, the insurer's legal position may be stronger. If such a limitation is breached, the insured may not be covered at all because they have breached the base terms of the underlying agreement.

Activity | Preamble and agreement

Modern insurance policies tend to combine the preamble and the agreement, and also express them in plain language.

Select two single-class insurance policies and review the policy text and identify wording you regard as forming the recital and the operative clause.

Basis of Settlement

The basis of settlement clause sets out how the insurer intends to treat the settlement of a claim. The basis of settlement clause should be placed close to the insuring clause.

EXAMPLE

Agreement and Basis of Settlement Clause

What is Covered

We will Cover You for loss of or Damage to the Business Contents caused by Burglary which happens at the Business Premises during the Period of Cover stated in the Schedule.

What is not Covered

We will not Cover You for loss of or Damage to:

- Glass or Signs as Defined and Covered in Section 8 Glass; or
- Money.

We will not pay for claims arising from:

- Burglary or theft in which You or any member of Your Family or Your Employees is/are involved other than loss or Damage committed by Your Employees following forcible and violent entry to the premises and not involving You or any member of Your Family as principle or accessory;

- loss of or Damage to Property in the open air;
- loss or Damage arising from Property stolen from a safe or security enclosure opened by the use of a key or by the use of a combination, or both, which has/have been left on the Business Premises whilst the Business Premises are either unattended or closed for business; or
- consequential loss of any kind.

Basis of Settlement

We will, at Our option, reinstate, repair or replace the lost or Damaged Property to a condition equal to but not better nor more extensive than its condition when new or, by agreement with You, pay You the Indemnity Value of the Property at the time of the loss or Damage.

Definitions

To reduce the possibility of policy wording ambiguity, insurers assign specific definitions to certain words or phrases. Typically, this is done in a purpose-built definitions section, wherein words or phrases applying across the entire policy are listed and explained. Such a section is usually located near the front of the policy wording.

When a particular word or expression is defined, the word or expression will have the same definition throughout the policy (unless otherwise indicated). Some insurers choose to emphasise words or phrases that have a special meaning in a policy by capitalising or otherwise highlighting them.

Terms that are often defined include:

- insured
- excess
- accidental damage
- buildings
- contents
- flood
- products
- property
- accessories
- modifications.

Explanations of more specialised definitions specific to a particular section of the policy are likely to be omitted from the definitions section of the policy document. Instead, these specialised definitions are located within the relevant section.

EXAMPLE

Varying Definitions of the Insured

Definitions of a word can differ significantly depending on:

- the insurer writing the contract;
- the time the contract was written;
- the jurisdiction in which the contract was written;
- the type of policy to which the definition is applied.

In a commercial insurance policy, an insured might be defined as:

> [...] the Company, Association, Insured Person(s) either individually or jointly, and other person(s), entities or corporation(s) named in the Schedule whom We have agreed to insure.

In a home insurance policy, an insured might be defined as:

> [...] the person(s) named in the Certificate of Insurance and any member of the insured's family ordinarily residing with the insured.

Exclusions

Exclusions are clauses included in policies with the intention of:

- eliminating cover available under another class of insurance
- eliminating cover for risks:
  - requiring special underwriting consideration
  - considered unsuitable for insurance
  - not needed by a specific organisation
- managing risks of fraud or dishonesty.

Each exclusion should have a clear heading to assist with quick identification and location. Exclusions are also commonly alphabetised to further assist with fast referencing.

Exclusions may be made on the basis of the:

- subject of insurance
- conduct of the insured
- cause of an insured event.

Exclusions relating to uninsured property are self-explanatory.

Exclusions relating to the conduct of the insured can be important and may also include the actions of those for whom the insured is responsible.

Exclusions relating to causes can be complex. Some causes are excluded because of the magnitude of the exposure. Other causes may be excluded because they are not intended to fall within the scope of the description in the policy but may possibly do so because of inclusive wording. In such cases, a properly articulated exclusion can place the intention of the agreement beyond doubt.

Some exclusions are standard in all basic wordings. If the insured is willing to pay an additional premium, some insurers may offer extended cover so that such typically excluded risks are actually re-included in the insurance agreement.

Exclusions can be separated into the following two types:

1. general exclusions
2. particular exclusions.

1. General exclusions

General exclusions may apply to all risks, across all sections of a policy. The most common general exclusions applying to most policies eliminate cover for events arising from:

- war and war-like activities
- nuclear material
- non-compliance with statutory obligations.

General exclusions (along with all of the general conditions and claims conditions) are presented together in the policy document to assist clients to distinguish between what is/is not covered in the policy.

The following table lists other general exclusions you are likely to encounter.

Note: These can be covered by specific policies.

General Exclusion	Description
Lawful seizure	the confiscation, nationalisation, requisition, destruction of or damage to property by or under the orders of any government, public authority or local or municipal authority or statutory authority
Pollution/ contamination	loss due to the discharge or escape of any contaminant, pollutant or harmful substance, including any solid, liquid, gaseous or thermal irritant or contaminant, smoke, vapour, soot, fumes, acids, alkalis, chemicals or waste, including waste materials to be recycled, reconditioned or reclaimed, or any clean-up costs in relation to any of the foregoing, unless the discharge or escape was sudden and accidental

(*Continued*)

(*Continued*)

General Exclusion	Description
Terrorism	loss due to terrorism, regardless of any other cause or event contributing concurrently or in other sequence, including any action taken in controlling, preventing, suppressing or in any way relating to any act of terrorism. In many countries, it is covered though national schemes and included in the policies.

2. Particular exclusions

Particular exclusions and conditions:

- relate to particular aspects of cover;
- restrict or limit one part of the policy's cover;
- do not affect the other parts of the policy's cover.

Particular exclusions should be included in the section of the policy in which the original cover is granted, along with all of the relevant claims conditions.

EXAMPLE

Burglary Policy Section with Particular Exclusions

What is covered?

We will cover you for loss of or to the business contents caused by burglary which happens at the business premises during the period of cover stated in the Schedule.

What is not covered?

We will not cover you for loss of or damage to glass, signs or money. We will not pay for claims arising from:

- burglary or theft in which you or any member of your family or your employees is/are involved other than loss or damage committed by your employees following forcible and violent entry to the premises and not involving you or any member of your family as principle or accessory;
- loss of or damage to Property in the open air;
- loss or damage arising from stolen from a safe or security enclosure opened by the use of a key or by the use of a combination, or both, which has/have been left on the Business Premises whilst the Business Premises are either unattended or closed for business; or
- consequential loss of any kind

Conditions

Conditions are the rules under which the policy operates. The legal remedy for a breach of a condition depends on when the condition applies. The following table lists three types of conditions.

Condition	Description
Precedent to the validity of the contract	must exist at the formation of the contract deemed essential to the validity of the contract breach or non-fulfilment of a condition precedent voids the policy ab initio, regardless of whether the condition is express or implied – for example, good faith must be observed
Subsequent to the formation of the contract	essential to the validity of the policy but which arises after information of the contract breach of a condition subsequent avoids the policy from the date of the breach which means the insurer is liable until the date of the breach
Precedent to liability	usually arises after an event which gives rise to a claim has occurred breach of a condition precedent to liability only entitles the insurer to decline liability for that particular claim and does not void the policy as a whole – for example, duty of care

There are many other types of policy conditions which vary according to the type of policy. Nevertheless, many conditions are common to most types of insurance contracts. Conditions can also be separated into two types:

1. general conditions
2. claims conditions.

1. General conditions

General conditions apply to all sections of the policy. The following table outlines common general conditions.

Note: Some countries have specific rules when there are multiple covers.

General Condition	Description
Insured's obligations	for example, to take reasonable care to avoid loss, to comply with statutory obligations
Alteration of risk	the insurer's written consent to be obtained when material changes to the risk occur

(*Continued*)

(*Continued*)

General Condition	Description
Other insurance	the insurer must be advised of any other insurance covering the property insured
Changes in policy	all changes are to be agreed in writing by the insurer
Cancellation	• sets out the rights of the insured and insurer to cancel the policy • the insured must give written notice of cancellation

2. Claims conditions

Claims conditions set out the procedures to be followed in the event of loss or damage that may lead to a claim. The claims conditions also set out the insurer's requirements with regard to:

- proceedings and negotiations
- subrogation
- sum insured and excess
- inspection of damaged property
- salvage
- false claims.

Claims conditions are commonly worded as duties imposed on the insured if they wish for a claim to be considered by the insurer.

Claims Cooperation

One of the most commonly imposed claims conditions relates to **claims cooperation** and requires the insured (and other people covered by the policy) to:

- take reasonable measures to avoid or diminish any policy covered:
  - loss
  - damage
  - liability
- supply all relevant information to the insurer to facilitate:
  - evaluations
  - investigations
  - prosecutions/defences.

Unauthorised Repairs for Property Insurance

It is also very common to include a claims condition relating to unauthorised repairs for property insurance. Such a condition typically imposes a duty on the customer to refrain from carrying out either unnecessary or permanent repairs until the insurer has the opportunity to inspect the damage.

Activity | Policy conditions

Choose any three insurance policies and prepare a comparison of policy conditions within each document. Prepare your analyses by:

- distinguishing between the general conditions and the claims conditions
- noting the commonalities and differences between the policies.

Additional Benefits

In return for a higher premium, insurers may provide additional cover by way of what are commonly referred to as additional benefits.

EXAMPLE

Additional Cover Under a Business Pack Burglary Section

The following is an example of the additional cover provided under a business pack burglary section.

Goods on consignment

We will pay You for loss of or Damage to goods which are held by You on consignment at the Business Premises and for which You are legally liable.

Our maximum liability under this additional benefit will be limited to $10,000 for any one claim.

In this example, the additional benefit provides additional cover not included in the main cover of the policy and is limited in the amount covered by the inclusion of a monetary limit.

Drafting of Wording

In a similar manner to the drafting of the policy wordings for exclusions and conditions, it is important that the drafting of the wording for additional benefits fits within the proper construct of the formal policy wording and that there are no ambiguities.

Endorsements/Policy Amendments

From time to time, customers may wish to make to their insurance policies. An endorsement is the formal record of a change to the insurer's standard contract terms or other details of the policy.

Occasions also arise where the risk acceptance is based upon a qualified or restricted form of cover due to either unusual or adverse features, or because of poor claims experience. If this is the case, the policy will be endorsed to reflect the qualification or restriction.

Endorsements are used to:

- effect changes in the details appearing on the policy schedule;
- extend, restrict or otherwise modify the cover provided in the basic policy;
- delete or modify an exclusion or condition.

Endorsements set down any changes, such as:

- increasing the sum insured
- deleting certain items (or including others)
- changing an insured's name
- limiting (or extending) cover.

Endorsements may be computer-produced and attached to the policy schedule or pre-printed on the policy, often with a computer-generated reference number.

EXAMPLE

Typical Business Pack Policy Limitations

A typical business pack policy might have the following limitations on some sections of cover:

- Limited cover may be given for liability assumed under contract. In their day-to-day business, the insured organisation is entering into contracts with suppliers and customers as a matter of routine.
- Public/products liability insurances do not normally cover liabilities voluntarily assumed by the customer, for example for undertakings contracted by the insured, unless specifically consented to by the insurer.
- Legal liability for property of third parties in care, custody or control of the organisation may be limited to € 5,000. For example, jewellers often have custody of expensive jewellery. If this jewellery were stolen, the policy would only cover items up to € 5,000. Many customers, for example dry cleaners or repairers, would require cover in excess of this amount.

- Under the business interruption section, damage at the premises of the supplier or manufacturer of goods may be limited to national suppliers or subject to a maximum of 20% of the gross income of the insured organisation. Many such clients import goods from overseas – they might have no cover or inadequate cover. Where cover does apply, it could be subject to the 20% limitation and this arbitrary percentage would not suit all customers.

After receiving and recording such advice, you should check the proposed alterations meet the insurer's underwriting acceptance criteria, as well as legislative and company requirements, before accepting them.

The policy alteration information should then be processed according to operating procedures and you should issue policy alteration advice to the client, together with notification of any new terms that differ from the original request. Often the practice is to issue the customer with an amended schedule incorporating the relevant change to the policy.

All monies received are processed or refunded according to operating procedures and legislative requirements. You should complete the process by updating information systems and accurately filing all relevant documentation.

If there is a conflict in wording between the wording of the printed policy and the endorsement, the wording of the endorsement takes precedence. Any ambiguity of wording is interpreted in favour of the policyholder.

Self-Help Question 9.1

1. A basis of settlement clause in a policy:

   a. sets out the conditions a customer must comply with in order to make a claim
   b. defines the manner in which indemnity will be provided, or
   c. both (a) and (b).

2. Which of the following best describes the purpose of the operative clause in a policy?

   a. to give the name and address of the insurer, identify the parties to the contract and set out the events insured and the period of insurance
   b. to identify the parties to the contract, set out the events insured, list general conditions and exclusions and set down the period of insurance

→

c. to identify the parties to the contract, set out the events insured and set out circumstances under which the insurer's promise will be activated
d. to set out the events insured, set out circumstances under which the insurer's promise will be activated and set down the period of insurance.

3. Particular exclusions are those that apply only to a particular section of a package policy. Is this statement true or false?
4. Categorise the following two fragments – commonly found in policy documents – indicating which is an exclusion and which is a condition.

   a. This insured event does not insure destruction or damage by burglary or theft except for such destruction or damage caused to a building when the building is owned by you but not occupied by you.
   b. Hazardous goods usual to trade and/or business are allowed to be stored in quantities and manner as permitted by statutory obligations, by-laws, regulations, public authority and safety requirements.

Answers to self-help questions are provided at the end of each section.

Summary

Please keep the following points from this chapter in mind:

- Insurance products can be categorised as risk or investment products.
- Domestic policies cover the personal property and/or of an individual.
- Commercial lines (or business) insurance is designed to protect both SME and large business corporations from common business perils.
- The two most common commercial insurance products are business packs and ISR policies.
- Business pack policies tend to be mostly for SMEs based on defined property and defined events.
- Defined events (risks or perils) for which cover is provided by the policy are specifically stated in the policy.
- ISR, or all risk, policies tend to be for larger organisations and use definitions that are more broadly inclusive in terms of both insured property and events.
- Contract works policies are designed to cover construction, engineering and complex installation projects, usually offering three distinct sections of cover.

- Commercial motor vehicle cover is relevant to anyone who operates a commercial vehicle – whether as a professional carrier or as part of their normal business operations.
- Liability policies are designed to protect people or organisations if their actions, negligence or property harms another person, for example, if a customer slips on a store's wet floor or a faulty product causes injury.
- Statutory classes are insurance products that are required by law, for example workers compensation and third party bodily injury for motor vehicles.
- Indemnity limits are the largest total amount the insurance company will pay for covered losses. They vary depending on the type and amount of cover and do not apply to statutory classes.
- An insurance policy is a legally binding contract between the insurance company and the policyholder. It details the insurer's and insured's rights, responsibilities and obligations.
- Policies differ from insurer to insurer, and from risk to risk.

Answers to Self-Help Questions

1. (b)
2. (d)
3. True – particular exclusions apply only to a particular aspect of cover, for example, loss or damage to money is excluded from the burglary section of the policy.
4. Exclusion, condition or insuring clause?

    a. Exclusion
    b. Condition

Chapter 10

Reinsurance

Introduction

Reinsurance is a key, if less known, element of the insurance industry that plays a significant role in enabling insurers to safely take on large risks. There are large sums of money involved in accepting certain risks, such as chemical or aviation risks, and without reinsurance, insurers that accept these risks would be putting the survival of their business on the line. The collapse of an insurer threatens the survival of an insured business, which would then be required to fund the loss itself.

This topic describes the purpose of reinsurance, the types of risks it will cover and the different ways in which reinsurance is transacted.

Learning Outcomes

By the end of this topic, you should be able to:

- describe the purpose and function of reinsurance;
- identify the differences between insurance and reinsurance;
- explain hard and soft market cycles and how they affect insurance;
- describe the difference between property insurance and non-property insurance and why this matters;
- describe the two main types of reinsurance and when each is used.

Risk Treatment, 207–223

Published under exclusive licence by Emerald Publishing Limited
doi:10.1108/978-1-83662-306-920251022

Definition of Reinsurance

In its simplest form, reinsurance is insurance for insurers. It is a specific branch of insurance that provides services to direct insurers that allow them to improve their covers by ceding some of their obligations to a reinsurer. Insurers **cede** risks and the insurer is then called the **ceding company**, or **transferor**. In the reinsurance contract, the reinsurer, or transferee, agrees to insure the ceding company against all or part of the risks it has underwritten based on the wording of the insurance contracts the parties signed. Reinsurance is more complex than insurance due to the international and diverse activities it encompasses.

When entering into insurance contracts, an insurer incurs substantial aggregated liabilities to policyholders. There are only two ways these liabilities can be managed, through:

- the use of the insurer's capital (where the entire risk is borne by the insurer), or
- (financial) risk transfer mechanisms such as reinsurance.

Reinsurance is an integral part of an insurer's process for managing risk. By spreading its liabilities, which were assumed under insurance policies that it issued to its customers, an insurer spreads its risks, thus lessening its exposure to adverse financial impacts arising from claims under those policies. Additionally, reinsurance offers insurers the capital they need to increase their underwriting capacities both in total values at risk and number of contracts, and number and importance of risks. However, the reinsurance contract does not limit the contractual obligations of the insurer regarding the insured; therefore the good standing of the reinsurer is a key factor for the insurer in choosing the reinsurer.

Thus, reinsurance helps an insurer achieve several practical business goals, such as ensuring large exposures, protecting policyholders' surplus from adverse loss experiences, and financing the insurer's growth. The reinsurance that an insurer obtains depends mainly on the constraints or problems the insurer must address to reach its goals.

When Is Reinsurance Required?

When an insurer accepts risk from customers, it needs to decide:

- how much of the risk it will retain itself – this is called the retention or the deductible;
- how much of the risk, if any, it will transfer by way of reinsurance.

Commonly, large risks, or risks that will expose an insurer to significant costs from a single event, such as a natural disaster, will be reinsured.

If reinsurance is required, the insurer will continue the risk management process started by the customer and will place a part of the risk it has accepted with another insurer. It will then pay that insurer, who is called the reinsurer, a share of the premium it has received from the customer.

In the event of a claim by the customer, the insurer and the reinsurer share the cost of the customer's claim in accordance with the terms of their reinsurance agreement.

The placement of reinsurance can be arranged with:

- specialised reinsurance companies (reinsurers) who handle only this type of insurance, and who do not accept business from the public, but only from other insurers;
- insurance companies who accept business directly from the public and who also act as reinsurers by accepting reinsurance business from other insurers.

In reinsurance terminology:

- the original insurer is called the **cedant**, or the ceding company (**cedant** arising from the word **cede**, meaning to yield);
- the company to which the reinsurance is ceded is called the **reinsurer**
- **cession** refers to a particular reinsurance transaction.

Global reinsurers, in particular, are exposed to problems of risk accumulation due to the many classes of business transacted in their various offices throughout the world. Reinsurers also use reinsurance as a risk management tool to protect their own risk exposures with other reinsurers. In those circumstances, the reinsurance placement is known as a **retrocession.** In that arrangement, the original reinsurer becomes the **retrocedant** and the second reinsurer is known as the **retrocessionaire**. The process may continue from there – that is, a reinsurance of a retrocession.

Throughout the process, the insurer may use a reinsurance broker to arrange and place their reinsurance program. The customer (the insurer) has reinsurance needs and the task of the reinsurance broker is to help the customer meet those needs through the most appropriate cover obtainable from suitable and financially secure reinsurers. This may be at the most economical price on offer, although this is often not the major consideration. Direct brokers perform this service for their customers – the original insurance customers – therefore, the roles are very similar in concept.

Both reinsurers and reinsurance brokers have specialist knowledge of the national and international insurance reinsurance marketplace in which they operate.

This process of risk transfer by way of insurance and reinsurance, and the insurance and reinsurance players, can be illustrated as follows:

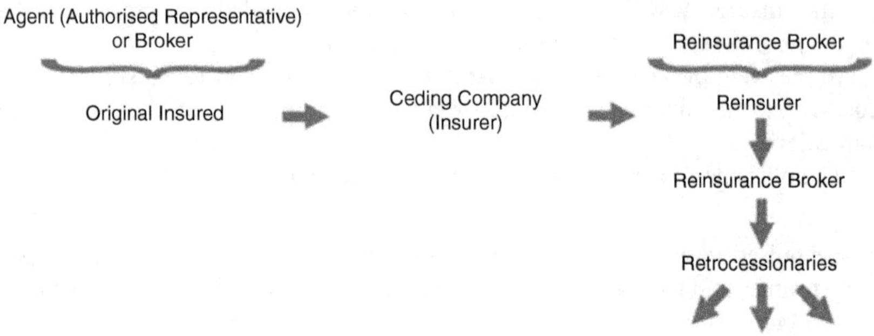

Although the figure depicts the reinsurance broker as having a role in placing the reinsurance between the insurer and the reinsurer, and again between the reinsurer and the retrocessionaires, it will often be the case that the insurer and the reinsurer will negotiate and place their own reinsurance arrangements without the assistance of a reinsurance broker.

This is similar to the way in which the original insurance might be placed – that is, with or without the services of an intermediary.

The two major types of reinsurance contracts are treaty and facultative reinsurance.

- **Treaty reinsurance** involves a reinsurance agreement that covers an entire class or portfolio of loss exposures; any of the primary insurer's individual loss exposures that fall within the treaty are automatically reinsured.
- **Facultative reinsurance** is similar to insurance, in that insurers select individual risks to be covered, and the reinsurer can choose to accept or reject any of the risks.

In simple terms, reinsurance contracts that cover more than one policy are called treaty reinsurance and those that can be purchased on an individual policy basis are known as facultative reinsurance.

Activity | Technical reinsurance terms

Cede, cedant, reinsurer, retrocession, retrocessionaire, retrocedant, **treaty and facultative** are just a few of the many technical words or terms that are used regularly in reinsurance.

Reinsurance involves its own technical language and you will need to understand the terminology used. As we have started to use some of this terminology, and will use more throughout the learning resource, refer now to the glossary, accessible via Study Centre. Take some time to read through it and familiarise yourself with the terms we will use throughout this subject.

Reinsurance Market

The reinsurance market is truly global. It follows the insurance and reinsurance cycle and reinsurance business works as part of this cycle. This section considers these aspects and how the marketplace has developed.

The Global Reinsurance Market

Most professional reinsurers operate on a worldwide basis in all of the world's main financial centres.

Although each country has professional reinsurers with offices that principally deal with local risks, the truly global aspect of reinsurance comes to the fore when placing catastrophe reinsurance programs, which will often use the financial resources of dozens of reinsurers throughout the world. Programs for special classes of reinsurance (such as marine, aviation and bloodstock) are often placed with specialist reinsurers.

The main **reinsurance centres** are Europe (including London, the largest market, Munich, Zurich, and Paris) followed by the US and Bermuda.

The Insurance and Reinsurance Cycle

In general, like the direct insurance industry, the reinsurance industry operates in a free and highly competitive global market. Insurance and reinsurance business tends to operate in cycles. Often these cycles will lead to talk of a **hard market** and a **soft market**.

In the initial stages of the cycle, insurance and reinsurance companies provide strong competition, often striving for **market share**. Competition becomes fierce with premium levels decreasing, often substantially – this is what is known as a soft market. As a result, profits are reduced and insurance and reinsurance business begins to become unprofitable.

When the insurance or reinsurance market has shrunk to the point of a capacity crisis (lack of insurers/reinsurers or affordable insurance/reinsurance), prices again rise and underwriting conditions harden (hence hard market) and the industry returns to profit. There is a return to stability, with profits maximised for both insurers and reinsurers.

As you can imagine, the fortunes of the reinsurance market are highly interdependent on the fortunes of the direct insurance market.

The Reinsurers' Business

Reinsurance relies on the principle of the worldwide spread of risk. This risk spread enables reinsurers to attract large premium volumes by doing business in all the world's markets. It also allows reinsurers to gain experience in difficult or unusual risks and form homogeneous portfolios of such risks worldwide even when there might be but one or two risks of a particular type in any national market. These factors combine to help the reinsurance industry provide significant additional support to local insurance markets.

Reinsurers insure catastrophe risks and other severe risks that normal insurers can't accept because of the potentially ruinous consequences of a major loss. A reinsurer must be able to provide appropriate cover to insurers while safeguarding their own business portfolio to ensure that it has not exposed itself to undue risk and is able to make a profit. It accomplishes this by balancing its portfolio through activities in many countries and involvement in all branches of insurance.

Reinsurers use the following means to safeguard their business activities:

- **underwriting policy** – guidelines are developed on the types of business that should be accepted, and the conditions of acceptance; direct insurers do the same;
- **retroceding** (further reinsuring) those risks that exceed their own capacity;
- **control of risk exposure** – reinsurers must keep track of all risks exposed to accumulation (especially natural hazards like earthquakes, bushfires and floods) as the reinsurer may be directly exposed through its own reinsurance or indirectly exposed through retrocession; again, direct insurers do the same.

From this, it should be clear that the business of **reinsurers** is similar to that of **insurers**.

Ultimately, the commercial viability of every reinsurer rests in large part on their ability to maintain good long-term relationships with each customer – the insurer. This allows them to share in the insurer's profitable years, and gives them the opportunity to underwrite more balanced portions of the direct insurer's business.

The Reinsurance Industry Marketplace

The marketplace for reinsurance has developed in a number of different ways and there is a range of reinsurance options now open to the insurer.

These include:

- professional reinsurance companies
- the Lloyd's market
- direct insurers
- insurance and reinsurance pools.

Professional Reinsurance Companies

Professional reinsurance companies are limited liability companies established for the sole purpose of transacting reinsurance business. They obtain their risk capital through normal commercial markets and shareholder investment and work either directly with insurers or through reinsurance brokers. The majority of reinsurers are professional reinsurance companies.

Generally speaking, these companies transact business around the world and gain much of their financial security from the spread of risk obtained in this way.

These companies range in size from the very large to the relatively small. Some specialise in certain types of reinsurance or business classes but most will transact all types and forms of reinsurance business.

Professional reinsurance companies can be based in any country in the world. In fact, in 2016, AM Best found that the top 10 global reinsurers wrote 72% of insurance premiums. The top 10 included Munich Re, Swiss Re, Hannover Re and Scor SE, all of which operate in Europe (where they're based), the Americas, the Asia-Pacific and Africa.

The Lloyd's Market

Lloyd's of London was established in the mid-1700s. Not a traditional insurance company, it can be described as an **insurance market**.

Traditionally the basis of the underwriting capacity of Lloyd's of London was a group of **names** – that is, individuals who placed their wealth at risk by accepting insurance. These names were later grouped into **syndicates** each with an underwriter who accepted business on behalf of the names at Lloyd's. The names were liable for losses to the extent of their personal wealth. Some of these syndicates specialise in accepting reinsurance businesses from around the world.

All business placed with these syndicates must be placed through a Lloyd's broker, who will arrange the necessary Lloyd's lead for each piece of business and the following Lloyd's markets. Each premium and claims transaction into this market must be processed through a Lloyd's broker.

In the 1980s, Lloyd's allowed limited liability companies to write business through these syndicates, providing **corporate capital** from limited liability companies writing reinsurance at boxes at Lloyd's in their own right. This is in addition to the London company market that has always existed side by side with Lloyd's.

Activity | Visit Lloyd's website

Visit the Lloyd's website at www.lloyds.com and read about Lloyd's.

- How was it founded?
- How does it operate?

It has an interesting history and you will often come across Lloyd's in your reinsurance activities and discussions with your professional colleagues.

Insurance and Reinsurance Pools

In many countries, national insurance pools have been established to provide local insurance market capacity for insurance coverage that is of national interest but is difficult to place. Aviation insurance is one example; others are nuclear, spacecraft and marine risks.

Generally, the objective of the pool is to retain part of the exposure for the risk, passing on a share of the risk exposure to foreign insurance pools or reinsurers in exchange for paying them a share of the premium.

Insurers in the local market will often participate in the risk, either in their own right or as a reinsurer to the pool.

An example of a pool in Australia is the terrorism insurance scheme administered by the Australian Reinsurance Pool Corporation. For details of the basis of the scheme go to www.arpc.treasury.gov.au.

An example of a pool in New Zealand is the Earthquake Commission. For details, go to www.eqc.govt.nz.

In both these instances, the capacity for these potentially enormous risks is provided by the respective governments.

Nuclear, aviation, satellite, energy and marine risks are typically dealt with in reinsurance pools, as are terrorism and aviation.

In France, the government has set up compulsory reinsurance agreements through CCR for natural events (catastrophes naturelles) and terrorism that are compulsory covered in all damage policies. For details, go to www.ccr.fr.

In several countries in Europe, there are similar arrangements for terrorism, but the exact cover and financial set-up vary from country to country.

Underwriting pools usually involve groups of insurers. The pool involves the insurers ceding all the business underwritten by them for the agreed class of business into a central fund. These insurers then share the overall premiums earned, costs incurred and claims incurred.

For example:

- Companies A, B, C and D agree to pool their resources on the marine portfolio.
- Each company will retain €100,000 and all premiums and costs will be shared evenly – that is, 25% to each company.
- This arrangement allows each company to accept risks up to €400,000 instead of the €100,000 dictated by their own financial resources.

When pools operate, the companies usually appoint a managing agent to handle all the underwriting, administration,

---

Self-Help Question 10.1

What are the main operational differences between the Lloyd's market and professional reinsurance companies?

Answers to self-help questions are provided at the end of each section.

Classifications

Traditionally, the different types of insurance business are grouped into four main classes:

- property
- liability (also referred to as casualty)
- marine
- aviation.

Reinsurance treaties usually follow these broad classifications.

Where policies include both material damage and liability sections (e.g. engineering insurance, or business packs covering material damage and public/products liability), it is usual practice for the material damage section of the original policy cover to be reinsured under a **property treaty**, and the liabilities under a **liability treaty**.

Property

Examples of property insurance include homeowners, commercial and industrial businesses, small to medium business and farm package policies.

Liability

Also referred to as casualty insurance, examples of liability business include motor vehicle third-party property damage liability, public liability, professional indemnity and employers' liability policies.

Marine

Examples of marine insurance include hull, cargo and marine liability policies.

Aviation

Examples of aviation insurance include hull, cargo and aviation liability policies.

Specialist Classes of Insurance

There are many other classes of insurance, such as:

- professional indemnity
- directors and officers liability
- health.

There are several other classes not mentioned here, but the general principles discussed in this resource in relation to general property and liability insurance cover are relevant to the reinsurance of these other classes of insurance.

Choosing the Method and Type of Reinsurance

It is generally feasible to use either of the two methods (proportional or non-proportional) and two types (facultative or treaty) of reinsurance for any class of insurance. However, the usual practice is to distinguish between property and non-property insurance.

The type of reinsurance appropriate for each class of insurance business will vary in accordance with the characteristics of that class.

Property Insurance

In all forms of property insurance, there is usually a sum insured that equates to the value at risk. In the average property portfolio, the distribution of losses will be such that the majority of losses experienced will be of low value.

In the first instance, property insurance classes are normally protected by proportional reinsurance. This is because a surplus treaty, often supported by a quota share, provides the most stable means of generating the underwriting capacity required by insurers operating in the commercial and industrial risks market.

The net account may also be protected on a risk excess of loss basis to guard against the occasional higher than normal single loss.

There will also almost invariably be catastrophe excess of loss protection against the aggregation of a number of losses arising from one event.

Non-Property Insurance

Non-property business classes are usually underwritten on a **limit of liability** per loss occurrence. There is no fixed value at risk apart from a reinsurance upper limit. Claims are projected to be fewer in frequency but larger in size.

For this reason, excess of loss reinsurance is the preferred method for insurance dealing with motor third-party property and bodily injury, public liability, professional indemnity and employers' liability and so on.

Proportional Reinsurance

Proportional reinsurance is the older of the two reinsurance methods, and possibly still the most commonly used method.

What Is Proportional Reinsurance?

As mentioned previously, proportional reinsurance is an arrangement whereby the reinsurer:

- is given (ceded) a proportion of the original premium by the insurer;
- agrees to pay the same proportion of each risk and each claim under the original policy of insurance which is covered by that agreement.

What classes of insurance does it apply to?

It is primarily used in insurance classes where the sum at risk is known, such as property insurance, that is:

- commercial fire
- industrial special risks (ISR)
- strata title risks
- home buildings and contents.

Proportional reinsurance is also commonly used for business interruption/loss of profits insurance which customarily follows the material damage cover under a commercial fire or ISR policy and can also be used to cover damage under the own damage section of motor vehicle or private pleasure craft policies.

Proportional Reinsurance Cover

With proportional reinsurance, it is standard practice for the reinsurance cover to follow the terms and conditions of the original insurance.

This is usually the case for treaty reinsurance but may not always be so for facultative reinsurance placements where the reinsurer may require more restrictive conditions to apply to hazardous risks than those that applied to the original insurance.

Attachment of Liability

Risks ceded to proportional treaties are reinsured on the basis of risks attaching during the treaty period – that is, the liability of the reinsurer commences at the same time as the cover under the original insurance (whether new business or renewal) – the inception date for the period of the original cover is within the treaty period. The reinsurer remains liable until the original policy cover has expired or is cancelled.

There are two instances where a reinsurer may be asked to cover risks written prior to the treaty inception, that is:

- on the replacement of a treaty with a previous reinsurer, or
- at the inception of a new treaty where there has been no prior reinsurance of the risks to be covered by the new treaty.

In the first situation, the new reinsurer is entitled to receive the amount of unearned premium from the previous reinsurer. In the second situation, the reinsurer is entitled to receive a similar adjustment from the insurer to cover this additional risk exposure. This is called a portfolio transfer, often referred to as a 'clean cut' portfolio transfer. In the absence of such a transfer (of premium and risk):

- In the first situation, the original reinsurer would be responsible for the run-off of claims under the then discontinued treaty.
- In the second situation, the treaty would only protect policies where the period of cover attached during the treaty period.

Note: Marine and aviation treaties are generally 'run-off' treaties; i.e. the treaty continues until all outstanding losses have been paid.

Proportional Reinsurance Claims

Any losses involving the reinsured risk will be settled (by the reinsurer) with the insurer in the same proportion as the risk accepted by the reinsurer.

For example, if the reinsurer has accepted 50% of the risk, it will have received 50% of the original insurance premium and will contribute 50% to all claims incurred under the original insurance for the risk. However, the ceding company will typically retain a cedant commission, so that the share of the premium the reinsurer receives will be less than 50%; for example, if the ceding commission is 10%, the reinsurer will receive half of 90% of the premium (45%) but still pay 50% of the claim.

Insurer Benefits

Benefits of proportional reinsurance include:

- spreading the risk
- increased financial capacity – risk acceptance
- financing – by way of exchange commission
- new classes of insurance – access to reinsurer's services and expertise
- improving the insurer's solvency position.

Types and Classes of Proportional Reinsurance

Proportional reinsurance can be used for both types of reinsurance (facultative and treaty) and, as previously mentioned, there are two classes of proportional reinsurance:

- quota share
- surplus and facultative obligatory (facultative treaty).

Non-Proportional Reinsurance

What Is Non-Proportional Reinsurance?

Unlike with proportional reinsurance, in non-proportional reinsurance, the insurer's premium and losses are not shared in the same proportion with the reinsurer.

Instead, the reinsurer calculates its own premium requirements based on the information available on the risks exposed to the reinsurance coverage above the deductible (excess) level, hence the term excess of loss.

This method of reinsurance arrangement does not operate with reference to the sums insured under the original insurance policies, but rather on the extent of the reinsurer's exposure to the frequency and severity of claims to the reinsurance cover.

Typically this type of reinsurance is arranged on what is referred to as an **excess of loss** (XL) basis and is the most commonly used treaty form of non-proportional business.

What Classes of Insurance Does It Apply to?

Non-proportional reinsurance is primarily used in portfolios where there are some small losses but there are occasional large losses that can materially affect the results of an individual portfolio.

This method of reinsurance can be used for property classes of insurance, such as:

- home buildings and contents
- commercial fire (including ISR) and business interruption
- motor vehicle own damage.

This method of reinsurance can also be used for liability classes of insurance, such as:

- public and products liability
- motor vehicle third-party property or personal injury
- professional indemnity insurance
- other general liability classes of insurance business
- marine and aviation insurance (all classes).

Non-Proportional Reinsurance Cover

Non-proportional reinsurance is an arrangement whereby:

- the insurer retains a pre-agreed amount of each loss, often referred to as the **deductible** or **retention**, and pays all claims that occur under the original policy up to that pre-agreed limit without recovery from the reinsurer;
- the reinsurer only pays claims for the amounts that exceed the insurer's **deductible**.

Unlike proportional reinsurance, the ratio of the sum insured protected by the treaty to the full sum insured under the original policy does not determine how premiums and losses are divided between the insurer and the reinsurer.

Furthermore, in the liability classes, there is no **sum insured** as such, but a **limit of liability**, so a surplus-type method would be impossible.

Instead, losses are apportioned according to the actual amount of loss incurred where the loss exceeds the insurer's treaty deductible.

The reinsurer agrees to indemnify the insurer if there is a claim that exceeds an agreed limit, the insurer's deductible (retention).

This claim might be in relation to:

- an individual risk (per-risk excess of loss);
- the total of a number of smaller claims all arising from the same event (prevent excess of loss);
- a portfolio of risks where the insurer wishes to stop its losses at a certain level (stop loss or excess of loss ratio reinsurance).

Non-proportional reinsurance can be likened to a motor vehicle policy covering loss of or damage to the vehicle. When the customer takes out the policy the cover provided often requires the customer to pay the first $500 (as an example) of any loss suffered during the currency of the policy. The insurer only pays any amount which exceeds the policy excess (or deductible).

Self-Help Question 10.2

1. What are the main differences between proportional and non-proportional reinsurance?
2. What types and classes of business are transacted on a non-proportional basis?

Answers to self-help questions are provided at the end of each section.

Reinsurance Cover Limit

An upper limit is placed on what the reinsurer agrees to bear. For reinsurance cover beyond that, another excess of loss treaty may be negotiated, or facultative protection can be purchased, or the insurer may bear that sum, the risk exposure, itself.

Attachment of Liability

Risks ceded to non-proportional treaties are generally reinsured on the basis of **losses occurring**: the loss date triggers the cover by both the insurer and reinsurer, meaning the loss must occur during the treaty period. The date the policy was written or renewed is irrelevant as long as the policy and the treaty were in force at the date of loss.

If the non-proportional treaty is cancelled the reinsurer will not be responsible for losses occurring after the date of cancellation.

Non-Proportional Reinsurance Claims

The reinsurer will only be involved in losses that exceed the insurer's deductible for the reinsurance arrangement. The insurer pays all amounts up to the level of the deductible.

Example

In a reinsurance arrangement with reinsurance cover of €900,000, an insurer deductible of €100,000 each and every loss and a loss of €75,000, the insurer pays the entire loss.

In the same example, if the loss were €300,000, the insurer is entitled to recover €200,000 from the reinsurer – what remains after the deductible.

In this example, the insurer can issue original policies up to a sum insured/limit of indemnity of a maximum of €1,000,000 before seeking additional reinsurance support.

Insurer Benefits

The main benefits of non-proportional reinsurance are:

- stabilising results – removing severe claims fluctuations in results
- spreading the risk
- increased financial capacity – risk acceptance
- financial security and solvency protection
- access to the reinsurer's claims services and expertise – liability classes of insurance in particular.

Types and Classes of Non-Proportional Reinsurance

Non-proportional reinsurance can be used for both types of reinsurance: facultative and treaty. As previously mentioned, the following three classes are non-proportional reinsurance:

- per-risk excess of loss
- per-event excess of loss
- stop loss or aggregate excess of loss for a period.

Summary

Please keep the following points from this topic in mind:

- In its simplest form, reinsurance is insurance for insurers. Despite functional similarities, it is more complex than insurance due to the international and diverse activities it encompasses.
- In general, like the direct insurance industry, the reinsurance industry operates in a free and highly competitive global market. Insurance and reinsurance business tends to operate in cycles.
- Reinsurance is an integral part of an insurer's process for managing risk. By spreading its liabilities an insurer spreads its risks, thus lessening its exposure to adverse financial impacts arising from claims.
- Reinsurance relies on risk spreading, which enables reinsurers to attract large premium volumes by doing business worldwide. It also allows reinsurers to gain experience in difficult or unusual risks and form homogeneous worldwide portfolios of such risks.
- Reinsurers insure catastrophe risks and other severe risks that normal insurers can't accept because of the potentially ruinous consequences of a major loss. A reinsurer must be able to provide appropriate cover to insurers while safeguarding their own business portfolio.
- In many countries, national insurance pools have been established to provide local insurance market capacity for insurance cover that is of national interest but is difficult to place. Generally, the objective of the pool is to retain part of the exposure for the risk, passing on a share of the risk exposure to foreign insurance pools or reinsurers in exchange for paying them a share of the premium.
- There are two main types of reinsurance.

  - Proportional reinsurance is an arrangement whereby the reinsurer is ceded a proportion of the original premium by the insurer and agrees to pay the same proportion of each risk and each claim under the original policy covered by that agreement. It is primarily used in insurance classes where the sum at risk is known, such as property insurance.
  - Non-proportional reinsurance is an arrangement whereby the insurer retains a pre-agreed amount of each loss, often referred to as the **deductible** or **retention**, and pays all claims that occur under the original policy up to that pre-agreed limit without recovery from the reinsurer and the reinsurer only pays claims for the amounts that exceed the insurer's **deductible**. It is used in the liability classes when there is no **sum insured**, just a **limit of liability**.

Answers to Self-Help Questions

Self-help question 10.1

Lloyd's comprises groups of names (private individuals) and companies who can provide risk capital. These names support a number of syndicates. Each syndicate is run by a managing agent and will have an underwriter who will accept business on behalf of its name or company. Some of these syndicates specialise in accepting reinsurance business from throughout the world.

Professional reinsurers obtain their risk capital through normal commercial markets and work either directly with insurers or through reinsurance brokers.

Self-help question 10.2

1. With proportional reinsurance, both the reinsurer's risk and premiums are proportional to those of the insurer. With non-proportional reinsurance, the reinsurer contributes to the insurer's losses only above the level of the insurer's deductible and determines premiums according to their exposure, independently of the insurer's premiums.
2. Non-proportional reinsurance can be used for both facultative and treaty business. Examples are:

   - per-risk excess of loss
   - per-event excess of loss
   - stop loss reinsurance.

Chapter 11

Captive (Re)insurance Companies

Introduction

A captive insurance or reinsurance company is a company subsidiary of one or several parent companies that is formed to handle the insurance of its mother companies.

Captives are companies that can provide insurance and/or reinsurance services to organisations in lieu of traditional insurance companies. They can only be formed in certain circumstances and must adhere to certain rules, much like traditional insurance companies.

Captives offer a number of benefits that can make them a more financially attractive and viable risk transfer solution. Key benefits include lower premiums and the ability to insure risks that traditional insurers cannot or will not insure. However, there are drawbacks too; these include the requirement to operate an insurance company with potentially limited knowledge and high establishment costs.

This chapter will describe how captives originated and why, and detail the positives and negatives of captives and the regulation that applies. It will also cover what is required when establishing a captive and the commercial rationale for doing so, and define the different types.

Learning Outcomes

By the end of this chapter, you should be able to:

- define captives;
- identify in which cases a captive will benefit an organisation and when they will become a liability;
- state which regulations apply and what is required under them;
- describe the different types of captives and the situations in which one would be better than another.

Risk Treatment, 225–237

Published under exclusive licence by Emerald Publishing Limited
doi:10.1108/978-1-83662-306-920251024

Definition of Captives

Modern risk financing is very different from strategies that were used 30 years ago. Captives emerged in the 1970s and were an alternative risk financing strategy to purchasing traditional insurance policies by the mid-1980s. A captive company is a company formed by an organisation (a group captive is one formed by a group of organisations) to insure one or more risks of the organisation. The captive may become a wholly owned subsidiary of the organisation, or a shared subsidiary of several organisations, but is operated as an independent insurer.

Depending on the context in which they operate – including risk category, legal and regulatory issues, and level of premium – captives can operate either as:

- an insurance company, which directly issues insurance policies to the operating entities of its parent company, manages and pay related claims, often with the assistance of a specialised service provider (third party administrator – TPA);
- a reinsurance company, which will reinsure all or part of the risk underwritten by a third-party insurer that issues the policies to the operating entities; the third-party insurer is called a front or fronting insurer.

One of the reasons put forward for an organisation to form a captive insurance company is to enable it to establish a contingency fund into which tax-deductible funds can be paid. The tax-deductible status of captives is outlined in various legislation, and is subject to scrutiny by tax authorities in many jurisdictions. Payments not used in the year paid can be rolled over to allow the contingency fund to accumulate. A significant incentive for using a captive is to gain better access to the wholesale insurance market, especially in tight market conditions. However, there are other major benefits to be drawn from a captive arrangement as listed below.

The main issue with establishing a captive is the need for the parent company to have enough financial strength to support the operating costs and regulatory capital requirements, as well as the potential underwriting losses. The retrocession programme of the captive will have to be designed so that it fulfils the risk appetite of the mother company. It is clearly a long-term investment proposal that must be assessed as such.

Over the last 30 years, the use of captives has grown with the establishment of rental captives and protected cell companies. Today's advanced risk financing strategies move beyond the use of captives with innovations such as:

- **integrated covers** – multiple insurance covers under one policy;
- **dual trigger policies** – usually a traditional insurance trigger such as property damage blended with a financial market trigger such as the price of a commodity dropping below a certain point;
- **catastrophe bonds** – the use of special purpose vehicles to access global capital markets for additional insurance capacity for earthquake and other natural hazards.

Each one of these risk pooling vehicles has complex legal and tax issues that may make one type of vehicle more, or less, attractive to an organisation over another. Irrespective of the type of captive, mutual pool or PCC, the following issues need to be considered:

- authenticity
- business case
- regulation
- overseas domiciles.

Authenticity

One of the reasons an organisation establishes a captive insurance company is to enable it to establish a contingency fund into which further funds can be paid that are tax deductible. If tax deductibility were not an issue, an organisation could simply operate a contingency fund as a captive within its own general ledger and not be bothered with the legal and regulatory requirements of forming captives.

An organisation must be careful to ensure that the formation of its captive creates a bona fide independent insurance company under the relevant legislation. If it is a bona fide independent insurance company, premiums paid into the company should be tax deductible, as with any other insurance premium expense. The constraints vary from domicile to domicile, also depending on the headquarters of the parent company, therefore the organisation must investigate in full all the conditions for a given captive project.

If the company were not deemed to be bona fide, then the premiums would be seen as an accumulation of reserves in a contingency fund and would not be tax deductible. Only the funds paid out of the captive to finance losses would be tax deductible. An organisation looking to establish a risk financing strategy such as a captive or a discretionary mutual fund should seek legal and tax advice.

Business Case

There are positives and negatives to be considered when establishing a captive insurance company. The negatives relate to the burden of regulation and other establishment and operating costs. However, these negatives are outweighed as an organisation increases in size.

The key reason for not establishing a captive insurance company is the cost. Costs are incurred because the following actions need to take place in order to establish a captive insurance company:

- formation of a company
- appointment and remuneration of directors
- appropriate capitalisation
- preparation of regulatory filings such as business plans, reinsurance strategies and actuarial reports
- claims handling
- appointment of a captive manager such as an insurance broker.

Because captives are generally formed and owned by general organisations, it's possible that the organisation will not fully understand how insurance companies work, or the legislative environment in which they operate. It can therefore be prudent to outsource the day-to-day management of the captive to an insurance professional.

The positive of establishing a captive is the lower overall cost of insurable risk. Insurance premiums are saved because the captive, as a bona fide insurance company, is able to directly access reinsurance markets, which bypasses some of the frictional costs of doing business with direct insurers. These frictional costs include direct insurers' administration and marketing costs and of course their profit margin.

A captive also provides additional flexibility and stability of insurance coverage. During periods where the insurance market is hard (very expensive and policy cover is restricted), a captive that has built up capital over time during a soft market (products are inexpensive and cover is open) may be able to continue to provide the same level of insurance cover to the parent organisation even though the general insurance market has withdrawn support.

The larger the organisation, the larger the captive and the better the economies of scale, resulting in more cost-effective captives or captive-related solutions. As with any such business decision, a cost-benefit analysis is required to ensure a captive solution is the most appropriate for the organisation.

The Commercial Case for a Captive

The following text is an excerpt from the information paper, 'FERMA information paper to OECD in order to propose captive (re)insurance guidelines to national tax authorities'.

Commercial Rationale

Documentation that would justify the commercial rationale of either forming or continuing a captive as a viable risk management tool includes some elements of the following list or any other demonstration of business rationale by the captive owner.

a. Total cost of risk ('TCOR') analysis showing how the captive framework can reduce TCOR for its parent group.
b. Total premium statement showing how the captive framework can save costs for its parent group by reducing total premiums paid outside the group, avoiding numerous local policies and potential duplications, accessing reinsurance and/or specialty capacity more directly, etc.
c. Risk Bearing Capacity analysis showing how the captive framework can add value to local subsidiaries by reducing deductibles for local operations against the optimal risk retention level determined at the group level, or against significant deductibles otherwise imposed by the insurance market.

d. Analysis explaining why the risk could not be retained on the balance sheet – financial, legal, IAIAS, cross border constraints, FX, etc.
e. Justification that standard insurance products in the marketplace are providing insufficient coverage against the group needs and that there is business-added value to build an extended coverage.
f. Justification that local insurance available to subsidiaries in their marketplace would be costlier at similar terms & conditions than the allocated cost resulting from the group captive programme.
g. Justification that premiums flowing in the captive framework are determined according to 'arm's length' principles and collected from numerous countries where the group has operations on a risk-based methodology.
h. Revenue statements showing how the captive framework enables the group to generate additional sources of revenue.
i. Analysis showing why insurance is utilised from a captive framework, and not from the traditional insurance market place, for business facilitation purposes (i.e. insurance as part of the business process vs risk transfer needs, for instance for Transport or Trade Credit insurance).
j. Analysis showing how the captive framework enables the group to reinforce its control over the risk exposures and the loss experience, derive better risk prevention programmes, reduce claims administration expenses and commissions, etc.

The Benefits of a Captive[1]

The objectives of creating a captive may vary from one group to the other. However, if the emphasis differs widely, some of the common reasons are the following:

- **To secure claims information data in a largely decentralised group**
  One of the most frustrating exercises for the risk management professional is to obtain reliable historical data on claims from the subsidiaries. This goal is not often mentioned in the literature concerning captives whereas it is often one of the most valuable advantages of the captive. The direct insurer documents and manages the claims but keeps the captive, the final payers, regularly informed of the statistical data for all subsidiaries; that information can be fed into the RMIS (risk management information system). This is one of the reasons why lower excess may prove useful to ensure more accurate information flows.
- **To obtain a better reward for prevention and reduction efforts deployed in the group thanks to premium conditions which are more responsive to better loss experience recorded inside the group**

[1]The content on these two pages reproduced from Condamin, L, Louisot, J and Naïm, P 2006, *Risk quantification: Management, diagnosis and hedging*, John Wiley & Sons Ltd, West Sussex, pp. 216–218.

The reinsurance agreement with the captive forces the direct insurer to isolate the claims history of the group from the other contracts in the books, thus creating an internal mutualisation that disconnects the group experience from the overall market claims ratio. Therefore, the risk manager will be shielded from automatic premium increases applied by the insurers to an entire market segment to balance their results. The impact on the tariffs is all the more important if the captive retention level is significant.

However, the organisation is not totally cut off from market fluctuations. It must fulfil its legal obligations and purchase all the compulsory covers. It relies heavily the on reinsurance markets to place its captive reinsurance program. At any time, the amount required in retrocession and the state of the market will influence the overall cost of risk.

- **To gain a direct access to reinsurance markets**

  For decades, the re-insurer was the 'bad guy', the hidden master of the destiny for the insured deciding on the fluctuations in insurance premiums that the underwriter had no choice but to pass on to the 'consumer'.

  The captive gives the risk manager a direct access to the reinsurance market, allowing him to better understand the mode of operation of the market, its expectations and anticipate on the cycles.

  The re-insurers, ever larger with the globalisation, merger movement, have fully integrated the captive phenomenon and its irreversibility. Most of them have set up specific departments to handle the captive reinsurance business and even provide risk management.

  Furthermore, this direct connection induces better knowledge of each group's risk management policies and their long-term effect on claims history. Furthermore, the dialogue that has been established provides the reinsurance underwriter a first-hand knowledge of the quality of the risk management policies conducted in large industrial groups.

- **To facilitate the standardisation of covers among the subsidiary**

  As mentioned earlier, the captive is a forum through which all information pertinent for risk management purposes in all the group subsidiaries flows. It is therefore ideally located to insure homogeneity of policies and covers worldwide.

  In some cases, the captive is the leader for all international master policies, for others only a re-insurer for a global program with a unique leader fronting worldwide, whenever possible.

- **To keep large cash flows within the group**

  The captive, being an insurance/reinsurance company, is allowed, indeed requested to set up appropriate reserves. Therefore, premium cash flows are kept within the group and invested to provide investment income that would otherwise go to the outside insurer. …

- **To create capacity to cover risks that the traditional market would not insure**

  Some risks cannot be insured through traditional markets, or only partially, or at prohibitive premium conditions thus the captive arrangement will allow 'creating underwriting capacity'. These events, although probabilistic in nature, are not insurable for some of the reasons listed below, and are often advanced by underwriters to refuse a risk:

- mutualisation is not possible – insufficient numbers of insurance prospects; or insufficient premium turnover to build a viable offer;
- no outlet on the reinsurer market to place excess cover;
- technical difficulty in appraising the risk (nature, new technology, new markets, etc.).

In the insurance industry, the phrase used for the availability of a cover is 'creating underwriting capacity'.

Listed below are a few of the risks, potentially catastrophic for the insured which, in case of an occurrence without outside sources of funds could hinder the survival of the organisation:

- pollution and damage to the environment
- product recalls
- image or reputation deterioration (and costs exposed to restoration)
- product liability (for some industries not favoured by the insurers)
- some 'acts of God'
- political and economical events (other than those insurable)
- and more generally any peril potentially significant for the insured and for which there is no established traditional market.

As mentioned before, with the captive, as with any reinsurer partner on the market, the risk manager has direct access to the reinsurance capacity. He can also establish reserves to face the long-term losses arising from otherwise uninsurable exposures. He can attempt a mutualisation through time if it is not open through space. In some cases, he can even use financial reinsurance to 'post-finance' some losses, thereby averaging the impact on cash flows and

Activity | The positives and negatives of forming a captive

There is plenty of information available on the internet that will help you form a more comprehensive list of reasons why an organisation may wish to form a captive or not. Compile your own list.

Read 'FERMA's views on captive insurance companies' on its website (www.ferma.eu) by searching for 'captives position paper' or by following this link: www.ferma.eu/app/uploads/2016/09/2016.09-FERMA-Statement-Captives.pdf

Make sure you also visit websites such as:

- www.cicaworld.com – the Captive Insurance Companies Association
- www.captive.com – a captive resource centre.

Regulation

Insurance and reinsurance are highly regulated businesses under the supervision of strong governmental bodies and a strict regulation at the European level (Solvency II) and captive companies have to meet the same set of supervisory requirements (i.e. corporate governance, minimum solvency level, fit-and-proper constraints for their management bodies, etc.)

Within EU domiciles, specific rules are applied to captives as they are regulated under the Solvency II regime, including the following:

- The captive has four key functions (risk management, actuarial, compliance and internal audit). These roles are pre-approved by the local regulator and generally performed by out-sourced service providers and individuals with the appropriate skills and experience.
- An actuarial opinion on technical provisions is required for the board, and prepared by the actuarial function annually. The actuarial function is also required to provide an opinion on underwriting policy, reinsurance and solvency capital requirements, and an own risk and solvency assessment report (ORSA) annually.

Overseas Domiciles

In the early days of captives, the use of a captive in a domicile with a low tax regime provided significant tax advantages, given corporate tax rates in excess of 30%. However, most countries soon after changed their tax rules so that any profits earned by subsidiaries (which include captive insurance companies) needed to be taken up in the accounts of the parent at the domestic tax rate. For example, if the tax rate in the overseas domicile is 10% and the domestic tax rate is 30%, an additional 20% tax on the profits of the captive is payable, even if the profits are not repatriated to the parent company and remain off-shore.

One of the key drivers of cost in establishing and maintaining a captive is regulation. For example, in Australia, a captive must comply with the same regulatory regime as a general insurance company selling home and contents insurance to consumers. This requires at least A$5 million of excess capital and there are stringent requirements regarding governance of the organisation, including business planning, risk and reinsurance management, independent actuarial sign-off and audit assurance. Consequently, many captives are formed off-shore where there is less regulation. For example, in Singapore, the minimum capital requirement is S$400,000 or around 10% of the Australian minimum requirement. In addition, there are less stringent requirements regarding actuarial sign-off and audit assurance because it is recognised that the failure of a captive is less of a risk than failure of a major insurance company.

Smaller organisations can take advantage of this strategy to set up a captive insurance company, because lower operating costs on a smaller capital base allow a much better return on the organisation's investment.

> **Activity | Discretionary mutuals (previously known as mutual discretionary funds) and protected cell companies**
>
> Return to your internet research of captives from the previous activity.
> Identify the main elements that distinguish discretionary mutuals and protected cell companies from pure captives.

Establishing a Captive

Organisations that decide to establish a captive need to provide certain information, including:

- details of key personnel, including owners, directors and service providers;
- insurers and reinsurers that will front the captive;
- what classes of business and cover the captive is intended to support and the liability limits of each;
- financial details, including:
  - how the captive will meet future credit requirements
  - a projected balance sheet (projecting balances)
  - a projected profit forecast
  - a projected cash flow
- investment and dividend strategies;
- details of what access it has to financial and other resources;
- actuarial reports (if appropriate);
- an outline of the legislation that applies in the various jurisdictions the captive will operate in, and confirmation that this legislation will not prohibit the transfer of risks to the captive's jurisdiction and does not require elements that are not part of the captive's business plan.

Classification

The main types of captives are classified as follows:

- Pure captives – when a single organisation forms a captive to only write only the risks of its owners, and/or the owner's affiliates.
- Group captives – when a group of organisations form their own jointly owned independent insurance company.
- Discretionary mutual funds (mutual pool) – formation of a discretionary fund by a group of organisations to pool risk in the same way as a group captive. The difference between a discretionary mutual fund and a group captive is that the fund is not a true insurance company because it is discretionary.

- Rental captives – an alternative to forming a captive is to rent a captive, which is to use the insurance licence of an existing insurance company. Rental captives are established specifically to provide captive services for a fee to any organisation that wishes to use them. This means that an organisation can have the tax benefits of a captive without having to set up their own insurance company. Also called rent-a-captives.
- Protected cell companies (PCC) – these companies are a form of rental captive except that each individual contractual arrangement with the insurance company (the protected cell company or PCC) is quarantined by legislation. That is, the funds placed into the PCC by an organisation to form a captive insurance cell to fund its own risk are quarantined from the insurance performance of the other cells of other organisations. Protected cell companies are designed to quarantine and protect the assets of each client of the PCC. PCCs do not exist in all countries, but they can be accessed in off-shore jurisdictions such as Bermuda and the Cayman Islands and in Europe, Malta, the Channel Islands and Luxembourg.
- Diversified captives – these are captives that write a limited number of risks for organisations that aren't its owner or an affiliate (compared to pure captives).
- Producer-owned reinsurance companies (PORCs) – these are captives or rental captives that directly reinsure risks underwritten by a connected insurance company. Essentially, the insurance company writes risks that the PORC reinsures. These captives' interests are more likely to conflict with the interests of organisations because the owners of the PORC have a vested interest in insuring the initial risk.
- Other types of captives were defined by A. M. Best as shown in the following table.

Type	Definition
Pure	Insurer that writes only the risks of its owners and/or affiliates.
Captive writing connected to business	Insurer that writes the risks of unaffiliated companies doing business with the insurer's owners and/or affiliates, in addition to the risks of its owners and/or affiliates.
Captive writing third-party business	Insurer that writes unrelated, open market risks, in addition to the risks of its owners and/ or affiliates.
Captive of insurer	Subsidiary of a commercial insurer and/or reinsurer that writes only risks assumed from its owners and/or affiliates.
Association captive	Insurer that is owned by a trade association or members of a common industry or trade association for the purpose of sharing risk among its members.

(*Continued*)

Type	Definition
Health care captive	Any type of captive writing coverage for hospitals, health maintenance organisations or managed care companies.
Multi-owner captive	Insurer that is owned by two or more unrelated parties for the purpose of writing the risks of its owners and/or affiliates.
Long-term (or life)	Any type of captive writing long-term (life) business.
Composite	Any type of captive writing a combination of long-term (life) business and general (non-life) business.
Rental captive	Insurer that contractually provides captive facilities for a fee to parties unrelated to the insurer's owners.
Agency captive	Insurer that is owned by one or more independent insurance agents to write high-quality risks that the agents control so the agents can participate in the profits generated by the business.
Finite	Any type of captive that writes related and/or unrelated risks involving: (i) clearly defined aggregate limits; and (ii) premiums that reflect the underwriter's anticipated investment income.
Captive not otherwise classified	Insurer that writes risks on a direct or reinsured basis that was formed to meet the insurance needs of its owner(s) whether it is IAIS Guidance Paper on the Regulation and Supervision of Captive Insurers Page 32 of 32 Approved in Budapest on 17 October 2008 formed under captive legislation or not.
Protected/ Segregated cell captive	Insurer that provides captive facilities for a fee to parties unrelated to the insurer's owners. The captive is established by legislation that legally protects, or segregates, each cell's assets so that liabilities of other cells cannot attach to them.
Sponsored captive	Insurer that is owned by one or more insurers, reinsurers and/or captive. Each participant is unrelated to the owner(s) and insures its own risks. Each participant has its assets protected in a separate cell within the facility so that one participant never pays for the losses or expenses of any other participant.
Branch captive	US domiciled subsidiary of an offshore captive that writes US employee benefits subject to ERISA legislation for the owner of the offshore captive.

(*Continued*)

(*Continued*)

Type	Definition
Risk-retention group	Multi-owner captives formed under the US Product Liability Risk Retention Act of 1981 or under the US Federal Liability Risk Retention Act of 1986 that writes only liability risks.
Governmental pool	Separate, legal, non-governmental, risk-bearing entity that is formed by one or more governmental agencies and/or subdivisions for the purpose of self-insuring its risks.
Group self-insurance pool	Separate, legal, risk-bearing entity that is formed by a trade association, common industry or other related group for the purpose of self-insuring the risks of its members.
Special purpose vehicle	Any type of captive that transfers insurance and non-insurance risks into the capital markets.
Trust	A fiduciary relationship created by agreement in which money from individuals and/or companies is held by a trustee to satisfy the legal obligations of the individuals and/or companies to injured third-party claimants.

Source: IAIS guidance paper on the regulation and supervision of captive insurers.

Summary

Please keep the following points from this chapter in mind:

- A captive company is a company formed by an organisation to insure one or more risks of the organisation. The captive becomes a wholly owned subsidiary of the organisation but is operated as an independent insurer.
- An organisation must be careful to ensure that the formation of its captive creates a bona fide independent insurance company under the relevant legislation.
- Captives can operate either as an insurance company or a reinsurance company.
- Over the last 30 years, the use of captives has grown with the establishment of rental captives and protected cell companies. Today's advanced risk financing strategies move beyond the use of captives with other innovations.
- The main issues with establishing a captive is the need for the parent company to have enough financial strength to support the operating costs and regulatory capital requirements, as well as the potential underwriting losses.
- The key reason for not establishing a captive insurance company is the cost. Other negatives relate to the burden of regulation and other establishment and operating costs. However, these negatives are outweighed as an organisation increases in size.
- The positive of establishing a captive is the lower overall cost of insurable risk. Insurance premiums are saved because the captive, as a bona fide insurance company, is able to directly access reinsurance markets, bypassing some of the costs of direct insurance.

- Other benefits of establishing a captive are:

    - to secure claims information data in a largely decentralised group
    - to obtain a better reward for prevention and reduction efforts thanks to premium conditions being more responsive to the loss experience of the group
    - to gain direct access to reinsurance markets
    - to facilitate the standardisation of covers among subsidiaries
    - to keep large cash flows within the group
    - to create capacity to cover risks that traditional market would not insure.

- The larger the organisation, the larger the captive and the better the economies of scale, resulting in more cost-effective captives or captive-related solutions.
- Captives, like insurance companies, are subject to regulation and legislation. Solvency II in Europe applies specific rules to captives.
- There numerous different types of captives that all play a slightly different role; some are specific to the parent companies, others write risks for other companies and some can be rented.

Chapter 12

Alternative Risk Transfer

Introduction

Traditionally, the main way of transferring risk was through insurance. However, insurance can be limited and expensive. Over the years, alternative risk financing techniques have been developed to address those limitations, and these days there are many more options available. One such relatively new method is captives, as explored in the previous topic, which enable organisations to insure risks that would otherwise have been uninsurable. Other methods, such as capital markets and contingent capital arrangements are described in the following topic.

This topic describes the alternative risk transfer techniques available and the situations in which each applies. It should be remembered that these are alternative not better techniques. Each situation needs to be analysed thoroughly so the risk transfer technique/s that will best address the risks involved can be applied.

Learning Outcomes

By the end of this topic, you should be able to:

- identify the shortcomings of other risk transfer methods and how these are addressed by the new alternatives;
- describe the differences between techniques and the situation in which they can and can't be used;
- identify the shortcomings of these alternatives and when other methods may be more suitable.

Risk Treatment, 239–253

doi:10.1108/978-1-83662-306-920251026

General Introduction to Capital Markets Products for Risk Financing[1]

Traditionally, the only role played by the capital markets in the insurance industry and in related risk financing matters was that of a purveyor of funds. The capital thus raised was used to underwrite risks. The question addressed here is how and when capital markets can be used as an alternative to traditional insurance or reinsurance markets.

Capital market products for risk financing currently used can be grouped into three categories:

- **Insurance-linked securities** are financial investments, most of the time in the form of bonds that have insurable risks embedded in them. The investor receives a higher return for the security as it includes a premium as a retribution for the embedded risk. Losses to the investor linked with the embedded risk benefits another organisation, which uses the proceeds to offset its insurable risks.
- **Insurance derivatives** are financial contracts valued on the base of the level of insurable losses that occur during a specific time period. An insurance derivative increases in value as specified insurable losses increase and, therefore, the purchaser of the derivative can use this gain to offset its insurable losses. The seller of an insurance derivative accepts insurable risks and receives a commensurate return for doing so.
- **Contingent capital arrangement** is an agreement entered into before losses occur that enables an organisation to raise cash by selling stock or issuing debt at prearranged terms following a loss that exceeds a certain threshold. The loss can arise from insurable risks such as property damage resulting from an earthquake or a liability loss resulting from pollution. The organisation agreeing to provide the contingent capital receives a commitment fee.

Securitisation

Securitisation means to create a marketable investment security based on the expected cash flows from a financial transaction. A financial institution can use securitisation to transfer income-producing assets off its balance sheet in exchange for cash. For example, a card issuer might securitise its credit card receivables, or a bank might securitise its mortgage receivables.

As an example of a mortgage securitisation, assume that a bank that extends loans to an individual who purchases homes would like to transfer its mortgage receivables (an asset) off its balance sheet. The bank could sell receivables for cash to an intermediary, usually called an **SPV** (special purpose vehicle). In turn, the SPV will issue securities to investors to finance the purchase of the assets.

---

[1]The content on these five pages is reproduced from ICMIF, Voice, see issue number 9. Sourced from Condamin, L, Louisot, J and Naïm, P 2006, *Risk quantification: Management, diagnosis and hedging*, John Wiley & Sons Ltd, West Sussex, pp. 225–230.

More generally, an organisation sells income-producing assets to a SPV in exchange for cash. The income-producing assets are taken off the organisation's balance sheet and reside in the SPV as collateral to securities sold to investors. The investors purchase the securities for cash and receive a return commensurate with the risk inherent in the income-producing assets that back the securities.

Insurance companies, including insurance or re-insurance captives, can participate in a number of ways linked to all classes of assets owned by such companies. However, what is referred to as insurance securitisation is a unique from of securitisation.

The concept of an insurance-linked security can best be explained through an illustrative example. An investor purchases a bond from an SPV that provides a higher interest rate than the risk-free interest rate (US treasury bonds), thus including a risk premium. The bond would be relatively free of credit risk as it is collateralised by liquid investments held by the SPV.

In return for the risk premium investors receive, returns are linked with a risk such as the occurrence of a hurricane during the term of the bond. The return to the investor will be reduced if a hurricane strike causes damages in excess of a stated level. When the threshold is exceeded, the return falls in direct proportion with the total loss incurred. The loss reference can be a given portfolio of an insurance company, an industry index or the losses of a given organisation (a captive).

In fact, there may be different classes (tranches) of bonds, usually three. Of course, these incur variable degrees of risk and the risk premium is proportional to the risk assumed. In increasing level of risk, they are:

- bonds with a guaranteed minimum return
- bonds with protected principal
- bonds with no guarantee (even for the principal).

Through this mechanism, the investor buying the bond is really underwriting an insurable risk that could be insured through a traditional insurance contract. It is a marketable security through a financial market. In other term, the process of insurance securitisation has securitised the risk of hurricane loss by linking the returns provided to investors in a marketable security.

In the case of insurance securitisation, the SPV plays a specific role that does not apply in other settings:

- The SPV transforms an insurable risk into an investment risk and vice versa.
- The SPV receives cash from both the investors and the organisation transferring the insurable risk. It holds cash as a collateral for its obligation to repay interest and principal on the insurance-linked securities and its obligation to pay any losses that occur.
- Depending on the jurisdiction involved, the SPV might qualify as an authorised insurer (or reinsurer), which enables the organisation transferring its risk of loss to treat the transaction as insurance (or reinsurance) for tax and accounting purposes. The main advantages of treating the transaction as insurance (or reinsurance) are that the losses do not have to be taken into account on the income statement or the balance sheet as they occur and that the 'premium' paid to the SPV is tax deductible at the time of payment.

Insurance Derivatives

A derivative is a financial contract that derives its value from the value of another asset, such as a commodity. A derivative can also derive its value from the yields on another asset or the level of an index, such as the Standard & Poor's 500 Index.

An insurance derivative is a financial contract that derives its value from the level of insurable losses that occur during a specific time period. The value of an insurance derivative can be based on the level of insurable losses experienced by a single organisation or on the level of an insurance industry index of insured losses.

The two major categories of insurance derivatives are swaps and options. These are routinely used by organisations to offset and hedge, their financial risks like interest rates and foreign currency exposures.

Swaps

A swap is an agreement between two organisations to exchange their cash flows based on the movements in the value of another asset, yields on an asset, or an index of values or yields. Thus, the swap derives its value from an underlying asset. The cash flows are exchanged back and forth between organisations on a continuous basis throughout the term of the swap.

An organisation can use a swap to transfer its insurable risk, in which case the swap is an insurance derivative. Insurance companies (or captives) can spread their risks through a swap arrangement. For example, one insurance company could exchange a portion of the cash flows (premiums and losses) arising from a hurricane exposure in the southwestern United States with a portion of the cash flows arising in another insurance company for tornado risks in the mid-western United States. Such a swap mimics a reinsurance contract. It could also be constructed to mimic an insurance contract.

A major advantage of swaps is that they cost less than insurance-linked securities. Their main disadvantage is that they are not collateralised therefore the issuer faces the risk that the other party (the counterpart) will not meet its obligation.

Insurance Options

An **insurance option** derives its value from insurable losses, either an organisation's actual insurable losses or an index of losses covered by a group of insurance companies. The value of an insurance option increases as the value of the underlying insurable losses increases. Therefore, an organisation can use a gain from an insurance option to offset its losses from insurable risk.

- **An over-the-counter option** is placed privately and is customised to meet an organisation's specific needs.
- **Exchange-traded options** are traded on an organised exchange, such as the Chicago Board of Trade.
- **A call option** gives the holder the right but not the obligation to buy an asset
- **A put option** gives the holder the right but not the obligation to sell an asset.
- The price at which the asset can be either purchased or sold is called the **strike price**.

Insurance options, like swaps, have the same cash flow characteristics as insurance policies. For a call option, imagine that the underlying asset is individual insurable losses and that the strike value (similar in concept to the price, but involving a value other than price) is set equal to the deductible or self-insured retention level under an insurance policy.

In this case, the call option is an insurance option that serves the same function as an insurance policy with a large deductible. The buyer of the call option pays a premium and receives cash when the value of the insurable losses exceeds the strike value, during the period of the option. The seller of the option is in the opposite position because he or she receives a premium and must pay cash if the value of insurable loss exceeds the strike value.

Contingent Capital Arrangements

Contingent capital arrangements are agreements entered into before losses occur and that enables an organisation to raise cash by selling stock or issuing debt at prearranged terms following a loss that exceeds a certain threshold. Therefore, in this type of transaction, the organisation does not transfer its risk of loss to investors. Instead, **after the loss has occurred**, it receives an injection of funds in the form of long-term debt or equity to pay for the losses.

The terms of the funds' injection are pre-agreed to; therefore, the organisation is usually able to receive more favourable terms than it would receive if it were to raise the funds after a large loss, assuming its weakened financial position would permit such a raise in the first place.

Investors in a contingent capital arrangement become creditors of, or equity investors in, the organisation following a loss. A contingent capital arrangement is set up as an option, so the organisation that purchases such an arrangement is not obligated to exercise the option even if the loss exceeds the threshold specified in the agreement.

In the case of equity, it may be compared with an insurance transaction. The indemnity received from the insurer in the event that a covered loss occurs is a 'free' injection of equity to restore previous stockholders to their financial position, at the cost of a reduction in current earnings (the insurance premium): it is a **pre-loss financing mechanism**. The insurer bears the risk of uncertainty associated with the exposure; thus it is a **transfer-financing tool**.

The equity contingent capital arrangement is much cheaper than insurance. The cost of the option is substantially smaller than the insurance premium, however the injection of equity capital is accompanied with a dilution of future earnings thus reducing the future earnings of current stockholders: it is a **post-loss financing mechanism**. As the current stockholders bear the risk of uncertainty involved with the exposure thus financed it is clearly a risk retention tool.

The contingent capital arrangement can take either of three forms:

- **Standby credit facility**

  A standby credit facility is an arrangement whereby a bank or another financial institution agrees to provide a loan to an organisation in the event of a loss. The credit is pre-arranged so that terms, such as the interest rate and principal repayment schedule are known in advance of a loss. In exchange for this credit commitment, the organisation taking out a line of credit pays a commitment fee.

This type of arrangement is referred to earlier in the presentation of retention risk financing instruments as **borrowing for losses** in connection with setting reserves.

- **Contingent surplus note**

  Surplus notes are specific to the statutory accounting rules applied to insurance companies in the USA (and where accounting rules similar to the US's apply). They are sold to investors and counted as policyholder surpluses rather than as a liability on an insurer's balance sheet. The main benefit of the surplus note is that it increases an insurer's assets without increasing its liability, whereas regular debt increases both similarly. Thus, a surplus note allows the insurer to increase its capacity to write business.

  Contingent surplus notes are prearranged so that the insurer has the option to obtain funds by issuing surplus notes at a pre-agreed rate of interest. Thus, the insurer can bolster its surplus following a loss.

  In the USA, they are made available to an insurer through a trust known as a contingent surplus note (CSN) trust. The trust receives funds from the investors and places them in liquid investments, such as US Treasury securities.

  The investors receive a higher interest rate than similar maturity securities. The cost to the insurer is this differential in rate, or risk premium granted to the investors. If it exercises its right to issue surplus notes, the insurer must repay interest and principal to the CSN trust over time so that funds are available to provide interest and principal repayments on the trust notes to the investors.

- **Catastrophe equity put option**

  Catastrophe equity puts are another way for an insurer (or a captive) or a non-insurance organisation to raise capital in the event of a catastrophic loss.

  As mentioned above, a put is a right to sell an asset at a predetermined price. In the case of a catastrophe equity put option it is the right to sell stocks at a predetermined price in the event of a catastrophic loss.

  The major advantage of this arrangement is that they make equity funds available at a pre-agreed-to price when an organisation needs them the most, and would be least likely to obtain it were it not pre-arranged, i.e. immediately following a catastrophic loss.

  If an organisation suffers a loss of capital due to a catastrophe, its stock price is likely to fall, lowering its price-earnings ratio and rendering equity financing more expensive: the dilution of future earnings for current stockholders, as exposed here above, would be much greater. Furthermore, the pre-agreed price sends a signal to the market and may well stop the fall of the stock price.

  A subsidiary question linked to the dilution is to know into which hands the new equity will fall. The sell must be carefully tailored to avoid too much new equity giving headway to a potential hostile takeover bid.

Case study – Drive-Smart

Drive-Smart is a medium-sized car hire organisation. It has a major motor vehicle accident every three or four years where a vehicle is written off. The cost of replacing a vehicle in any one year would significantly impact on Drive-Smart's cash flow. To cope with the financial risk of vehicle loss, Drive-Smart set aside funds from operating cash flow each month. This strategy gives Drive-Smart a financial solution to vehicle loss. If no vehicle loss occurs, Drive-Smart accumulates the funds they have retained as reserves for future incidents.

Alternative Risk Transfer (ART) Methods

In addition to captives and related structures, there are other risk financing strategies that are used globally. In most cases, they can be utilised with or without the formation of a captive insurance company. These include the following:

- integrated programs or basket covers
- dual trigger policies
- finite or blended risk policies
- contingent capital
- weather derivatives
- insurance-linked securities.

Integrated Programs or Basket Covers

This strategy is used when one insurance policy is arranged for an organisation to cover a range of insurance lines usually over a timeframe of three or more years. This offers the insured an advantage in that it reduces the likelihood of a gap in cover. For example, such a gap may occur between a professional indemnity policy and a general liability policy where there can be disputes as to whether any loss occurred due to negligent advice (the professional indemnity policy) or due to a faulty product (the general liability policy). This type of dispute may occur when advice was given about the use of a product and it is uncertain whether the advice was the problem or the product itself was faulty.

The timeframe of three or more years allows for the insured to benefit from more stable pricing in what is often a volatile insurance market.

Dual Trigger Policies

These policies require two events to occur for a claim to be made. The events are usually unrelated; for example, a fire loss at the same time as interest rates exceeds a certain level. Dual trigger policies are used to protect organisations from extremely rare events which could prevent the organisation from operating.

For example, an organisation's financial position is already hampered by very high interest rates on their floating rate debt and at the same time they are unable to grow their business to earn additional profit to cover the debt due to a fire loss.

Financial Reinsurance and Finite Risks[2]

The first generation of alternative risk financing mechanisms was used by both insurers and insured. It is mostly articulated around two concepts both taking into account the time value of money: one being mostly a post-financing technique (financial reinsurance) and one a pre-financing technique (finite risk). Using capital markets to address potential risk financing needs has become known as risk securitisation.

As far as financial reinsurance and finite insurance/reinsurance products are concerned, their impact on the reinsurance programmes for captives and pools alone justifies the understanding of their mechanisms by any risk management professional.

Gathered under the same topic, the two concepts are clearly distinguished in specialised circles. 'Finite risk' applies to a specific amount of cover of future losses over a policy period, typically several years. 'Financial reinsurance' applies to the purchase by an insurer or a reinsurer of past losses, already incurred but not already paid for. Readers interested in large corporations involved in the global economy will need to get much more familiar with these approaches that are often needed to build enough capacity to cover professional indemnity or environmental liabilities that can far exceed the world's traditional insurance markets' capacities.

Readers interested only in small and medium size organisations may skip the presentation of these products, which require a sizeable stake!

[…] The major specificity, however, lies in the present value approach to losses and the post-financing mechanism. A key factor in placing financial reinsurance is therefore the forecasting of future cash outflows linked with incurred losses. Both amounts and timing are essential in this process, as interest is the major risk transferred in the transaction.

The 'aggregate limit' is stated in monetary terms for the reported claims portfolio transferred and the premium paid upfront by the transferee is reduced to take into account the interest earned on the funds while the reinsurer pays the losses over the period.

It should be noted that this mechanism provides the insurer (or the captive) an improvement on his balance sheet. A portfolio of losses is written out of his

---

[2]The content on these two pages reproduced from Condamin, L, Louisot, J and Naïm, P 2006, *Risk quantification: Management, diagnosis and hedging*, John Wiley & Sons Ltd, West Sussex, pp. 223–225. Copyright © 2006 John Wiley & Sons Ltd, The Atrium, Southern Gate, Chichester, West Sussex PO19 8SQ, England. All Rights Reserved.

liabilities for the amount of the full reserve while, on the asset side, only the present value of the set reserves is paid. Therefore, he gains an immediate improvement in his current results and safety ratio.

During the 1990s, financial reinsurance has become more present in the markets and its products have diversified and become more sophisticated. However, the key question remains the extent to which the reinsurer shares in the actual development risk for reported losses, starting with no share at all in the original version stated above.

The most common product, which risk managers in large organisations could find useful is detailed here. It could be used especially to outsource post-financing for exposures not insurable in the traditional insurance markets.

Integration of interest on investment: interest earned on the investment of the premium is an essential part of the contract and is recognised as such. Traditional reinsurance does not ignore this aspect and in many branches negotiations between insurers and reinsurers take into account interest earned on long tail claims (automobile liability for bodily injuries, product liability, workers compensation, etc.). However, they do not appear explicitly in the terms of the contract.

Contractual limit for insurer liability: the object of the contract is to cover claims already reported at their estimated outstanding cost (reserve) and, occasionally, it may be extended to IBNR (incurred but not reported) that appear in the insurer (or the captive reinsurer) books. However, the reinsurer liability is strictly limited to the transferred claims and to the reserve deemed correct at the time of transfer. All financial reinsurance contracts therefore contain an 'aggregate limit', i.e. the maximum that the reinsurer will pay to or on behalf of the insurer over the period.

Profit and loss sharing: financial reinsurance contracts also include a mechanism that allows the insurer to get back part of the premium should the claims close for less than the reserves set up. The insurer is responsible for any excess and the sharing of this excess may constitute an underwriting risk for the reinsurer. In some cases, the aggregate limit is set at a level that includes a line of cover in excess of current reserve to allow for long-term claims development. This is more like a line of 'excess of loss' traditional reinsurance added to the first layer of pure financial reinsurance. …

Long-term commitment: Financial reinsurance is by essence a long-term approach and supposes a long-term commitment for both parties. It can be an additional tool to protect insurance lines that traditional reinsurance would exclude from cover. The principle is a full payment for incurred losses allowing only for the risk of timing of the outflows to be transferred. The reinsurer is more a financial institution than a traditional reinsurer. Fully analysing the exposures involved and expecting a portfolio effect to 'mutualise' the risks.

Finite or Blended Risk Policies

Finite risk refers to an arrangement where an insurer issues an insurance policy to an organisation that usually covers several years; however, all of the insurance risk is to be funded by the insured via a deposit of cash to the insurer and/or a promise to repay any losses. The risk to the insurance company is that claims are made early in the policy period and the client is unable to repay any claims made. Blended risk policies involve a combination of full risk transfer to the insurer and some self-funded risk by the insured.

Truly finite risk policies are not actually insurance policies and hence they should not be treated as such in the accounts of the insured. They should be treated as an investment or debt, depending on whether the account with the insurer is in surplus or deficit.

Finite insurance policies can be used by insurers as well as corporations by way of reinsurance finite risk policies. Finite reinsurance policies have been the subject of many problems globally; for example, certain companies have made debt facilities look like reinsurance and others have treated pure finite risk contracts as insurance policies.

Some countries will have guidelines on when a blended finite risk policy has sufficient risk transfer to be deemed an insurance policy. Expert independent advice should be sought by any organisation contemplating such an arrangement.

Contingent Capital

Contingent debt and equity are viable risk-financing strategies. In essence, these strategies concern arranging financing such as senior debt, surplus notes, preferred shares and sub-prime debt where the facilities are put into place at pre-agreed terms based on an insurable trigger such as a major earthquake or cyclone loss. Swiss Re is a prominent reinsurance company, and according to one of its publications (Sigma No.4/2005, p. 23), contingent capital strategies are structured and priced using a blend of insurance and capital market techniques and the insured gains lower-cost access to capital at times when it is especially needed.

It is not necessary to enter into an insurance contract to have available contingent debt. One commonly used risk financing method is to have available a line of credit. Under this arrangement, an organisation enters into a contract with a bank that will allow it to draw down some or all of a loan based on pre-agreed terms and conditions. The organisation will pay the bank a fee for holding this facility available, as the bank must retain some capital against all of its contingent debt facilities in case one or more are drawn down.

Weather Derivatives

A derivative is a contract covering a speculative risk where the parties succeed or fail based on an underlying index such as the interest rate on government bonds or the amount of rain falling over a period. The term, 'weather derivative' evolved to identify derivative contracts based on weather-related triggers such as heat, cold, rain and snow.

These contracts are entered into by organisations that wish to hedge an exposure to the weather. Typically, these are organisations such as energy utilities and ski resorts that are dependent on the weather for their financial prosperity and survival.

The existence of a weather derivatives market depends on an independent body that measures temperatures, rainfall, wind and snowfall and can create appropriate indices on which derivative contracts can be based.

Weather Derivative Instruments

Weather derivatives are likely to have more and more practical use in certain countries over the coming decades. Three weather derivative instruments are described below:

- swap option
- call option
- put option.

Swap option – an agreement between two organisations (referred to as counter-parties to the one transaction) where future cash flows are exchanged. One counter-party trades an uncertain cash flow (an index that floats) for a certain cash flow (a fixed price). A common example is that one party exchanges a floating interest rate for a fixed interest rate. The party seeking certainty pays a premium to the party offering the hedge against a floating index.

Call option – an agreement between two counterparties where one party pays an initial contract fee (equivalent to an insurance premium) to the other party to form a contract that allows the first party to buy certain security at a predetermined price – the strike price. For example, an airline may buy call options on aviation fuel six months in advance to provide certainty about their cost of fuel when they are selling tickets six months in advance. If, in six months, the cost of fuel is lower than the strike price for the option, the airline would not exercise its right to buy at the higher price. It provides protection from upward movement in a market.

Put option – an agreement between two counterparties where one party pays an initial contract fee (equivalent to an insurance premium) to the other party to form a contract that allows the first party to sell a certain security at a predetermined price – the strike price. For example, a cotton farmer may buy 'put options' on raw cotton six months in advance to provide certainty about the price received at harvest time. If, in six months, the price of cotton is higher than the strike price for the option, the farmer would not exercise the right to sell at a price lower than the current market price. It provides protection from downward movement in a market.

Derivatives contracts detail the total value of the underlying security to be swapped, bought or sold, in addition to the strike price for the option. In weather trading, the total value is determined by the variation in temperature, snow or rainfall from the agreed strike price for the option. For example, the contract may be for €1 million per 10 mm of rain difference from a strike price of 150mm of rain over a certain period.

Self-Help Question 12.1

What is the main advantage of a swap option for an energy utility hedging its exposure to low temperatures in summer?

What kind of protection does a call option on temperature provide for an organisation manufacturing woollen products such as winter jackets and jumpers?

What kind of protection does a put option on rainfall provide for a farmer?

Answers to self-help questions are provided at the end of each section.

Insurance-Linked Securities (ILS)

Insurance-linked securities are based on the principle of securitisation, which was first developed in the residential mortgage and credit card receivables market. According to Fisher and Shaw, securitisation is defined as follows:

> Securitisation – securitisation is the packaging of designated pools of loans or receivables with an appropriate level of credit enhancement and the redistribution of these packages to investors.

Investors buy the repackaged assets in the form of securities or loans which are collateralised (secured) on the underlying pool and its associated income stream. Securitisation thereby converts illiquid assets into liquid assets.

The growing importance of ILS is illustrated in a recent article entitled 'UK government seeks to attract ILS market with new regulations', published in **Intelligent Insurer**:

> The UK government has brought in new regulations that have created what it calls a competitive regulatory and tax regime for Insurance Linked Securities (ILS) which will ensure that UK gets a share of this rapidly growing market.
>
> ILS allow insurance and reinsurance firms to transfer risk to the capital markets, meaning that risk can be managed more effectively for businesses and consumers.
>
> The products are sometimes known as catastrophe bonds and are normally used to insure against extreme risks, such as earthquakes and hurricanes.
>
> Over $80 billion of these securities have been issued to date, with over $10 billion issued in 2017 alone. According to the UK government, this is a rapidly growing market with research showing that it could grow to an estimated $87 billion by 2019.

Catastrophe Bonds

In insurance-linked securities, an illiquid risk (for example, exposure to earthquake damage) is converted to a liquid security, often referred to as a catastrophe bond that can be traded in global capital markets.

The following diagram depicts how a catastrophe bond operates for an insurance company obtaining reinsurance protection for natural hazard risk. The structure is identical for an organisation that is not an insurance company; however, the organisation would be referred to as the insured rather than the reinsured in the diagram below.

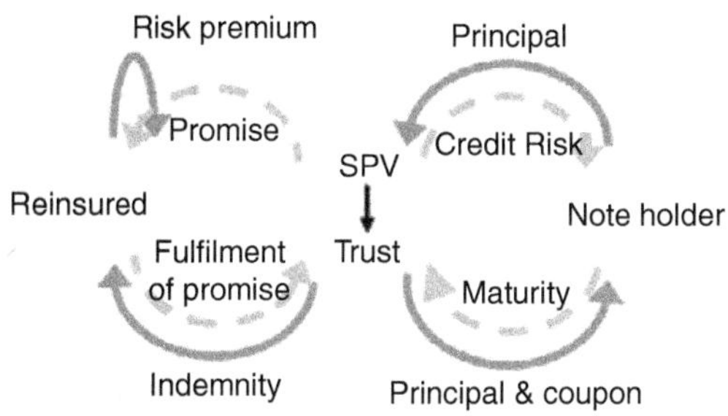

Catastrophe Bond Diagram
©St Paul Re 2001

Usually, a catastrophe bond involves establishing a SPV that issues commercial bonds to investors. The SPV enters into an agreement with the insurance company that it will pay a sum of money based on a certain trigger such as a certain size earthquake event in a certain location. The SPV receives cash from the issuing of the bonds and retains it in a trust account that is invested in a safe security such as government bonds.

If the defined catastrophe event does not occur, the cash flows are in favour of the investor/note holder (the holder of the catastrophe bond) and the investor makes a set return. If the catastrophe bond is triggered by an event, the cash flows are against the investor and the investors may lose their upside or even their capital depending on the contract.

Types of Triggers for Catastrophe Bonds

The two types of triggers for catastrophe bonds are:

- Indemnity trigger – this is when the bond is triggered once the insured (or reinsured in the case of an insurance company) suffers a certain level of loss from an event such as an earthquake or hurricane.
- Non-indemnity or parametric trigger – this is where the bond is triggered by a specified event. For example, a trigger may be described as 'an earthquake measuring more than 8.1 on the Richter scale with epicentre located within 50km radius of the insured premises'.

Advantages of Trigger Types

- The advantage of an indemnity trigger for an insured is that there is more certainty that their losses will be covered; however, investors fear the insured can affect the loss outcomes via the claims management process.
- The advantage of a non-indemnity trigger for an insured is that there will be more interest from investors and hence more capacity and perhaps a lower price. The disadvantage is that an event such as an earthquake may occur but not be strong enough to trigger the bond, with more damage caused than the insured anticipated and funds not available to rectify it.

Pricing of Bonds

Another element of catastrophe bonds that risk managers need to consider is the way that bonds are priced. The insured engages an independent modelling firm to model the natural hazard risk to provide an indication of how likely the bond is to be triggered. The bond is then rated by a rating agency to give it a bond rating equivalent to other bonds such as corporate or government debt that have similar levels of probability of default. That is, an investor is inclined to pay the same amount for a corporate bond rated AA+ as they would for a catastrophe bond rated AA+, as there is a similar likelihood of loss for both bonds.

The driving forces for advanced risk financing strategies are often related to enterprise risk management. As organisations identify risk exposures that are not currently insured, the insurance market is often tested to see whether it is able and willing to cover the risk or risks identified. This is when an underwriter needs to apply the principles of insurance and insurable risk, and principles of treasury risk management, to new risks to determine whether the risks can be insured profitably. Examples of enterprise risks that are generally not covered by insurance include the value of intangible assets such as brand value and goodwill on the balance sheet.

In Europe, these advanced techniques, although often considered in brokers' offers, are not often used, due to the reasonable rating and availability of conventional insurance programmes, except in the case of global European-based companies, or for subsidiaries of US-based conglomerates. Many of these advanced strategies require teams of analysts pouring over data and building complex models before a deal can be structured. The cost is often prohibitive unless the organisation is very large and financially strong and the executive team and directors have an understanding of these options.

Summary

Please keep the following points from this topic in mind:

- Traditionally, capital markets in the insurance industry and in related risk financing matters only purveyed funds. The capital thus raised was used to underwrite risks. These days, capital markets can be used as an alternative to traditional insurance or re-insurance markets.

- Capital market products for risk financing currently used can be grouped into three categories:

  - Insurance-linked securities
  - Insurance derivatives
  - Contin**gent capital arrangement**

- Securitisation means to create a marketable investment security based on the expected cash flows from a financial transaction. A financial institution can use securitisation to transfer income-producing assets off its balance sheet in exchange for cash.
- A derivative is a financial contract that derives its value from the value of another asset, such as a commodity. A derivative can also derive its value from the yields on another asset or the level of an index:
- The two major categories of insurance derivatives are swaps and options.
- Contingent capital arrangements are agreements entered into before losses occur that enable an organisation to raise cash by selling stock or issuing debt at prearranged terms following a loss that exceeds a certain threshold.
- The contingent capital arrangement can take any of three forms:

  - **Standby credi**t facility
  - Contingent surplus note
  - Catastrophe equity put option

- In addition to captives and related structures there are other risk financing strategies that are used globally. In most cases, they can be utilised with or without the formation of a captive insurance company. Examples are integrated programs or basket covers, finite or blended risk policies and insurance-linked securities.

Answers to Self-Help Questions

Self-help question 12.1

1. The main advantage of a swap option for an energy utility hedging its exposure to low temperatures in summer is that it obtains a guaranteed minimum amount of revenue in case energy demand is consistently low over an extended cool summer.
2. A call option on temperature provides a manufacturer of woollen products protection against a period of extended high temperatures. For example, the manufacturer would buy a call option on minimum temperature over the winter
3. A put option on rainfall provides protection for a farmer against a period of extended low rainfall. A farmer would buy a put option on rainfall to protect against a level of rainfall over the growing season that would result in a very low crop yield or no crop at all.

Chapter 13

International Insurance Market

Introduction

To improve their insurance coverage and cost efficiency, many global firms have developed international insurance programmes.

An international programme of insurance is a programme that covers risk in several countries. It aims at covering gaps, complying with the legal and regulatory environment, and being a model of transparency.

The problem is complex as the regulators in each country are observing closely this question, and that they are particularly strict when it comes to compliance with local norms (laws and regulation).

Learning Outcomes

By the end of this chapter, you should be able to:

- understand how and why to develop an international programme of insurance;
- understand the legal and regulatory context for the development of an international programme of insurance;
- list the pros and cons of an international programme of insurance;
- understand the main concepts associated with the international programmes of insurance.

Risk Treatment, 255–265

Published under exclusive licence by Emerald Publishing Limited
doi:10.1108/978-1-83662-306-920251029

The Role of Reinsurance in the International Insurance Market

Risk management professionals need to be aware of the importance of reinsurance. Every insured organisation depends on the financial stability of its commercial insurers. Because commercial insurers usually rely on reinsurance to mitigate the potentially adverse effects of a single large loss or an aggregation of smaller losses, any disruption to an insurer's reinsurance network, such as the bankruptcy of a major reinsurer, can threaten an organisation's risk financing program. Furthermore, an organisation's risk management professional sometimes deals directly with reinsurers, for example, when he or she purchases reinsurance for a captive insurance subsidiary or places excess insurance layers directly into the reinsurance market. To understand the importance of reinsurance to a risk financing program, the risk management professional should have a solid understanding of the sources and types of reinsurance.

International Insurance Programmes

An international programme is an insurance programme that includes covers for more than one country.

Context and Challenges

The configuration of an international insurance programme must be constantly updated, as it will not be in any way static. In some situations, it will be possible to find answers to limits but no conditions, and vice versa. There are situations in which identified feared gaps and other undesired circumstances will be present, and it will be necessary to analyse whether the organisation can live with them.

Risk management professionals must be aware of the context in which they are operating, including the organisation's strategy in terms of positioning, taking into account, for example, that the mere existence of commercial offices is not enough to justify the creation of an international insurance programme. For this reason, it is essential to be attentive to the evolution of the local insurance markets taking into account the countries involved, including the behaviour of local colleagues who will always try to bypass the international programme regulation, if only for the sake of simplification. On the other hand, it is advisable to have a single mediator in the same sector so that all the participants are aligned in the search for the major interests.

The key consideration is the necessity to build programmes that protect the patrimonial and personal assets of the organisation, and the programmes will vary depending on risk location. The following questions should be considered:

- What is the nature of our risks?
- Is it necessary to establish an insurance programme?
- Are there other options?
- What are the legal and tax implications?

The first version of an insurance programme involves building an initial pragmatic and complete commercial version of the future programme with an objective analysis of the exposures that will avoid surprises. It is necessary to try and reach an appropriate balance so that the premiums are contained, while also optimally managing claims, identifying and avoiding the possible.

It is useful when developing an international insurance programme to map out the covers to visually check that coverage is adequate. Metaphorically speaking, the objective is to erect a building with different heights, representing the covers and limits for each country depending on local needs and requirements, with the resulting profile like skyscrapers of different heights: some professionals have called it the Manhattan Skyline of the international insurance programmes.

If the corporate risk management department doesn't comply with local obligations, an unavoidable increase in the costs will occur unless an efficient programme is put in place. Accordingly, making adequate decisions in this matter will improve corporate risk management, eliminating covers not needed, reducing overall costs and confirming that the success of an international insurance programme resides in the close supervision to ensure proper local services.

Compliance Issues and Consistency of Cover Worldwide

Compliance with all required local regulations that apply to the issuance of an international insurance programme is essential, keeping in mind that all practical questions relative to this situation must be taken into account.

When these considerations are taken into account, it is essential to stress that it may prove difficult to comply with all the norms of a market that does not rest on a global regulation, where the legal and regulatory context is based on a variety of local and multicultural dispositions. The answers to the question of compliance depend on the decisions of the risk manager. They could always be asked to explain their position, to justify beforehand the additional cost associated with the development of an international programme. Therefore, it will always prove necessary to develop a cost-benefit analysis for such a programme.

The final goal of top management is to obtain homogenous insurance covers worldwide; and this requires providing specific answers to the following questions:

- Do we understand the location of the risks and the regulatory environment of the countries involved? How can the development of an international programme be affected by regulatory and tax issues, specifically the requirement for local policies?
- What is the most effective way the risk manager can handle these issues, taking into account the current situation of the organisation, and its present and future strategy?
- What are the issues stemming from participating in a joint venture with local partners when the organisation transfers to them the bulk of risk management decisions?
- How can the use of local insurers be valued, specifically their financial stability and solvency margin?

- How could all these issues impact the organisation's capacity to conduct business in its sector?

The key objective of creating an international insurance programme is to maximise the insurance capacity, minimise the cost and maintain the control of the risks that are managed through the placement of adequate covers.

Main Concepts Associated with International Programmes of Insurance

The terminology used in the market often leads to confusion and problems, perhaps due to the translation of the English expressions (admitted or registered), taking into account that those concepts are not uniformly applied in all countries and their definitions can vary. This is why it is essential to have a common understanding of all those terms and their specificities.

'Admitted' Policy

Policy issued by an insurer licensed in the country where the risk covered is located. It is important to keep in mind that the insurer's licence may cover all lines or a limited number of lines that will be specified in the licence.

'Non-admitted' Policy

Policy issued by an insurer not licensed in the country where the risk covered is located. This non-admitted policy may be totally prohibited, or allowed under some circumstances defined here below.

'Non-admitted' Permitted Policy

The following expressions are equivalent: non-admitted permitted; non-admitted/not prohibited; permissible unlicensed coverage (PUC). The country's legislation authorises an insurer not licensed in the country to insure risks domiciled in the country.

Depending on the location, this can apply only to a limited number of branches or to all of them. It is possible to issue insurance programmes with covers in excess and difference in limits or difference in conditions (DIC/DIL).

Examples of countries non-admitted permitted are: Canada (provided the local tax on insurance premium is acquitted), Chile, El Salvador, Slovakia, Israel, New Zealand, Paraguay, Peru, Samoa and Trinidad y Tobago.

'Non-admitted' Prohibited Policy

The following expressions are equivalent: non-admitted/not permitted; non-admitted/prohibited. The country's legislation does not authorise, or expressly prohibits, an insurer not licensed in the country to insure risks domiciled or located in the country. The legislation also does not authorise, or expressly prohibit, a policy to be issued by an insurer outside of the country where the risk is located.

Issuing policies under such circumstances would be in breach of the local law, and risks fines and sanctions that include suppositions that tax legislation is breached, with the additional issues like the handling of claims under this format. Only locally registered companies are allowed to do business in the country, and there is a major risk for the insurer, as well as for the policyholder of policies issued illegally as there are tax consequences. Furthermore, it should be stressed that in 85% of countries non-admitted cover is forbidden, or severely restricted.

For example, Brazil is a non-admitted prohibited country, therefore policies issued by an insurer not licensed or authorised in Brazil are prohibited, and international programmes with policies in DIC/DIL (see below) do not comply with the existing legislation.

Other non-admitted prohibited countries include: Algeria, Argentina, Aruba, Bahamas, China, Costa Rica, Ecuador, The Philippines, Honduras, India, Japan, Jordan, Malaysia, Mauritania, Morocco, Mexico, Nicaragua, Nigeria, Mozambique, Russia, Senegal, Tunisia, Tanzania, Uruguay and Venezuela.

Note: There are also regulations that prohibit an unlicensed insurer from operating but have no provisions concerning a local insurer choosing to place the cover with an insurer abroad (for example as part of the co-insurance).

- Downside of such a situation:
  - Possible breach of the local regulation and no access to public pools
  - Possible problems for the payment of local taxes, and tax implications for the claims compensation
  - Complex claims management
- Upside (benefits):
  - Covers aligned with the worldwide level
  - Costs contained
  - Absolute control over covers scope

Self-Insurance Provisions (Reserve)

This is not permitted in some countries, specifically when it comes to compulsory insurances. Additionally, in some cases, the contractual agreements with third parties explicitly require proof of the existence of an insurance contract.

Other terms can be found in international insurance programmes including:

Unauthorised Alien Insurer

Under the *Insurance Act 1973* in Australia, all people and companies intending to conduct insurance business must obtain authorisation from the Australian

Prudential Regulation Authority (APRA) to do so. In 2008, the law was amended to make it clear that all companies conducting insurance business must be authorised by APRA, even if they are authorised in an overseas jurisdiction and even if that business is being conducted through an intermediary.

The exemption to this law is that if the business cannot be placed by an authorised company, it can be provided by an unauthorised foreign insurer. Instances where this exemption applies include:

- atypical risks (e.g. specific insurance for hazardous properties or health research);
- high-value insured (e.g. a policyholder that has annual revenue or assets of $200 million or more, or that employs 500 or more people);
- other risks that cannot be reasonably placed in Australia (e.g. risks that no Australian insurer will insure or that will only be insured under highly unfavourable terms).

In the US, the law requires that a non-admitted insurer (one outside the US) be considered in the same way that it would be considered in that insurer's country of origin.

Surplus Lines Insurer

This is a concept used in the USA to refer to insurers in states where they have lines in excess that can be used by other interested parties in other states. Put simply, this essentially means insurers can be included in a list where they are allowed to provide covers only when the covers cannot be offered by the 'admitted' market. In the USA, these are insurers not licensed in a given state but that fulfil all the requirements to sell insurance in the state. The insurance issued by extraterritorial companies is usually more expensive and offers less cover than that offered by licensed insurers, with the additional obligation to use the services of a broker.

Furthermore, in the USA, a company must secure authorisation to write covers in each state. The insurers must be approved by the State Insurance Commissioner regarding conditions and taxes applicable.

There are tools that can help risk management professionals gain a clearer understanding of these issues, including databases created by insurers and brokers, for example, AXCO, which describes the principal characteristics in each country in terms of regulation, with the objective to help define the best insurance solution to comply with all local legislations.

DIC/DIL

The initials DIC/DIL (difference in conditions/difference in limits) refer to the establishment of an international master programme that complements local covers with increased limits, or better conditions.

- Difference in conditions covers (DIC) The master policy provides covers to the organisations domiciled in other countries, with respect to the local policies issued in those countries, when the terms and conditions of the covers in the master policy exceed those of the local.

- Difference in limits cover (DIL) The master policy provides covers to the organisations domiciled in other countries, with respect to the local policies issued in those countries, for the portion of the claim that exceeds the maximum compensation in the local policy, up to the limits of the master policy.

The DIC/DIL approach was traditionally used before the introduction of the FIC (financial interest clause) for the development of international programmes. When DIC/DIL policies function perfectly, they represent an ally of great value in the freedom of service countries or the non-admitted permitted jurisdictions; however, they may create problems in non-admitted prohibited countries as they do not comply with the local legislation, therefore in these situations it is advisable to refrain from using them.

It is also important to keep in mind that rebuilding after suffering damage is never based solely on an insurance solution. The solution is in the hands of the organisation as with any other entrepreneurial project. It is necessary to take into account that the local programmes must establish limits in accordance with the technical criteria appropriate for the risk they protect, so that any gap in the covers is avoided and that the cover complies with local compulsory insurance (countries with compulsory insurance impose minimums when it comes to some forms of contracts). It is important to also ensure that playing around the local legislation does not affect the organisation's reputation when a claim arises.

Freedom of Service (FOS)

The initials FOS (freedom of service or freedom to provide services) refer to those countries where it is legally possible to operate under a freedom of service, meaning those belonging to the European economic area (EEA), which covers the EU, including Ireland, Liechtenstein and Norway.

The regulation is stated in article 5 of the CEE Directive 92/49 from the Council of June 18, 1992 relative to the authorisation delivered in these matters in the EEA. The result is clear: insurers registered in the EEA can apply for EU registration, and the European Insurance market has responded to this.

In those countries, there is freedom to establish insurance programmes by insurance companies authorised and domiciled in one of the member states of the EEA that offer their services from their headquarters or through local branches in other member states, assuming risks or acquiring policies in other states while complying with the local legal and tax dispositions in each country.

Insurance companies wishing to operate in FOS in one or several states must notify the relevant authority in their member state of origin. They will also have to inform the said authorities of any change introduced in the frame of their activities. Then the state of origin has a month to inform the authorities in the state where the freedom of service will be executed. This information must include the name of the company as well as the nature of the activities that will be conducted and the nature of the risks to be covered.

When it comes to insurers from countries that are not members of the EEA, the country concerned will be considered as non-admitted prohibited and not licensed to operate in the countries mentioned (for example, US insurers without authorisation will not be allowed to issue programmes for their European subsidiaries from the US). Therefore, the insurance issued from outside the European Union ('non-admitted') is considered as legally prohibited as FOS is applicable only to countries belonging to the EEA.

Financial Interest Clause (FIC)

The initials FIC refer to a clause that appeared after the DIC/DIL clauses as part of the evolution of the international programmes in the process of searching for solutions that comply with the regulatory and tax local dispositions. With this clause, once the claim has arisen, the mother company owner of the international programme will be entitled to compensation by the carrier of the programme (the insurer), according to the limit and conditions of the contract, in which the parameters of the financial interest of the mother company (A) located in a country (A1) have been clearly defined if their damages occur in one of its subsidiaries (B) located in a different country (B1).

The FIC clause will compensate the interest as defined in the policy prior to the claim, not the actual damage suffered, which means that the basic elements to be considered for the valorisation of this interest must be set in the contract as well as any other connected elements (for example, assessors in charge), otherwise, controversies could arise on these issues with a great risk of ending in the courts of law. It is always complex to define the concept of financial interest and how to compute a loss of this type.

Limits and Problems with Master Policies and Local Legislation

The master policy cannot provide cover under the conditions non-admitted prohibited to an organisation domiciled in a foreign country if the local legislation does not allow the cover, but it can provide cover to the leading insured (mother company) for its own financial interest in its local subsidiaries. The leading insured is the only insured and the local subsidiary does not appear as 'insured' in the master policy. In the case of a claim, the policyholder receives directly in its own country the compensation according to the terms and conditions of the master policy.

This clause has proven controversial, specifically when the mother company wants the funds received through it to be channelled to the subsidiary that suffered the damage even when it is domiciled in a non-admitted prohibited jurisdiction (this issue was not originally envisioned as the funds were meant to remain at headquarters).

Finally, the current schemes for international insurance programmes, with possible structures (integrated or not-integrated local policies, mix solutions, etc.) and master policies in relation to determined geographical areas are still to be tested and full compliance with all laws and regulations is never assured.

Regarding the characteristics of the local issuances and the realities of 'good local standards' confronted with the master policy content, difficulties may arise when replicating locally the conditions of the master policy when in a non-admitted country where the local market does not offer the same cover extensions. It is important to remember the tax implications of a mother-subsidiaries programme when attempting to complement the local conditions, including the payment of the insurance premium tax, and taking into account the importance of the internal premium allocation process, as it may be questioned by the local regulator.

> **Activity | International insurance**
>
> To learn more about how these concepts interconnect, read the article entitled 'What is a financial interest in clause in a reinsurance contract' availableat: www.irmi.com/articles/expert-commentary/reinsurance-financial-interest-clause

Designing a Programme

An international insurance programme scheme, depending on the local circumstances and always taking into account the specificities and final decisions of risk managers, could be envisioned as follows:

- local policies in the countries where it is necessary or compulsory with premium in line with each country depending on the local market balance;
- master policy, if the system above is not sufficient, with DIC/DIL clauses in countries non-admitted permitted and the FIC clause for those that are non-admitted prohibited.

Local legislations are multiple and varied, and they also impact the management of claims, with a majority of countries in the non-admitted prohibited category.

The DIC/DIL clause and the FIC clause and their functions were described earlier in this block, especially in connection with the tax policy and the other financial mechanisms of the company.

When designing an international insurance programme, best practice is to aim for simplicity and use communication as a key element. A detailed analysis of the advantages and disadvantages of each situation, and co-operation with the broker, insurer and internal teams involved are essential to developing a guide to critical situations and problems so that the risk manager can assess, evaluate and make the best final decisions in the search for the optimal solution.

Another important element is the use of technical criteria adequate to establish the transfer pricing, so that the internal allocation of the premium can be justified as well as the payment of indemnities.

Considerations and Caveats When Building an International Programme

A number of issues must be given serious consideration to avoid the major pitfalls in international programmes:

- A final legal responsibility when establishing international insurance programmes rests with the insurers, the intermediaries (brokers) or the policyholders as determined by the legislation of the country involved (tax, legal, etc.).
- The intermediary's responsibilities depend on the stipulations of the applicable legislation on a case-by-case basis in the country involved while the relations between the policyholder and the intermediary are governed by the service level agreement signed between the two parties.
- Several international teams (risk management, legal, taxes, finance, etc.) must get involved in the elaboration of an international insurance programme. Other departments of the organisations in the countries involved in the programme will be solicited too, since it is not possible to finalise the process only on the contributions of the headquarters' risk management team.
- A great many international insurance programmes have not delivered as expected due to tax issues (errors in the consideration of taxes involved at the premium and at the indemnity levels). It is advisable to include in an international insurance programme a tax guarantee clause that implies the insurer will get involved should a problem arise on tax issues.
- It is not possible to have identical policies in all the countries, therefore it is important to refer to local standards, taking into account that in some countries the denomination 'all risks' does not exist in the way it is understood generally, with a reference only to 'named perils'; and there are also other idiomatic interpretations that can lead to confusion. In the case of participation as a shareholder, the possible compensation applied through an FIC clause must not be limited in the conditions of the policy to the extent of the holding; the financial interest must be defined, not as share in the capital of an organisation, but as what is necessary to maintain a good operation of the organisation.

Summary

Please keep the following points from this chapter in mind:

- The objective when creating an international insurance programme is to maximise the insurance capacity, contain the costs and maintain control over the risks through the placement of adequate covers.
- There are grey areas in these issues so that, in each situation, decision-makers can only make the decisions that best suit the situation.
- Fines and sanctions that apply to the insurer, intermediary or client, generally in this order, vary depending on the local legislation for the country involved.

- The problem of the local certificate of insurance issuance is a very important theme as a wrong interpretation of the local legislation could end up in court. On the other hand, it is important to note that those documents certify only the cover provided, not the financial interest.
- The multinational companies that use international insurance programmes for their global operations must take into account the international regulations relative to the insurance covers, and study them with sufficient care, as there are jurisdictions where non-admitted policies can be prohibited.
- The evidence of a lack of harmonisation worldwide is provided by the diversity of norms. The main differences are on the tax and regulatory areas, and the reality is met with the proper legislation. No solution has proven perfect or definitive for this issue. It may prove necessary to include in the master policy some covers specific to countries where they would be required.
- There are currently more than 140 non-admitted prohibited countries. In recent years, there has been an increasing follow-up of the existing local regulations to enforce the obligation of local insurance and limit premium export in order to build a local insurance market, and get revenues also through the local taxes applicable.
- Organisations can exclusively purchase local insurance policies in each country where they have activities; however, this approach may result in cover gaps, high costs and a loss of control from headquarters. On the other hand, buying only global policies could expose them to the risk of fines and sanctions in the countries where admitted policies are required.
- Those that are in favour of local programmes stress that local programmes are preferable for their bringing solutions for the legal and tax issues in the country were they are issued, allowing a better evaluation of the exposures, bringing evidence of the insurance to satisfy local authorities, and a faster settlement of claims, opening access to local pools (and compulsory covers). Finally, the main argument is that the more significant the insured local exposure, the more a local policy is needed.
- Compulsory insurance always must be managed through local policies. With regard to legal and tax issues, it is always necessary to make sure that the terms and premium of the insurance are sufficient for the risk exposure.
- There are countries that allow foreign placement of a necessary cover when the local market does not offer it. This issue must be analysed on a case-by-case basis to ensure compliance with the relevant legal environment.

Decisions about insurance covers always have an element of taxation that must be taken into account, therefore the tax department in the organisation must be involved in the decision-making process. Traditional international insurance programmes must be adapted to follow the development of these issues taking into account the modifications in the local legislation.

References and Recommended Reading

Standards and Handbooks

British Standards Institute, BS 25999-1:2006, *Business continuity management code of practice.* (Replaced in 2014.)

International Organization for Standardization and International Electrotechnical Commission, ISO/IEC 27031:2011, *Information technology – Security techniques – Guidelines for information and communication technology readiness for business continuity.*

International Organization for Standardization, ISO 22301:2012, *Societal security – Business continuity management systems – Requirements.*

International Organization for Standardization, ISO 22313:2012, *Societal security – Business continuity management systems – Guidance.*

National Fire Protection Association, NFPA 1600:2005, *Standard on disaster/emergency management and business continuity/continuity of operations programs.*

Standards Australia, HB 292:2006, *A practitioners guide to business continuity management*, Standards Australia/Standards New Zealand.

Standards Australia, HB 293:2006, *An executive guide to business continuity management*, Standards Australia/Standards New Zealand.

Print Material

Cannon-Bowers, J, Tannenbaum, S, Salas, E and Volpe, C 1995, *Defining competencies and establishing team training requirements*, in Guzzo, R and Salas, E (eds), *Team effectiveness and decision making in organisations*, Wiley, New Jersey.

Elliot, D, Swartz, E and Herbane, B 1999, *Business continuity management – Preparing for the worst*, Incomes Data Services, London.

Kraakman, R H 1986, 'Gatekeepers: The anatomy of a third-party enforcement strategy', *Journal of Law, Economics and Organization*, 2(1).

Online Material

Allianz Global Corporate & Specialty 2015, 'Global claims review 2015: Business interruption in focus'. www.agcs.allianz.com/assets/PDFs/Reports/AGCS-Global-Claims-Review-2015.pdf (site accessed 6 July 2017).

Bank for International Settlements (BIS), 'Basel III'. www.bis.org/bcbs/basel3.htm (site accessed 28 July 2017).

Business Continuity Institute (BCI) 2005, https://www.bcm-institute.org/

Business Continuity Institute (BCI) 2013, 'Good practice guidelines'. www.thebci.org/index.php/resources/the-good-practice-guidelines (site accessed 6 July 2017).

Business Continuity Institute (BCI) 2016, 'BCM legislations, regulations & standards'. www.thebci.org/index.php/resources/knowledgebank/cat_view/17-regulations-standards-guidelines/45-other/177-bci-resources?orderby=dmdatecounter&ascdesc=DESC (site accessed 1 August 2017).

Coffee, J 2002, 'Understanding Enron: It's about the gatekeepers, stupid', Columbia Law & Economics Working Paper No. 207. http://papers.ssrn.com/sol3/papers.cfm?abstract_id=325240 (site accessed 16 April 2007).

Coffee, J 2004, 'Gatekeeper failure and reform: The challenge of fashioning relevant reforms', Berkeley Program in Law and Economics Working Papers Series. http://respositories.collib.org/blewp/arti60 (site accessed 16 April 2007).

Snowden, D and Boone, M 2007, 'A leader's framework for decision making', *Harvard Business Review*, November. https://hbr.org/2007/11/a-leaders-framework-for-decision-making (site accessed 4 August 2017).

Toyota Case Study

Sites accessed 4 August 2017

ABC News 2014, 'Toyota to pay $1.2b for hiding deadly "unintended acceleration"'. http://abcnews.go.com/Blotter/toyota-pay-12b-hiding-deadly-unintended-acceleration/story?id=22972214

Motor Trend 2010, 'A chronology of how the world's largest and most profitable automaker drove into a PR disaster'. www.motortrend.com/news/toyota-recall-crisis

Wikipedia '2009–11 Toyota vehiclerecalls'. https://en.wikipedia.org/wiki/2009%E2%80%9311_Toyota_vehicle_recalls

Fukushima Case Study

CNN 2017, '2011 Japan earthquake – tsunami fast facts'. http://edition.cnn.com/2013/07/17/world/asia/japan-earthquake--tsunami-fast-facts/index.html (site accessed 4 August 2017).

The National Diet of Japan 2012, 'The official report of the Fukushima nuclear accident independent investigation commission: Executive summary'. www.nirs.org/wp-content/uploads/fukushima/naiic_report.pdf (site accessed 4 August 2017).

UNIS 2014, 'Press release: Increase in cancer unlikely following Fukushima exposure – says UN report'. www.unis.unvienna.org/unis/en/pressrels/2014/unisous237.html (site accessed 4 August 2017).

References and Resources

Print Resources

Condamin, L, Louisot, J and Naïm, P 2006, *Risk quantification: Management, diagnosis and hedging*, 1st edn, John Wiley & Sons Inc., West Sussex.

Fisher, M and Shaw, Z 2003, *Securitisation: For issuers, arrangers and investors*, 2nd edn, Euromoney Books, London.

Vaughan, E and Vaughan, T 2008, *Fundamentals of risk and insurance*, 10th edn, John Wiley & Sons Inc., New Jersey.

Online Resources

Aon Risk Solutions 2016, 'Base Erosion & Profit Shifting (BEPS): Exploring why captive insurance companies are legitimate risk management solutions adding value to their owners', July. www.aon.com/attachments/risk-services/BEPS-July-2016-White-Paper-Final.pdf (site accessed 20 July 2017).

Bests' Special Report 2016, '*Global reinsurance – Segment review: Remaining relevant*', September. www.bestweek.com/europe/promo/GlobalReinsuranceSegmentReview.pdf (site accessed 19 July 2017).

FERMA 2017, '*FERMA information paper to OECD in order to propose captive (re)insurance guidelines to national tax authorities*', June. www.ferma.eu/app/uploads/2017/06/2017.06-FERMA-Information-Paper-on-Captive-reInsurance-Guidelines.pdf (site accessed 9 August 2017).

IAIS 2008, 'IAIS Guidance paper on the regulation and supervision of captive insurers', October (site accessed 20 July 2017).

Intelligent Insurer 2017, '*UK government seeks to attract ILS market with new regulations*', Intelligent Insurer, July. www.intelligentinsurer.com/news/uk-government-seeks-to-attract-ils-market-with-new-regulations-12595 (site accessed 7 August 2017).

PWC 2012, '*Laying the foundations for the future of insurance reporting*', November. www.pwc.com/insurance (site accessed 20 August 2017).

Recommended Readings

Armit, T and Marvell, S 2001, 'Maintaining and exercising business continuity plans', in Hiles, A and Barnes, P (eds), *The definitive handbook of business continuity management*, John Wiley and Sons, UK.

Brown, L (Editor-in-Chief) 1993, *The new shorter Oxford English dictionary*, 4th edn, Oxford University Press, UK.

Campbell, R 1999, *Crisis control – Preventing & managing corporate crises*, Penguin Group, Australia.

Evans, D 2012, *Risk intelligence: How to live with uncertainty*, 1st edn, Simon & Chuster, New York.

Goemans, T 1992, *Crisis management: Handling the unexpected, the unknown and the undesired*, KPMG Management Consulting.

Hearle, D, in Gottschalk, J 2002, *Crisis management*, Capstone Publishing, Minnesota.

Kramer, H T 1980, '*The nature of reinsurance*', *Reinsurance*, 1st edn, Strain, R (ed.), College of Insurance, New York.

Little, A D 1984, in Gottschalk, J, 2002, *Crisis management*, Capstone Publishing, Minnesota.

Mitroff, I, Pearson, C and Harrington, K 1996, *The essential guide to managing corporate crises: A step-by-step handbook for surviving major catastrophes*, Oxford University Press, UK.

Musson, D and Jordan, E 2002, *Managing for failure – The Macquarie University survey of business and computer contingency planning in Australia*, Macquarie Graduate School of Management, Australia quoted in Standards Australia/Standards New Zealand Handbook HB 221:2004 *Business continuity management*.

Swiss Re 2005, '*Sigma N°4: Innovating to insure the uninsurable*'.

Appendix: Hillsborough Disaster

Introduction

The Hillsborough disaster was a deadly human crush that occurred on 15 April 1989, at Hillsborough, a football stadium in Sheffield, England, resulting in the loss of 96 lives.

The Disaster

Liverpool F.C. were involved in their 17th FA Cup semi-final, to be played against Nottingham Forest F.C. at Hillsborough, the home of Sheffield Wednesday F.C. – FA Cup semi-finals are traditionally played at neutral venues so as not to favour either club involved. Liverpool and Nottingham Forest had played at the semi-final stage at the same ground the previous year without incident.

As a risk treatment, most stadiums had placed high steel fencing between the spectators and the pitch, in response to hooliganism which had plagued the sport for years. Hooliganism was particularly virulent in England, where it often involved pitch invasions and/or the throwing of a variety of missiles. Hooliganism was not a factor at Hillsborough on the day of the disaster, but the fencing was later identified as one of the main factors leading to the disaster as it prevented fans from escaping the crush. The part of the stadium where the problem occurred was also a 'terrace' area, a cheaper standing section without seats that was determined to be a major contributing factor to the disaster. Terraces were frequently divided by further fencing into sections called pens to aid crowd control.

Hillsborough Stadium was segregated between the opposing fans as was customary at all large matches, the Liverpool supporters being assigned to the Leppings Lane End. Kick off was scheduled for 3.00 p.m. but due to a variety of factors including traffic delays on the route to Sheffield from Liverpool many of the Liverpool supporters were later than usual arriving. Between 2.00 p.m. and 2.45 p.m., there was a considerable build-up of fans in the small area outside the turnstiles at the Leppings Lane End, all eager to enter the stadium before the match started. A bottleneck developed with more fans arriving than were able to enter the stadium. The risk of overcrowding had been identified by the stadium operators because the stadium included crush barriers and the use of police and stewards to direct the crowd.

Unfortunately, with an estimated 5,000 fans trying to get through the turnstiles, the police decided to open a set of exit gates which did not have turnstiles to control the influx of fans. Failure to control the fans was the most significant reason for the disaster. Not manning the entrances to central pens 3 and 4 on the terraces meant that hundreds, or possibly thousands of people entered the already overcrowded pens and they were not aware of the crush they were creating at the front of the pens. The risk treatment of using turnstiles, police and stewards to control the crowd, failed.

Even at this point, there was still much confusion among the authorities at the match. Senior police initially assumed that they were witnessing a pitch invasion and responded by sending in reinforcements to keep people off the pitch rather than helping the fans out of the crush.

The crush ultimately took the lives of 96 people, with 766 fans receiving injuries. Tony Bland survived for nearly four years in a persistent vegetative state before he became the 96th victim. Following the disaster, Lord Justice Taylor was appointed to conduct an inquiry into the disaster. Taylor's inquiry sat for 31 days and published two reports, one interim report that laid out the events of the day and identified that the most significant failure was the inability of police and stewards to control the crowd; also the unseated terraces allowed overcrowding. One final report made general recommendations on football ground safety. As a result of the inquiry, fences in front of fans were removed and stadiums were converted to become all-seated. This became known as the Taylor Report.

www.ingramcontent.com/pod-product-compliance
Lightning Source LLC
Jackson TN
JSHW052038250325
81415JS00003B/4
* 9 7 8 1 8 3 6 6 2 3 0 7 6 *